# JAVASCRIPT FUNDA

# BASICS

By ROBERT PETERSON

# JAVASCRIPT FUNDAMENTALS AND BASICS

ROBERT PETERSON

2019

## Contents

### 1.1 BASICS OF JAVA SCRIPT

3

## 1.1 BASICS OF JAVA SCRIPT

### What is JavaScript?

- Was designed to add interactivity to HTML pages
- Is a scripting language (a scripting language is a lightweight programming language)
- JavaScript code is usually embedded directly into HTML pages
- JavaScript is an interpreted language (means that scripts execute without preliminary compilation)

5

**What can a JavaScript do?**

- JavaScript gives HTML designers a programming tool
- JavaScript can put dynamic text into an HTML page
- JavaScript can react to events
- JavaScript can read and write HTML elements
- JavaScript can be used to validate input data
- JavaScript can be used to detect the visitor's browser
- JavaScript can be used to create cookies

6

**How to put a JavaScript code into an HTML page?**

- Use the <script> tag (also use the type attribute to define the scripting language)

```
<html>
<head>
<script type="text/javascript">
...
</script>
</head>
<body>
<script type="text/javascript">
...
</script>
</body>
</html>
```

8

**Where Do You Place Scripts?**

- Scripts can be in the either *<head>* section or *<body>* section
- Convention is to place it in the *<head>* section

```
<html>
<head>
<script type="text/javascript">
....
</script>
</head>
```

9

**Referencing External JavaScript File**

- Scripts can be provided locally or remotely accessible JavaScript file using *src* attribute

```
<html>
<head>
<script language="JavaScript"
        type="text/javascript"
        src="http://somesite/myOwnJavaScript.js">
</script>
<script language="JavaScript"
        type="text/javascript"
        src="myOwnSubdirectory/myOwn2ndJavaScript.js">
</script>
```

**10**

# JavaScript Language

**JavaScript Variable**

- You create a variable with or without the var statement

    var strname = some value

    strname = some value

- When you declare a variable within a function, the variable can only be accessed within that function
- If you declare a variable outside a function, all the functions on your page can access it
- The lifetime of these variables starts when they are declared, and ends when the page is closed

**12**

**JavaScript Popup Boxes**

- Alert box
  - > User will have to click "OK" to proceed
  - > alert("sometext")
- Confirm box
  - > User will have to click either "OK" or "Cancel" to proceed
  - > confirm("sometext")
- Prompt box
  - > User will have to click either "OK" or "Cancel" to proceed after entering an input value
  - > prompt("sometext","defaultvalue")

13

## JavaScript Language

- Conditional statement
  - > if, if.. else, switch
- Loop
  - > for loop, while loop
- try...catch
- throw

**JavaScript Functions (which behave like Java methods)**

**More on Functions in other Presentation**

**JavaScript Funcitons**

- A JavaScript function contains some code that will be executed only by an event or by a call to that function
  - > To keep the browser from executing a script as soon as the page is loaded, you can write your script as a function
- You may call a function from anywhere within the page (or even from other pages if the function is embedded in an external .js file).
- Functions can be defined either <head> or <body> section
  - > As a convention, they are typically defined in the <head> section 16

**Example: JavaScript Function**

```
<html>
<head>
<script type="text/javascript">
  // If alert("Hello world!!") below had not been written within a
  // function, it would have been executed as soon as the page gets loaded. function displaymessage() {
        alert("Hello World!")
  }
</script>
</head>


<body>
<form>
<input type="button" value="Click me!"
onclick="displaymessage()" >
</form>
</body>

</html>
```

17

## JavaScript Events

**Events & Event Handlers**

- Every element on a web page has certain events which can trigger invocation of event handlers
- Attributes are inserted into HTML tags to define events and event handlers
- Examples of events
    - A mouse click
    - A web page or an image loading
    - Mousing over a hot spot on the web page
    - Selecting an input box in an HTML form
    - Submitting an HTML form

    - A keystroke

19

**Events**

- onabort - Loading of an image is interrupted
- onblur - An element loses focus
- onchange - The content of a field changes
- onclick - Mouse clicks an object
- ondblclick - Mouse double-clicks an object
- onerror - An error occurs when loading a document or an image
- onfocus - An element gets focus

- onkeydown - A keyboard key is pressed

**Events**

- onkeypress - A keyboard key is pressed or held down
- onkeyup - A keyboard key is released
- onload - A page or an image is finished loading
- onmousedown - A mouse button is pressed
- onmousemove - The mouse is moved
- onmouseout - The mouse is moved off an element
- onmouseover - The mouse is moved over an element
- onmouseup - A mouse button is released

**Events**

- onreset - The reset button is clicked
- onresize - A window or frame is resized
- onselect - Text is selected
- onsubmit - The submit button is clicked
- onunload - The user exits the page

**onload & onUnload Events**

- The *onload* and *onUnload* events are triggered when the user enters or leaves the page
- The onload event is often used to check the visitor's browser type and browser version, and load the proper version of the web page based on the information
- Both the onload and onUnload events are also often used to deal with cookies that should be set when a user enters or leaves a page.

**onFocus, onBlur and onChange**

- The onFocus, onBlur and onChange events are often used in combination with validation of form fields.
- Example: The *checkEmail()* function will be called whenever the user changes the content of the field:
  <input type="text" size="30" id="email"
  onchange="*checkEmail()*">;

**Example & Demo: onblur**

```
<html>
<head>
<script type="text/javascript">
    function upperCase() {
        var x=document.getElementById("fname").value
    }   document.getElementById("fname").value=x.toUpperCase()
</script>
</head>

<body>

Enter your name:
<input type="text" id="fname" onblur="upperCase()">

</body>
</html>
```

**onSubmit**

- The *onSubmit* event is used to validate all form fields before submitting it.
- Example: The *checkForm()* function will be called when the user clicks the submit button in the form. If the field values are not accepted, the submit should be canceled. The function *checkForm()* returns either true or false. If it returns true the form will be submitted, otherwise the submit will be cancelled:

  <form method="post" action="xxx.html"

  onsubmit="return *checkForm()*">

**Example & Demo: onSubmit**

```
<html>
<head>
<script type="text/javascript">
    function validate() {
    } // return true or false based on validation logic
</script>
</head>

<body>
        <form action="tryjs_submitpage.htm" onsubmit="return validate()">
            Name (max 10 chararcters): <input type="text" id="fname" size="20"><br />
            Age (from 1 to 100): <input type="text" id="age" size="20"><br />
            E-mail: <input type="text" id="email" size="20"><br /> <br />
            <input type="submit" value="Submit">
        </form>
</body>
</html>
```

**onMouseOver and onMouseOut**

- onMouseOver and onMouseOut are often used to create "animated" buttons.
- Below is an example of an onMouseOver event. An alert box appears when an onMouseOver event is detected:
  <a href="http://www.w3schools.com" onmouseover="alert('An onMouseOver event');return false">
  <img src="w3schools.gif" width="100" height="30"> </a>

# JavaScript Objects

**JavaScript Object**

- JavaScript is an Object Oriented Programming (OOP) language
- A JavaScript object has properties and methods
    - Example: *String* JavaScript object has *length* property and *toUpperCase()* method

```
<script type="text/javascript">

var txt="Hello World!"
document.write(txt.length)
document.write(txt.toUpperCase())

</script>
```

**30**

**JavaScript Built-in Objects**

- String
- Date
- Array
- Boolean
- Math

**JavaScript Object vs. Java Object**

- Simlarities
    > Both has properties and methods
- Differences
    > JavaScript object can be dynamically typed while Java object is statically typed
    > In JavaScript, properties and methods are dynamically added

32

# JavaScript Objects; 3 Different Ways of Creating JavaScript Objects

**Creating Your Own JavaScript Objects**

- 3 different ways
  - Create a direct instance of an object by using built-in constructor for the *Object* class
  - Create a template (Constructor) first and then create an instance of an object from it
  - Create object instance as Hash Literal

**Option 1: Creating a Direct Instance of a JavaScript Object**

- By invoking the built-in constructor for the Object class

```
personObj=new Object(); // Initially empty with no properties or methods
```

- Add properties to it

```
personObj.firstname="John";
personObj.age=50;
```

- Add an anonymous function to the *personObj*

```
personObj.tellYourage=function(){

    alert("This age is " + this.age);

}

// You can call then tellYourage function as following

personObj.tellYourage();
```

**Option 1: Creating a Direct Instance of a JavaScript Object**

- Add a pre-defined function

```
function tellYourage(){
    alert("The age is" + this.age);
}
personObj.tellYourage=tellYourage;
```

- Note that the following two lines of code are doing completely different things

```
// Set property with a function
personObj.tellYourage=tellYourage;
// Set property with returned value of the function
personObj.tellYourage=tellYourage();
```

36

**Option 2: Creating a template of a JavaScript Object**

- The template defines the structure of a JavaScript object in the form of a function
- You can think of the template as a constructor

```
function Person(firstname,lastname,age,eyecolor) { this.firstname=firstname;
        this.lastname=lastname;
        this.age=age;
        this.tellYourage=function(){
            alert("This age is " + this.age);
        }
}
```

37

**Option 2: Creating a template of a JavaScript Object**

- Once you have the template, you can create new instances of the object

  myFather=new Person("John","Doe",50,"blue"); myMother=new Person("Sally","Rally",48,"green");

- You can add new properties and functions to new objects

  myFather.newField = "some data"; myFather.myfunction =

  function() { alert(this["fullName"] + " is " + this.age); }

38

## Option 3: Creating JavaScript

## Object as a Hash Literal

- Create *personObj* JavaScript object

```
var personObj = {
        firstname: "John",
        lastname: "Doe",
        age: 50,
        tellYourage: function () {

            alert("The age is " + this.age );
        }
        tellSomething: function(something) {

            alert(something);
        }
}


personObj.tellYourage();
```

```
personObj.tellSomething("Life is good!");
```

# JavaScript Objects: Hash (Associative Array)

**JavaScript Object is an Associative Array (Hash)**

- A JavaScript object is essentially an associative array (hash) with fields and methods, which are keyed by name

```
{
    firstname: "John",
    lastname: "Doe",
    age: 50,
    tellYourage: function () {
        alert("The age is " + this.age );
    },
    tellSomething: function(something) {
        alert(something);
    }
}
```

- The following two lines of code are semantically equivalent

  *myObject.myfield = "something";*

  *myObject['myfield'] = "something";*

41

# JavaScript Objects:
# Classes, Objects, Inheritance

**JavaScript has No built-in concept of Inheritance**

- JavaScript has a concept of objects and classes (like in Java) but no built-in concept of inheritance (unlike in Java)
  - Every JavaScript object is really an instance of the same base class, a class that is capable of binding member fields and functions to itself at runtime

43

# JavaScript Objects: prototype

**prototype**

- A prototype is a property of every JavaScript object
- Functions and properties can be associated with a constructor's property
- When a function is invoked with *new* keyword, all properties and methods of the prototype for the function are attached to the resulting object

**prototype**

```
// Constructor of the MyObject function
MyObject(name, size){
      this.name=name;
      this.size=size;
}
// Add a function to the prototype
MyObject.prototype.tellSize=function{
      alert("size of " + this.name+" is " + this.size);
}

// Create an instance of the object. The new object has tellSize() method. var myObj=new MyObject("Sang",
"30 inches");
myObj.tellSize();
```

46

# JavaScript Objects: Functions Again

**A function is a first-class JavaScript Object**

- Functions are a bit like Java methods
  - > They have arguments and return values
- A function is a first-class object in JavaScript (unlike in Java)
  - > Can be considered as a descendant of Object
  - > Can do everything a regular JavaScript object can do such as storing properties by name
  - > Function objects can have other function objects as methods

48

**A function can take Variable arguments**

- You can call *myfunction()* or *myfunction(20)*

```
function myfunction(value){
    if (value){
        this.area=value;
    }
    return this.area;
}
```

49

# JavaScript Objects: Context

# HTML DOM Objects

**HTML DOM**

- The HTML DOM defines a standard set of objects for HTML, and a standard way to access and manipulate HTML documents
- All HTML elements, along with their containing text and attributes, can be accessed through the DOM.
  - The contents can be modified or deleted, and new elements can be created.
- The HTML DOM is platform and language independent
  - It can be used by any programming language like Java, JavaScript, and VBScript

52

**HTML DOM Objects**

- Anchor object
- Document object
- Event object
- Form and Form Input object
- Frame, Frameset, and IFrame objects
- Image object
- Location object
- Navigator object

**HTML DOM Objects**

- Option and Select objects
- Screen object
- Table, TableHeader, TableRow, TableData objects
- Window object

54

## Document Object

**Document Object: Write text to the output**

```
<html>
<body>

<script type="text/javascript">
document.write("Hello World!")
</script>

</body>
</html>
```

**Document Object: Write text with Formatting to the output**

```
<html>
<body>

<script type="text/javascript">
   document.write("<h1>Hello World!</h1>")
</script>

</body>
</html>
```

57

**Document Object: Use getElementById()**

```
<html>

<head>
<script type="text/javascript">
    function getElement() {
        var x=document.getElementById("myHeader")
    }   alert("I am a " + x.tagName + " element")
</script>
</head>

<body>
<h1 id="myHeader" onclick="getElement()">Click to see what element I am!</h1> </body>

</html>
```

**Document Object: Use getElementsByName()**

```
<html>
<head>
<script type="text/javascript">
    function getElements() {
        var x=document.getElementsByName("myInput")

        alert(x.length + " elements!")
    }
</script>

</head>

<body>
<input name="myInput" type="text" size="20"><br />
<input name="myInput" type="text" size="20"><br />
<input name="myInput" type="text" size="20"><br />
<br />
<input type="button" onclick="getElements()" value="How many elements named
    'myInput'?">
</body>

</html>
```

**Document Object: Return the innerHTML of the first anchor in a document**

```
<html>
<body>

<a name="first">First anchor</a><br />
<a name="second">Second anchor</a><br /> <a
name="third">Third anchor</a><br /> <br />

InnerHTML of the first anchor in this document:
<script type="text/javascript">
    document.write(document.anchors[0].innerHTML)
</script>

</body>

</html>
```

**Document Object: Access an item in a collection**

```
<html>
<body>
<form id="Form1" name="Form1">
Your name: <input type="text">
</form>
<form id="Form2" name="Form2">
Your car: <input type="text">
</form>

<p>
To access an item in a collection you can either use the number or the name of the item:
</p>

<script type="text/javascript">
document.write("<p>The first form's name is: " + document.forms[0].name + "</p>")
document.write("<p>The first form's name is: " + document.getElementById("Form1").name + "</p>")
</script>

</body>
</html>
```

# Event Object

**Event Object: What are the coordinates of the cursor?**

```
<html>
<head>
<script type="text/javascript">
    function show_coords(event) {
        x=event.clientX
        y=event.clientY
        alert("X coords: " + x + ", Y coords: " + y)
    }
</script>
</head>

<body onmousedown="show_coords(event)">
<p>Click in the document. An alert box will alert the x and y coordinates of the cursor.</p>
</body>

</html>
```

**Event Object: What is the unicode of the key pressed?**

```
<html>
<head>
<script type="text/javascript">
    function whichButton(event) {
    ;   alert(event.keyCode)

</script>
</head>

<body onkeyup="whichButton(event)">
<p><b>Note:</b> Make sure the right frame has focus when trying this example!</p> <p>Press a key on
your keyboard. An alert box will alert the unicode of the key
    pressed.</p>
</body>

</html>
```

64

**Event Object: Which element was clicked?**

```
<html>
<head>
<script type="text/javascript">
function whichElement(e) {
   var targ
   if (!e) var e = window.event
   if (e.target) targ = e.target
        else if (e.srcElement) targ = e.srcElement
   if (targ.nodeType == 3) // defeat Safari bug
        targ = targ.parentNode
   var tname
  tname=targ.tagName
} alert("You clicked on a " + tname + " element.")
</script>
</head>

<body onmousedown="whichElement(event)">
<p>Click somewhere in the document. An alert box will alert the tag name of the element you clicked on.</p>

<h3>This is a header</h3>
<p>This is a paragraph</p>
<img border="0" src="ball16.gif" width="29" height="28" alt="Ball">
</body>
</html>
```

**65**

**Event Object: Which event type occurred?**

```
<html>
<head>

<script type="text/javascript">
   function whichType(event) {
  }  alert(event.type)
</script>
</head>

<body onmousedown="whichType(event)">

<p>
Click on the document. An alert box will alert which type of event occurred. </p>

</body>
</html>
```

# 1 What is a Programming Language?

## Key Points

- A programming language is a set of codes that we can use to give a computer instructions to follow.
- Popular and well-known programming languages include Java, C++, COBOL, BASIC, LISP and more. Most popular programming languages consist of words and phrases that are similar in form to the English language.
- A well-written program will be easily readable by anyone with a little programming experience, regardless of whether they have any direct experience of the language in question. This is because modern programming languages share a large number of common concepts. In particular, they all have a notion of **variables**, **arrays**, **loops**, **conditionals**, and **functions**. We will meet these concepts again in more depth later in the course.
- Traditionally, programming languages have been used to write (for the most part) "stand-alone" applications. Things like Microsoft Word, Mozilla Firefox and Lotus Notes are all examples of such applications. Once installed on a PC, these applications run without necessarily requiring any other software to be installed alongside them.
- Web Applications differ from these traditional applications in many respects, but the most striking is that they all run **inside your web browser**.

Examples of popular web applications are things like Google, Hotmail, Flickr, GMail and any of the vast array of "weblogging" systems.

---

- These applications are also written using programming languages, but as a rule they are built using multiple, interdependent technologies. These technologies are easily (though not completely) broken down into two categories: **server-side** and **client-side**.

# 2 Server-side vs. Client-side

## Key Points

- The World Wide Web is built on a number of different technologies.
- For most users, the web starts and ends with their choice of **web browser**. The browser is said to define the **client-side** of the web, with the browser, the computer it is running on, and the user surfing the web being collectively referred to as **the client**.
- Consider a client who has decided to visit the web site at **www.google.com**. The first thing that happens is that the client will make a request to Google's **web server** for the default page of that web site.
- The **web server** is an application running on a computer owned by Google. Like the client, the server application and the computer on which it runs define the **server-side** of the web, and are collectively referred to as **the server**.
- When the server receives the request from the client for a particular page, its job is to retrieve the page from the computer's files and **serve** it back to the client. In many cases, this operation is a very simple procedure involving little or no work on the part of the server.
- However, using a programming language like PHP, Perl or Java, we can cause the server to either modify the page it finds before it passes it back to the client, or even to generate the page entirely from scratch. This is referred to as a **server-side** application. The

page passed back to the client looks (to the client) exactly the same as any other page that has not been modified.

---

- An example of a **server-side** application might be to insert the current date and time into a page. This would mean that each time the page was requested (say, by using the browser's refresh button), a new time value would be added to the page.
- Once the client has received the page from the server, it displays the page and waits for the user to request another page. As soon as the page reaches this state, it has moved beyond the control of the server. No **server-side** application can now alter the contents of the page without the client having to make another trip back to the server to get a new (and possibly updated) copy of the page.
- However, all modern browsers allow for the running of **client-side** applications. These are small applications which are **embedded** within the HTML code of the page itself.
- **Server-side** applications ignore any **client-side** applications that they find while modifying pages to send to the client, so in general the two types of application cannot easily "talk" to each other.
- However, once the client has received a **client-side** application, it can begin to modify the page **dynamically**, without the need to go back to the server.
- An example of a **client-side** application might be a clock on a web page that updated every second.
- An unfortunate side effect of **client-side** applications is that all the code must be sent to the client for running, which means that the application's inner workings are available for anyone to see. This makes it impractical for checking passwords, or doing anything else that could cause confidential information to be released into the wild.

- In addition, all modern web browsers afford the user the opportunity to switch off **client-side** applications altogether. On top of this, the way the same **client-side** application is run will vary from browser type to browser type.
- Despite these drawbacks, **client-side** applications (or **scripts**, as they are better known due to their general brevity) remain the best way to provide web users with a rich environment when developing web applications.

---

- In short, the two technologies each have their strengths and weaknesses:
- **Client-side** scripts allow the developer to alter pages dynamically, and to respond to user actions immediately rather than having to wait for the server to create a new version of the page. However, there are security and **cross-browser compatibility** issues to be aware of, and these are often non-trivial.
- **Server-side** applications allow the developer to keep her code secure and secret, thus allowing for more powerful applications to be created. In addition, since the server running the code is always a known quantity, applications that run successfully in one browser will run successfully in all browsers. However, despite all this power, there is no direct way for a **server-side** application to alter a page without having to force the **client-side** to load another page. This makes it completely impractical for things like drop-down menus, pre-submission form checking, timers, warning alerts and so forth.

# 3 About JavaScript

## Key Points

- **JavaScript** is an interpreted, client-side, event-based, object-oriented scripting language that you can use to add dynamic interactivity to your web pages.
- **JavaScript** scripts are written in plain text, like HTML, XML, Java, PHP and just about any other modern computer code. In this code, we will use **Windows NotePad** to create and edit our **JavaScript** code, but there are a large number of alternatives available. **NotePad** is chosen to demonstrate **JavaScript's** immediacy and simplicity.
- You can use **JavaScript** to achieve any of the following:

  Create special effects with images that give the impression that a button is either highlighted or depressed whenever the mouse pointer is hovered over it.

  Validate information that users enter into your web forms

  Open pages in new windows, and customise the appearance of those new windows.

  Detect the capabilities of the user's browser and alter your page's content appropriately.

  Create custom pages "on the fly" without the need for a server-side language like PHP.

And much more…

---

- **JavaScript** is *not* **Java**, though if you come from a Java background, you will notice that both languages look similar when written. **Java** is a full featured and comprehensive programming language similar to C or C++, and although **JavaScript** can interact with **Java** web applications, the two should not be confused.
- Different **web browsers** will run your **JavaScript** in different, sometimes incompatible ways. In order to work around this, it is often necessary to use **JavaScript** itself to detect the capabilities of the browser in which it finds itself, and alter its operation depending on the result.
- To revisit the original definition in this chapter, note the following points:

  **Interpreted** refers to the fact that **JavaScript** code is executed (acted on) as it is loaded into the browser. This is a change of pace from **compiled** languages like Java, which check your program thoroughly before running a single line of code, and can have many implications that can catch you out if you are from a non-interpreted programming background.

  **Client-side** has been defined already in the previous chapter.

  **Event-based** refers to **JavaScript's** ability to run certain bits of code only when a specified **event** occurs. An event could be the page being loaded, a form being submitted, a link being clicked, or an image being pointed at by a mouse pointer.

  **Object-oriented** signals that **JavaScript's** power to exert control over an HTML page is based on manipulating **objects** within that page.

If you are familiar with **object-oriented programming**, you will be aware of some of the power that this can bring to the coding environment.

---

- One final note: While **JavaScript** is a programming language, HTML (the language of the World Wide Web) is *not*. HTML is a **Markup Language**, which means that it can be used to mark areas of a document as having special characteristics like headers, paragraphs, images, forms and so on, but it cannot perform any logical processing on its own. So while **JavaScript** is often written alongside HTML, the rules of one do not necessarily have any bearing on the other.

# 4 A Tour of JavaScript

## Key Points

- Let's start with a quick tour of the major features of **JavaScript**. This chapter is intended to be a showcase of what **JavaScript** can do, not an in depth investigation into the deeper concepts, so don't worry too much if you get lost or don't understand the code you're typing in!

## Project

- Our **JavaScript** is all going to be written using **NotePad**. Open **NotePad** and save the resulting empty document in your user drive as `chapter_4.html`.

- Begin by creating a basic HTML page in your blank document. It doesn't have to be anything fancy – the following will be more than sufficient:

```
<html>
<head>
   <title>Chapter 4: A Tour of ↵
  JavaScript</title>
</head>

<body>

<h1>A Tour of JavaScript</h1>

</body>
</html>
```

/ / As a convention, when the notes intend that you should enter code all on one line, they will use an arrow as above ↵ *to indicate that you should not take a new line at that point. With HTML, this is rarely important, but with* ***JavaScript****, a new line in the wrong place can stop your code from working.*

---

- Save your new webpage, and view it in your web browser. For the moment, use **Internet Explorer** to view this page. To do this, find your saved file on your user drive, and double-click on it. This will open the file in **Internet Explorer** by default, and let you see the header you've just created.

- So far, we haven't done anything beyond the scope of HTML. Let's add some **JavaScript** to the page.

- There are (generally speaking) **three** places in a web page where we can add **JavaScript**. The first of these is between a new set of HTML tags. These `script` tags take the following form:

```
<script language="JavaScript" ↵
  type="text/JavaScript">
... code ...
</script>
```

- The `script` element above can be placed virtually anywhere you could place any element in an HTML page – in other words, in either the `head` element or the `body` element. It is most commonly placed in the former, though this is usually so that all your code can be easily found on the page.

- Note too that there is no arbitrary limit on the number of `script` elements that can be contained in an HTML page. There is nothing stopping you from having a hundred of these dotted around your pages, except perhaps prudence.

  Let's add our opening and closing script tags to the head element of the page, like so:

```
<html>
<head>
   <title> ... </title>
```

```
  <script language="JavaScript" ↵
 type="text/JavaScript">
  </script>
</head>
```

…

Save the file, and then try refreshing your page in the browser window. Note that nothing has happened. This is what we expected – all we have done so far is to set up an area of the page to *hold* our **JavaScript**.

Go back to **NotePad** and enter the following text between the opening and closing **`script`** tags:

```
window.alert("Hello world!");
```

Save your changes, and again refresh your page in the browser window. Welcome to the world of **JavaScript**!

Go back to notepad and remove the **`window.alert`** line you just added. Now add the following, slightly more complex code:

```
if ( confirm("Go to
   Google?") ) {
   document.location = ↵
"http://www.google.com/";
}
```

Again, save your changes and refresh the page. For those with an eye to future chapters, this is an example of a **conditional** statement, where we ask **JavaScript** to check the **condition** of something (in this case, our response to a question) and then to alter its behaviour based on what it finds.

Now, both of these bits of **JavaScript** have run uncontrollably when the page has loaded into the browser. In most cases, we will want to have more control over when our **JavaScript** does what we ask it to.

This control is the domain of **events**. In a browser, every element of an HTML document has associated with it a number of **events** that can happen to it.

Links can be **click**ed, forms can be **submit**ted, pages can be **load**ed and so on.

Modify the previous lines of JavaScript in your **script** element to match the following:

```
function go_to_google() {
  if ( confirm("Go to
    Google?") ) {
    document.location = ↵
"http://www.google.com/";
  }
}
```

---

Be careful with your brackets here!

Save and refresh, and note that nothing happens this time. This is because we have enclosed the previous action (popping up a question and acting on the response) within a **function**. A **function** is a block of code that is given a name – in this case, the name is `go_to_google()` – and is only run when that name is "called". It can be useful to think of **functions** as magic spells that can be invoked when their name is said.

To invoke this spell, we need to choose an element on the page to trigger it. A natural candidate is a link element, so add the following HTML to the **`body`** section of your page:

```
<p>A quick <a href="#">test</a>.</p>
```

The # link is a common HTML trick that allows us to create a "link to nowhere".

Save and refresh, and check that the link appears on the page, and that it goes nowhere when clicked.

Now, we want to have our page ask us if we want to "Go to Google?" when we click on that link. Here's how

Take the link element, and modify it as follows:

```
<a href="#"
onclick="go_to_google();">test</a>
```

Save and refresh, and then click on the link. This is an example of an **event handler**. When the link is clicked (**`onclick`**), our browser says the "magic words" **`go_to_google()`**, and our **function** is invoked.

For our final trick, add the following code to the **body** section of the page, after the paragraph containing the link:

```
<body>
...
<script language="JavaScript" ↵
  type="text/JavaScript">
document.write("<h2>Here's
  another ↵ header!</h2>");
</script>
```

Note that the line of code should be all on one line!

---

Save the page and refresh the browser. Note that we now have a new line of text on the page – another header! We've used **JavaScript** to create HTML and tell the browser to display it appropriately. In this example, **JavaScript** has done nothing that we couldn't have done with a line of HTML, but in future chapters we will see how we can use this to write the current date and more.

# 5 Objects, Properties and Methods

## Key Points

Generally speaking, **objects** are "things". For example, a piano is an **object**.

**Properties** are terms that can describe and define a particular **object**. Our piano, for example, has a colour, a weight, a height, pedals, a keyboard and a lid.

Note from the above that an object's properties *can be properties themselves*. So we have the case where a piano lid is a property of the piano, but is also an object in its own right, with its own set of properties – for example, the lid has a colour, a length, and even a *state* of either open or closed.

If **objects** are the nouns of a programming language and **properties** are the adjectives, then **methods** are the verbs. **Methods** are actions that can be performed on (or by) a particular object. To continue our piano example, you could play a piano, open its lid, or press the sustain pedal.

Many programming languages have similar ways of referring to objects and their properties or methods. In general, they are *hierarchical*, and an object's relationship with its properties and methods, as well as with other objects, can often be easily seen from the programming notation.

In JavaScript, we use a "dot notation" to represent objects and their properties and methods. For example, we would refer to our piano's colour in the following way:

```
piano.colour;
```

---

If we wanted to instruct JavaScript to play the piano, we could write something as simple as:

```
piano.play();
```

A clear example of object hierarchy could be seen if we decided to open the lid of the piano:

```
piano.lid.open();
```

Or even more so if we wanted to press the sustain pedal of the piano:

```
piano.pedals.sustain.press();
```

Note that in some of the examples above, we have brackets () after each set of words, and in some we don't. This has to do with making sure that JavaScript can understand what we say.

JavaScript works with objects throughout its existence in a web browser. All HTML elements on a page can be described as objects, properties or methods. We have already seen a few of these objects in our previous introductory chapter:

```
document.write(...);
document.location;
```

In these examples, **`document`** is an object, while **`write`** is a method and **`location`** is a property.

In these lines, we see a clue about the use of brackets in these statements. We use brackets to signify to JavaScript that we are talking about an object's **method**, and not a property of the same name.

Brackets also allow us to pass certain extra information to an object's method. In the above example, to write the text "Hello world!" to a web page document, we would write the following JavaScript:

```
document.write("Hello World");
```

Each method can do different things depending on what is put in the brackets (or "passed to the method as an argument", to use the technical term). Indeed, many methods can take multiple "arguments" to modify its behaviour. Multiple arguments are separated by a comma (,).

---

23 A JavaScript instruction like those shown here is referred to as a JavaScript **statement**. All statements should end in a single semi-colon (;). JavaScript will often ignore missed semi-colons at the end of lines, and insert the semi-colon for you. However, this can cause some unexpected results. Consider the following:

```
document.write("<h1>
               Hello World!
            </h1>");
```

In many other languages, this would be acceptable. However, JavaScript will often interpret something like this as the following:

```
document.write("<h1>;
Hello World!;
</h1>");
```

This interpretation will generate an error, as JavaScript will complain if you end a statement without ensuring that any terms between quotes have matching pairs of quotes. In this example, the first line's "statement" is cut short, and JavaScript will fall over.

For this reason, it is recommended that all your statements should end with semi-colons.

# 6 Assigning Values to Properties

## Key Points

While objects and methods allow us to **do** things on a page, such as alter the content or pop up dialogue boxes to interact with the user, in many cases we will want to alter the value of one of an object's properties directly. These cases are akin to painting our piano green.

Given our discussion on methods so far, we might expect to be able to alter our object's properties by using a method – for example, the following would seem logical:

```
piano.paint("green");
```

In many cases, that is exactly what we will do. However, there are two drawbacks here. The first is that, within this course, the majority of objects that we discover are built into and defined by our browser. If we rely on using a method to alter an object's property, we are also relying on the fact that the method exists in the first place.

A much more direct way to solve this problem is to access the object's properties directly. For example:

```
piano.colour =   "green";
```

Here we are no longer using a method to perform an action, we are using what is known as an **operator**. In this case, the operator has the symbol "=", and is known as the **assignment operator**.

Within JavaScript, we can use this operator to great effectiveness. For example, we could alter the title element of a document (the text that is displayed in the top bar of the browser's window) dynamically. This could be done when a user clicked on a part of the page using an event handler (more later on this), or could be set to automatically update each minute to show the current time in the page title. The code we would use for this task is simple:

```
document.title = "a new title";
```

There are many assignment operators in JavaScript. Some of the more common are shown in the table below:

| Assignment | Function |
|---|---|
| x = y | Sets the value of x to y |
| x += y | Sets the value of x to x+y |
| x -= y | Sets the value of x to x-y |
| x *=y | Sets the value of x to x times y |
| x /=y | Sets the value of x to x divided by y |

Not all assignment operators work with all types of values. But the addition assignment operator works with both numbers and text. When dealing with numbers, the result will be the sum of the two numbers. When dealing with text (technically called **strings**), the result will be the **concatenation** of the two strings:

```
document.title += "!";
```

will cause the symbol “!” to be appended to the end of the current document title.

## Project

Open your previous project file, and save it under the name **`chapter_6.html`**.

Remove any existing JavaScript from your script tags, but leave the tags in place ready for some new JavaScript.

---

Use your text editor to change the value of the title element of the page as follows, then load your page into a browser and view the result:

```
<title>With a little help from</title>
```

Now, add a statement to our script element to add the following text to the end of the current title:

```
"ROBERT PETERSON!";
```

Reload the page in your browser and note the title bar of the window.

If the display looks odd, consider your use of spaces…

All we have so far is an example that does nothing more than HTML could manage. Let's introduce a new method of the **window** object to help us to add a little more dynamism and interaction to the script. Change the value of the title tag as follows:

```
<title>Chapter 6: Assigning
Values to Properties</title>
```

Now, remove your previous JavaScript statement and insert the following:

```
document.title = ↵
  window.prompt("Your
  title?", "");
```

Reload your page and consider the result.

We have come across the **window** object before. Our demonstration of the **alert** method in chapter 4 could have been more properly written as:

```
window.alert("message");
```

In many cases, we can omit certain parts of our object/property/method hierarchy when writing our code. We will discuss this again later.

---

To understand what is going on with our **prompt** method, we can write down a method **prototype**. This is a way of describing a method's arguments in such a way that their effect on the method is more self explanatory. A prototype for the prompt method of the window object might look like the following:

```
window.prompt( message, default_response
);
```

So, we can see that the first argument defines the text that appears as the question in the prompt dialogue box. The second argument is a little less clear. Try your code with different values and see what difference your changes make.

Finally, we note that this prompt method somehow takes the information typed into the box and passes it to our JavaScript assignment. Say someone typed "Hello World" into the box. It would have been as if our assignment had actually been:

```
document.title = "Hello World";
```

When this sort of passing of values occurs, it is said that the method has **returned** the value passed. In this case, we would say that "the prompt method has returned the value 'Hello World'", or that "the return value of the prompt method was 'Hello World'".

Return values will become very important when we deal with event handlers later on.

# 7 About Comments

## Key Points

Repeat after me : Comments are important. Comments are **important**. **Comments are important**.

Adding comments to your code is always good practice. As the complexity of your scripts grows, comments help you (and others) understand their structure when you come to view the code at a later date.

A lot of code created quickly is said to be "write only" code, as it suffers from an inherent lack of structure or commenting. Debugging such code, or reusing it months later, becomes maddeningly impossible as you try to remember what a certain line was supposed to do, or why using certain values seems to stop your code from working.

Comments are completely ignored by JavaScript and have no effect on the speed at which your scripts run, provided they are properly formed.

Comments *can* slow the loading of your page, however – many coders keep a "development" copy of their code fully commented for editing, and remove all comments from their code when they finally publish it.

There are two types of comment in JavaScript – single line comments, and multi-line comments.

Single line comments begin with two forward-slash characters (//), and end with a new line:

```
   this is a comment

alert("hello"); // so

is this
```

---

Single line comments in JavaScript can also use the HTML comment format that you may be familiar with:

```
<!-- this is a comment

alert("hello");
```

Note two things: firstly, this use of the HTML comment format **does not** require a closing **-->** tag. Secondly, this is only a one line comment, unlike its use in HTML, which comments all lines until the closing comment tag.

You can add multiple-line comments by enclosing the comment block between /* and */. For example:

```
/* all of this text is going to be
ignored by JavaScript. This allows
us to write larger comments
without worrying about having to
individually "comment out" each
line */

alert("Hello World");

/* a one line, "mult-line" comment */
```

As well as adding narrative to your script, you can use comments to remove code from your pages without having to delete the code. For example:

```
  this was the old message
  alert("Hello World");
  and this is the new message
alert("Hello everyone!");
```

This can be very useful if you are trying to track down an error in your code – you can "comment out" each suspect line in turn until you manage to get your code working again.

**Project**

Open your previous project file, and save it under the name **`chapter_7.html`**.

Add the single line comment

**`This is my first comment`**

to the beginning of your script.

---

Add a multi-line comment to your script, replacing your previous single line comment. The multi-line comment should describe what your script does at present.

# 8 Hiding Scripts from Older Browsers

## Key Points

Very old browsers don't understand JavaScript. There are very few such browsers in use today, but two factors force us to continue to consider environments that may not be able to cope with our JavaScript code.

Firstly, all modern browsers allow users to control whether JavaScript code will be run. In many cases, users will not have any say over their company policy, and may not even know that their work machine has had JavaScript disabled.

Secondly, not all of your visitors will be using browsers that can make any use of JavaScript. Braille displays, screen readers and other non-visual browsers have little use for many JavaScript tricks. In addition, search engines like Google will ignore any JavaScript you use on your pages, potentially hiding important content and causing your pages to remain un-indexed.

Browsers that don't support JavaScript are supposed to ignore anything between the opening and closing script tags. However, many break this rule and will attempt to render your code as HTML, with potentially embarrassing consequences.

However, we can use the fact that `<!--` denotes a single line comment in JavaScript but a multi-line comment in HTML to ensure that our code is seen by a JavaScript-savvy browser, but ignored as commented-out HTML by anything else:

```
<script>
<!-- hide   from older browsers

... your code

  stop hiding
code --> </script>
```

This prevents older browsers from displaying the code, but what if we want to replace this with some comment. For example, let's say we had a bit of code that displayed the time of day and greeted our user by name. Without JavaScript and using the method above, there would simply be a blank on the page where the greeting should have been.

We can use the <noscript> tag to cause our code to "fail gracefully" where JavaScript has been disabled or is unavailable. The contents of this element will be ignored where JavaScript is understood, and displayed anywhere else. For example:

```
<noscript>
   <h1>Welcome to our site!</h1>
</noscript>

<script>
<!-- hide   from older browsers

... code to customise header

  stop hiding
code --> </script>
```

### Project

Open your previous project file, and save it under the name

**chapter_8.html**.

Add two lines to your code to ensure that it will not confuse older browsers or browsers where the user has disabled JavaScript.

---

Add a noscript element to explain what your JavaScript does. It is generally considered “bad form” to instruct your user to “upgrade to a better browser”, as this can insult many people who use assistive devices – consider this form of advice to be similar to the advice that tells a blind person “to get some glasses”.

Instead where possible you should use the noscript element to provide content that adequately replaces the scripted content with a suitable replacement. For example, if you use your JavaScript to build a navigation panel on your page, the noscript element should contain a plain HTML list that does the same job.

# 9 Automatically Redirecting the User

## Key Points

We have already briefly seen the use of browser redirection in chapter 4.

To formulate the idea more completely, in order to redirect the user to a different page, you set the **location** property of the **document** objects.

As we saw in chapter 6, we can use the assignment operator here. For example:

```
document.location =
"http://www.bbc.co.uk/";
document.location =
"chapter_4.html";
```

## Project

Open your previous project file, and save it under the name **`chapter_9_redirect.html`**.

Save another copy of the file, this time called **`chapter_9.html`**.

Make sure both files are saved in the same folder, and that you have **`chapter_9.html`** open in your editor.

Remove all script from between the script tags, except for your browser hiding lines. Make sure that the script tags are still in the head section of the page.

Now, add a single statement to this script that will automatically redirect the user to the page

**chapter_9_redirect.html** as soon as the page is loaded into a browser.

---

Finally, add a header tag to the body section of the page containing the text "You can't see me!".

Close this page, don't check it in a browser yet, and open the page **`chapter_9_redirect.html`** in your editor.

Remove all JavaScript from this page (including your script tags) and ensure that only HTML remains on the page.

Add a header tag to the body section of the page containing the text "But you can see ME!".

Save this page, and load the page **`chapter_9.html`** into your browser.

Experiment with various positions for the script tags on **`chapter_9.html`** to see if you can make the header appear before the redirection.

## 10 Alert, Prompt and Confirm

### Key Points

So far, we have seen brief examples of **alert**, **prompt** and **confirm** dialogue boxes to request a response from the user, and to pause all code in the background until the request is satisfied.

All of these boxes are the result of methods of the **window** object. This object is the highest level object that JavaScript can deal with in a browser. As such, all other objects on a page (with a few exceptions) are actually properties of the window object.

Because of this ubiquity, its presence is assumed even if it is omitted. Thus, where we technically *should* write:

```
window.document.write("…");
```

it is equally valid to write:

```
document.write("…");
```

as we have been doing.

Similarly, instead of writing:

```
window.alert("…");
```

we can happily write:

```
alert("…");
```

The prototypes of the three methods are:

```
window.alert( message );
window.confirm( message );
window.prompt( message, default_response
);
```

Alert will always return a value of "true" when it is cleared by clicking "ok".

Confirm will return either "true" or "false" depending on the response chosen to clear the box.

Prompt will return either the value typed in, "null" if nothing is typed in, and "false" if the box is cancelled.

### Project

Open your previous project file, and save it under the name **chapter_10.html**.

Clear the previous redirection code, and ensure that the script tags have been returned to the head section of the document.

Add a new statement to the script on the page that will display the following message before the rest of the page is shown:

```
Welcome to my website! Click OK to
continue.
```

Check your page in your browser.

We will use **alert**, **confirm**, and **prompt** throughout this course. Take a moment to try each of them in turn on this page, each time stopping to review your changes.

Use the write method of the **document** object to check the return values of each method. For example:

```
document.write(alert("hello world"));
```

Make sure that you place this particular snippet of code in script tags within the body area of the page, as we are generating text output to be rendered by the browser. Also, note the use (or not) of quotes here. More next chapter!

---

# 11 Variables and Operators

## Key Points

We have been introduced to the concepts of **objects** and their various **properties** and **methods**. These inter-related concepts allow any web page to be broken down into little snippets of information or **data**, which can then be accessed by JavaScript and, in many cases, changed.

However, what if we want to create our own storage space for information that doesn't necessarily have a page-based counterpart? For example, what if we wanted to store the previous value of a document's title property before changing it, so it could be retrieved later, or if we wished to store the date time that the page was loaded into the browser for reproduction in several places on the page, and didn't want to have to recalculate the time on each occasion?

**Variables** are named containers for **values** within JavaScript. They are similar to object properties in many ways, but differ importantly:

In a practical sense, variables have no "parent" object with which they are associated.

Variables can be created ("declared") by you as a developer, and can be given any arbitrary name (within certain rules) – object properties, however, are restricted by the definition of the parent object. It would make no sense, for example, for our piano object in the previous chapters to have a propeller property!

Variable name rules are straightforward – no spaces, names must start with a letter. Examples of valid variable names are:

**BrowserNa**
**me**
**page_name**
**Message1**
**MESSAGE1**

In many browsers, JavaScript is **case-sensitive**, which means that the last two variables in the example above are **distinct variables**. It is a good idea to pick a particular naming style for your variables, and to stick to it within your projects.

At the simplest level, variables can store three different types of value:

**Numbers**
e.g. 1.3324, 3.14159, 100000, -8 etc.

**Strings**
e.g. "ROBERT PETERSON, week 3", "Hello World" etc.

**Boolean**
**Values** e.g.
true, false

Note that strings can contain numbers, but the following variable values are **not** equivalent:

1.234 and "1.234"

The latter is a **string value**. This becomes important. Consider:

1+2 = 3
"a" + "b" = "ab"
"1" + "2" = "12"

Some developers use their own naming convention with variable names to denote the type of value expected to be contained in a given variable. This can often be helpful, but is in no way required by JavaScript (c.f. JavaScript comments)

For example, **strMessage** might indicate a string variable, where **numPageHits** might indicate a numerical value in the variable.

---

**Variable assignment** is accomplished in the same way as object property assignment. When a variable is assigned a value for the first time, it is automatically created. This is different from other programming languages, where a variable must be created explicitly first, before it can be loaded with a value.

Some examples of variable assignment follow:

```
numBrowserVersion = 5.5;
```

```
numTotal += 33;
```

```
Message = "Hello!";
Message = "Goodbye";
Message = 3;
```

Note that the last three examples show that variable values can be altered after their initial assignment, and also that the type of value stored in a variable can be altered in a similar manner.

Once a variable has been created and a value stored within, we will want to be able to access it and perhaps manipulate it. In a similar manner to object properties, we access our variables simply by **calling them:**

```
Message = "Hello World!";
alert(Message);
```

Note that we do not use quote marks around our variable names. The above code is different from:

```
alert("Message");
```

for hopefully obvious reasons.

As well as using variables for storage and access, we can combine and manipulate them using **operators**. For example:

```
a =
12;
b =
13;
c       b; //  i
=  a + c       s  now 25
     += // c
c    a; is      now 37
        "
c =b + Hello!"; // c is now "13 Hello!"
```

Our last example may have been unexpected – we added a number to a string and got a string as a result. JavaScript is smart enough to realise that a number cannot be “added” to a string in a numerical sense, so it converts the number temporarily to a string and performs a **concatenation** of the two strings. Note that **b** remains **13**, not **“13”**.

A table of operators:

| **Operator** | **Function** |
|---|---|
| x + y | Adds x to y if both are numerical – otherwise performs concatenation |
| x – y | Subtracts x from y if both are numerical |
| x * y | Multiplies x and y |
| x / y | Divides x by y |
| x % y | Divides x by y, and returns the remainder |
| -x | Reverses the sign of x |
| x++ | Adds 1 to x AFTER any associated assignment |
| ++x | Adds 1 to x BEFORE any associated assignment |
| x-- | Subtracts 1 from x AFTER any associated |

|  |  |
| --- | --- |
|  | assignment |
| --x | Subtracts 1 from x BEFORE any associated assignment |

## Project

Open your previous project file, and save it under the name **`chapter_11.html`**.

Clear the previous JavaScript code, and ensure that the script tags are contained in the body section of the document.

Assign the message

**`"Welcome to my web site"`**

to a variable called **`greeting`**.

Use this variable to create an alert box containing the message, and also to produce a header on the page without having to retype the message.

Test this page in your browser.

Now, modify your code to create two variables, **`var_1`** and **`var_2`**.

Assign the value "Welcome to" to **`var_1`**, and the value "my web site" to **`var_2`**.

Create a third variable **`var_3`**, and assign to it the value of **`var_1 + var_2`**. Then use an alert box to check the resultant value of **`var_3`**.

Test this page in your browser.

If the text in the alert box does not appear as expected, consider the use of spaces in the variable assignments, and correct the error.

Now, modify your code to produce the same result but without requiring a third variable.

Clear all statements from the current script tags.

Add two statements to the script which assign the **numbers `100`** to one variable and **`5.5`** to another.

Use **`document.write`** to show the effects of each of the operators given in the table on page 34 on the two numerical values.

Substitute one of the numerical values for a text string and repeat the procedure. Note the differences.

# 12 Comparisons

## Key Points

Comparison operators compare two values with each other. Most commonly, they are used to compare the contents of two variables – for example we might want to check if the value of **`var_1`** was numerically greater than that of **`var_2`**.

When you use a comparison operator, the value that is **returned** from the comparison is invariably a **Boolean** value of either **`true`** or **`false`**. For example, consider the following statements:

```
var_1 = 4;
var_2 = 10;

var_3 = var_1 > var_2;
```

In this case, the value of **`var_3`** is false. Note that the **Boolean** value of false is not the same as the text string **`"false"`**:

```
var_4 = false;   // Boolean value
var_5 = "false"; // Text string
```

Common comparison operators are given below:

| Comparison | Function |
|---|---|
| X == y | Returns true if x and y are equivalent, false otherwise |
| X != y | Returns true if x and y are **not** equivalent, |

| | |
|---|---|
| | false otherwise |
| X > y | Returns true if x is numerically greater than<br>y, false otherwise |

| | |
|---|---|
| X >= y | Returns true if x is numerically greater than<br>or equal to y, false otherwise |
| X < y | Returns true if y is numerically greater than<br>x, false otherwise |
| X <= y | Returns true if y is numerically greater than<br>or equal to x, false otherwise |

To reverse the value returned from a comparison, we generally modify the comparison operator with a `!` (a "bang"). Note that in many cases this is not necessary, but can aid comprehension:

```
var_1 !> var_2;
var_1 <= var_2;
```

both of these are equivalent, but one may make more semantic sense in a given context than the other.

### Project

Open your previous project file, and save it under the name **`chapter_12.html`**.

Ensure that your two variables both have numerical values in them and not strings.

Use an alert box to display the result of a comparison of your two variables for each of the comparison operators listed above.

Substitute one of the numerical values for a text string and repeat the procedure. Note the differences.

# 13 Conditionals

## Key Points

Up until now, our JavaScript projects have been unable to alter their behaviour spontaneously. When a page loads with our JavaScript embedded within, it is unable to do anything other than what we expect, time and again.

The only difference we have seen is in the use of a prompt box to alter what is shown on a page. However, the page essentially does the same thing with the text provided, regardless of what text is typed in.

What would be really handy would be to give JavaScript a mechanism to make decisions. For example, if we provided a prompt box asking the visitor for their name, it might be nice to have a list of "known names" that could be greeted differently from any other visitors to the site.

**Conditional statements** give us that ability, and are key to working with JavaScript.

A conditional statement consists of three parts:

A test (often with a comparison operator, or **comparator**) to see **if** a given condition is **true** or **false**.

A block of code that is performed if and only if the condition is **true**.

An optional block of code that is performed if and only if the condition is **false**.

---

- These three parts are represented in JavaScript as follows:

```
if ( conditional_test )
  {
  JavaScript statement;
  JavaScript statement;
  JavaScript statement;
  ...
  }
else
  {
  JavaScript statement;
  JavaScript statement;
  JavaScript statement;
  ...
  }
```

- Everything from the first closing curly bracket (or **brace**) is optional, so the following is also a valid conditional prototype:

```
if ( conditional_test )
  {
  JavaScript statement;
  JavaScript statement;
  JavaScript statement;
  ...
  }
```

- In this case, if the **`conditional_test`** does not return **true**, nothing happens.
- An example of complete conditional statement is as follows:

```
if ( var_1 > var_2 )
  {
  alert("Variable 1 is greater");
  }
else
  {
  alert("Variable 2 is greater");
```

```
}
```

---

- Note that the above condition is not necessarily always correct. Consider the case where **`var_1`** is equal to **`var_2`**. In that case, the above code will produce the message that "Variable 2 is greater", since **`var_1 > var_2`** returns **false**. In this case, we want to add an additional condition to the **`else`** branch of code:

```
if ( var_1 > var_2 )
  {
  alert("Variable 1 is greater");
  }
else
if ( var_1 < var_2 )
  {
  alert("Variable 2 is greater");
  }
```

- In this case, equality will produce no output, as neither of the conditions will return true. For completeness, we could add a final else branch to the statement:

```
if ( var_1 > var_2 )
  {
  alert("Variable 1 is greater");
  }
else
if ( var_1 < var_2 )
  {
  alert("Variable 2 is greater");
  }
else
  {
  alert("The variables are equal");
  }
```

- Note that in this case, we don't have to check for equality in the final branch, as if **`var_1`** is neither greater than nor less than **`var_2`**, then – numerically at least – the two must be equal.

- We can continue adding as many else if statements as required to this stack.

---

- If you only have one statement following your conditional test, the braces may be omitted:

```
if ( var_1 > var_2 )
  alert("Variable 2 is greater");
```

  However, if you later want to add further statements to this conditional branch, you will have to add braces around the block, and this can lead to confusion. It is recommended that you use braces to enclose all blocks of conditional code.

- Consider the following block of code:

```
if ( var_1 > 4 )
  {
  var_2 = var_1;
  }
else
  {
  var_2 = 4;
  }
```

- This code is rather long, but achieves comparatively little – **var_2** is equal to **var_1** or **4**, whichever is greater.

- A more compact way of writing this could be:

```
var_2 = 4;
if ( var_1 > var_2 )
  {
  var_2 = var_1;
  }
```

- However, an even more compact way of writing this could be to use the **ternary operator**:

```
var_2 = (var_1 > 4) ? var_1 : 4;
```

- In the above statement, the conditional is evaluated and, if true, the value returned is the value between **?**

and : symbols, or if false, it is the value between the : and ; symbols.

### Project

- Open your previous project file, and save it under the name **`chapter_13.html`**.
- Clear all JavaScript code from your script tags.
- Create two variables and assign numerical values to them.

- Use a conditional statement to show alert boxes declaring which variable is the greater of the two.
- Consider the following code:

```
var_3 = (var_1 > var_2);
```

- Use this code in your script to simplify your conditional checking code.
- Now, use a prompt box to ask your visitor their name. Assign this name to **`var_3`**.
- Check to see if the name typed in is your own name. If it is, use **`document.write`** to display a personalised greeting on the page. Otherwise, display a generic greeting.
- Use multiple else if branches to check the typed name against the names of some of your friends. Create personalised messages for all of them.
- There may be a way to simplify your conditional greeting code to use only one **`document.write`** statement. See if you can figure out how. Hint – how might you use a variable called **`greeting`**?

### Project 2

- In many cases, the brevity of your conditional statements will rely on your ability to formulate the right "questions" to consider when performing your tests. Try to make your solution to the following problem as concise as possible.
- Clear all of your current code from the script tags.
- Ensure that your script tags are currently situated in the body section of the page.

- Create a variable called **exam_result** and store a numerical value of between **0** and **100** in it.

---

- Use an **`if`** statement and multiple **`else if`** statements to check the value of this variable against the following exam grading scheme, and print out the appropriate message to the page:

| Exam Result | Result Message |
| --- | --- |
| 90 or more | Excellent. Pass with Distinction. |
| Between 70 and 89 | Well Done. Pass with Honours |
| Between 55 and 69 | Just passed. |
| 54 or below | Failed. Do better next time. |

- Test your result in your browser. Vary the value of **`exam_result`** and check the value shown in the browser. For extra practise, try to use a prompt box to make changes to your **`exam_result`** variable as easy to achieve as possible.

# 14 Looping

## Key Points

- The letters **i**, **j** and **k** are traditionally used by programmers to name variables that are used as counters. For example, at different stages of the program, **i** may contain the numbers 1, 2, 3 etc.

- In order to achieve a "counting" effect, you will need to **increment** or **decrement** the value of your counting variable by a set value. Here are some examples:

```
i = i + 1;

i = i - 1;

i = i + 35;

incr = 10
i = i + incr;
```

- To keep things concise, we can use the following shortcuts:

```
i++; // equivalent to i = i + 1;
i--; // equivalent to i = i + 1;
```

- Counting in JavaScript, like many other programming languages, **often begins at zero**.

- In many cases, this makes a lot of sense, as we will see. However, it can often cause confusion. Consider starting at 0 and counting up to 10. In that case, we may have actually counted 11 items:

  - (1)
  - (2)
  - (3)
  - (4)
  - (5)
  - (6)
  - (7)
  - (8)
  - (9)

  10 (11!)

- If you wanted to give an instruction to someone to perform a repetitive action, you might say that you wanted them to continue the action for a certain number of times. If someone were performing an action 300 times, for example, they might do something like the following to ensure that their count was accurate:

- Write the number 1 on a bit of paper.

- After each action, erase the number on the bit of paper and increment it by 1.

- Before each action, check the number on the bit of paper. If it is less than **or equal to** 300, perform the action.

- Alternatively, they might decide to start counting at 0. In this case, the procedure would be identical, but the check before each action would be to make sure that the number was **strictly less than** 300.

- In JavaScript, we say almost the same thing. The following code will display the numbers 1 to 100 on the page:

```
for    ( i = 1; i <= 100; i++ )
  {
  document.write("<p>" + i " </p>");
  }
```

---

- The **for** statement tells the browser that we are about to perform a **loop**. The layout here is very similar to a conditional statement, but in this case we have much more information in the brackets. Where our conditional had one JavaScript statement to describe its action, a **for loop** has three:

- An initialiser – this sets up the initial counting condition, in this case `i = 1`.

- A conditional – this is identical to our conditional statements earlier, and must return **true** or **false**. If it returns **true**, the loop continues, otherwise it exits.

- An incrementer – this defines the action to be performed at the end of each loop. In this case, i is incremented by a value of 1.

- The key difference between a conditional and a for loop is that the condition is constantly being changed and re-evaluated. It is possible to create an infinite loop by making the conditional non-reliant on the count value – for example:

```
for    ( i=0; 5 > 4; i++ )
```

will always perform the script in the braces, and will probably cause errors in the browser.

- Note too that it is very common to start counting at zero in JavaScript. The reason for this is that it is often desirable to count **how many times** an operation has been performed.
Consider the following:

```
for    ( i=1; 1 < 2; i++ )
```

- In this case, the loop will run once, but the value of `i` will be 2, as after the first run, `i` will be incremented to 2, and will then fail the test and so the loop will exit. If we use the following:

```
for    ( i=0; 1 < 1; i++ )
```

Then the loop will run once, and the value of **i** afterwards will be 1, as we might hope.

## Project

- Open your previous project file, and save it under the name **chapter_14.html**.
- Clear all JavaScript code from your script tags.

- Write a series of statements to produce a multiplication table as follows:

## The 12x Multiplication Table

1 × 12 = 12

2 × 12 = 24

3 × 12 = 36

4 × 12 = 48

5 × 12 = 60

6 × 12 = 72

7 × 12 = 84

8 × 12 = 96

9 × 12 = 108

10 × 12 = 120

11 × 12 = 132

12 × 12 = 144

- The following exercise is more of an HTML example, but demonstrates an important facet of using JavaScript (or, indeed, any programming language) to produce well-formatted text.
- Modify your previous code to make your page's content appear in the centre of the page. Put your multiplication table in an HTML table to make sure that the equals signs, multiplication signs and so forth line up in neat columns:

## The 12x Multiplication Table

| | | | | |
|---|---|---|---|---|
| 1 | × | 12 | = | 12 |
| 2 | × | 12 | = | 24 |
| 3 | × | 12 | = | 36 |
| 4 | × | 12 | = | 48 |
| 5 | × | 12 | = | 60 |
| 6 | × | 12 | = | 72 |
| 7 | × | 12 | = | 84 |
| 8 | × | 12 | = | 96 |
| 9 | × | 12 | = | 108 |
| 10 | × | 12 | = | 120 |
| 11 | × | 12 | = | 132 |
| 12 | × | 12 | = | 144 |

- As a hint, here is a look at the table cells involved:

## The 12x Multiplication Table

| | | |
|---|---|---|
| 1 | × 12 = | 12 |
| 2 | × 12 = | 24 |
| 3 | × 12 = | 36 |
| 4 | × 12 = | 48 |
| 5 | × 12 = | 60 |
| 6 | × 12 = | 72 |
| 7 | × 12 = | 84 |
| 8 | × 12 = | 96 |
| 9 | × 12 = | 108 |
| 10 | × 12 = | 120 |
| 11 | × 12 = | 132 |
| 12 | × 12 = | 144 |

# 15 Arrays

## Key points

- In many cases, variables will completely satisfy our data storage needs in JavaScript. However, in a large number of cases, we may wish to "group" variables into a collection of related items.
- Take, for example, days of the week. In each day we perform a number of tasks, so we could want to record each task as a separate item under a group called, say, Monday's Tasks.
- In JavaScript, to achieve this we would store each task in a separate variable, and then group those variables together into an **array**.
- An **array** is a special type of JavaScript object that can store multiple data values – unlike a variable, which can only store one data value at a time.
- It could be helpful to think of an array as a row of mail boxes in an office, just as you might think of a variable as a single, solitary mail box.
- The boxes in an array are numbered upwards, starting at box number 0 – note that counting begins at 0 here, just as we discussed in the previous chapter. The number assigned to each box is known as its **index**.

- In order to use an array in JavaScript, you must first create it. There are a number of ways to create arrays in JavaScript. The simplest follows:

  ```
  arrDays = new Array();
  ```

  This statement creates a new, empty array called arrDays. We can call arrays just like we can variables, but with a few minor adjustments.

- If you already know how many elements a given array will have, you can declare this explicitly:

  ```
  arrDays = new Array(7);
  ```

  This modification creates an array with 7 empty boxes. However, arrays will expand and contract to the required size in JavaScript, so the cases where you will need to state the size of the array are rare.

- More useful, however, is the ability to "fill" the boxes of an array when you create it. For example:

  ```
  arrDays = new Array("Monday","Tuesday");
  ```

  We now have an array with two elements. The first (element 0) has a value of "Monday", while the second (element 1) has a value of "Tuesday". We need not restrict ourselves to string values in arrays – Boolean, numerical and string values are allowed, as in arrays. It is even possible to assign other arrays to array elements – more on this later.

- The most often-used way of creating an array is to use "square bracket" notation. Square brackets play a large role in the use of arrays, so this is often the easiest method to remember:

  ```
  arrDays = ["Monday","Tuesday"];
  ```

  This is identical to the previous example.

- To access an array's elements, we first call the array's name, and then specify the number of the element in square brackets, like so:

  ```
  alert(arrDays[0]);
  ```

  Note the lack of quotes around the 0 here. This line of code is equivalent to:

  ```
  alert("Monday");
  ```

  assuming the array is defined as in the previous examples.

- Not only can we access the value of an array element using this notation, but we can also **assign** the value as well:

  ```
  arrDays[2] = "Tuesday";
  arrDays[3] = "Wednesday";
  ```

- If you wish to add an element to an array **without** knowing the index of the last element, you can use the following code:

  ```
  arrDays[] = "some other day";
  ```

- As we will see, arrays are actually just special JavaScript objects, and have properties and methods associated with them. The most important property that every array has is its length property:

  how_many_days = arrDays.length;

- As well as properties, arrays have very useful methods. If you wished to sort your array alphanumerically, you could use the array's sort method thus:

  arrDays.sort();

  Note that the sort method works on the actual array itself, over-writing the current values. So, if you had an array with each day of the week as an element, calling its sort method would mean that **`arrDays[0]`** was then equal to "Friday", not "Monday".

## Project

- Open your previous project file, and save it under the name **`chapter_15.html`**.

---

- Clear all JavaScript code from your script tags.
- Write a few JavaScript statements that will present the months of the year on the page in alphabetical order. You should use the following technique to achieve this:
- Store the names of the months of the year in an array.
- Use an array method to sort the array elements alphanumerically.
- Use a **for** loop to *iterate* through each array element in turn, and print the value of the element to the screen (hint, consider the use of **`array[i]`**, where **`i`** is the for loop's counter).
- The above method (the use of a **for** loop to iterate through a series of array elements) is one of the first common programming techniques we have discussed in this course. Its usefulness cannot be overstated, as it allows us to perform repetitive tasks on a series of related elements *without necessarily knowing what those elements might be when we wrote the code.* It can be applied to form elements, cookies, page elements, pages, windows, and just about any other collection of object that you might wish to manipulate with JavaScript.
- To reinforce this generalism, if you have not used the **`array.length`** value in your loop, consider its use now. To prove that you have created a more generic loop, try the code with an array of days instead of an array of months, and see if you have to change any of the looping code.

## 16 Associative & Objective Arrays

### Key Points

- We have already seen that we can access array elements by their index:

```
arrDays = ["Monday", "Tuesday"];

• print "Monday" to
the page
document.write(arrDays
[0]);
```

- However, it might be more useful to be able to **name** our array elements. By default, an array will be created as a **numeric** array. We can also create an **associative** array:

```
arrDays = new Array();

arrDays["Monday"] = "Go to the
dentist"; arrDays["Tuesday"] =
"Attend JavaScript class";
arrDays["Wednesday"] = "JavaScript
homework";

• remind you of
Wednesday's task
alert(arrDays["Wednesday"
]);
```

- This looks a lot like our previous discussion of objects and properties. In fact, since an array *is* actually an object, we can access its elements as though they were properties:

```
// remind you of
Wednesday's task
alert(arrDays.Wedensday);
```

---

- Note a subtle difference here – in our previous, numeric array examples, the names of the week days were the **values** of our array elements. Here, the names of the week days are the **indexes** of our elements. Avoid the following common error:

```
arrDays = ["Monday","Tuesday"];
arrDays["Monday"] = "Go to work";
```

```
• this is actually
equivalent to arrDays =
new Array();
```

```
arrDays[0] = "Monday";
arrDays[1] = "Tuesday";
arrDays["Monday"] = "Go to work";
```

```
// and arrDays.length is now 3, not 2
```

## Project

- Open your previous project file, and save it under the name `chapter_16.html`.
- Clear all JavaScript code from your script tags.
- Write a new script which creates a new, seven element associative array called Week:
- Use the days of the week as indexes for each element of the array.
- Assign a task to each day of the week as each associative element is created.
- Use a for loop to display a calendar on the page, as follows:

**Monday:** task
**Tuesday:** task

etc…

- Modify your code to use a prompt box to ask the visitor to choose a day, and display on the page the task allotted to that day.

---

## 17 Two Dimensional Arrays

### Key Points

- Referring back to our mailbox analogy, where our array could be pictured as a row of mailboxes, each with its own contents and label, a two dimensional array can be thought of as a series of these rows of mailboxes, stacked on top of each other.
- In reality, a **two dimensional array** is simply an array in which each element is itself an array. Each "sub array" of a two dimensional array can be of a different length – in other words, the two dimensional array doesn't have to be "square".
- You can access the contents of each sub array by using two pairs of square brackets instead of just one. An example will illustrate this best:

```
array_1 = ["element", "element 2"];
array_2 = ["another element", 2, 98,
true];

array_3 = [array_1, array_2];

alert(array_3[1][3]);// displays "98"
```

- While you can't mix numerical and string indexing systems in a single array (i.e. an array cannot be both numerical *and* associative), you can have both associative and numerical arrays in two dimensional arrays. For example, consider the above recast as follows:

```
array_3 = new Array();
```

```
array_3["firstArray"] = array_1;
array_3["secondArray"] = array_2;

alert(array_3["secondArray"][3]);
   //displays "98" again
```

---

- Similarly, we can happily use our "objective" notation for associative arrays:

```
alert(array_3.secondArray[3]);
  //displays "98" yet again
```

### Project

- Open your previous project file, and save it under the name **`chapter_17.html`**.
- Building on your previous project, create a number of new, seven element associative arrays to represent 4 separate weeks.
- Combine these 4 weeks into a four element array to represent a month.
- Modify your previous code to take a week number and print out all that week's activities to the page.
- Modify one of your week arrays to consist not of single elements, but of arrays of hours from 8am to 5pm. This then represents a *three dimensional array*. We can extend arrays to be ***n-dimensional***, where ***n*** is more or less arbitrary.
- Finally, alter your code to prompt the user for **three** values – a week, a day and an hour. Store these values in three separate variables, and use those variables to display the requested task, or else to display an error message if a task cannot be found.

# 18 String Manipulation

## Key Points

- Throughout your use of JavaScript in a production environment, you will often use it to read values from variables, and alter a behaviour based on what it finds.
- We have already seen some basic string reading in the section on comparisons where we test for equality. However, this all-or-nothing approach is often not subtle enough for our purposes.
- Take the case where we want to check a user's name against a list of known users. If the user enters their name as "Karen", for example, that will be fine if **and only if** they spell the name precisely as we have it recorded, including capitalisation etc. If the user decides to type in her full name, say "Karen Aaronofsky", the code will not recognise her.
- In this case, we want to see if the text "Karen" appears at all in the string. We call this **substring searching**, and it can be incredibly useful.
- One of the simplest substring searches is done by using the **indexOf** method. Every string-type variable has this method associated with it. Consider this code:

  ```
  var_1 = "Karen Aaronofsky";
  var_2 = var_1.indexOf("Karen");
  ```

  In this case, the value of **var_2** will be 0 – remembering that JavaScript begins counting at 0!

- If we were to search for a surname here:

  ```
  var_1 = "Karen Aaronofsky";
  var_2 = var_1.indexOf("Aaronofsky");
  ```

  **var_2** will have a value of 6.

- Finally, if the search were to "fail", so say we searched for the name "Anisa" as a substring, the value of **var_2** would then be -1.

- Note that this is more flexible, but still presents an issue if the user forgets to capitalise any of the substrings that we are searching for – in JavaScript, "Karen" does not equal "karen".

- In order to get around this, we might want to ensure that capitalisation is not taken into account. A simple way to achieve this is to force strings into lowercase before the check is performed:

  ```
  real_name = "Karen";
  name = prompt("Your name?","");

  real_name =
  real_name.toLowerCase();
  try_name =
  try_name.toLowerCase();

  if ( try_name.indexOf(real_name) > -1 )
  {
    alert("Hello Karen!");
  }
  else
  {
   • note we use the original,
   • non-lower-cased
   name here
   alert("Welcome " +
   name);
  }
  ```

- There are a number of string methods we can use to perform “value checks” on strings. A few are printed in the following table:

| Method | Behaviour |
| --- | --- |
| String.indexOf(“str”) | Returns the numerical position of the first character of the substring “str” in the String |
| String.charAt(x) | Returns the character at position x in the string – the opposite of indexOf |

---

| | |
|---|---|
| String.toLowerCase() | Returns a copy of the string with all capital letters replaced by their lowercase counterparts |
| String.toUpperCase() | Returns a copy of the string with all lowercase letters replaced by their capital counterparts |
| String.match(/exp/) | Returns true or false based on a **regular expression** search of the string |

- The final method here deserves some comment. What is a **regular expression**?
- A **regular expression** is a standard way of writing down a "pattern" of characters that is easily recognisable. For example, consider a typical email address:

  jonathan@relativesanity.com

- An email address follows a "pattern" which makes it instantly recognisable as an email address to a human. Wouldn't it be handy if we could define that pattern in JavaScript for a browser to use? Regular expressions allow us to do just that.
- Let's look at our email address again. We can break it down to a "prototype" email address as follows:

  [some letters]@[some more letters].[a few more letters]

- Of course, it's slightly more complex than that – there are some characters which aren't allowed to be in certain parts of the email address (no spaces, for example), but this lets you see the idea of breaking this string up into required “chunks”.

- Now, to convert this to a regular expression. Just as we use quote marks to denote (or “delimit”) string values in JavaScript, to signify a regular expression, we use forward slashes: /. Our email address regular expression might look like this:

  ```
  /^.+@.+\..+$/
  ```

- This warrants some discussion. Let’s look at this a character at a time:
- / denotes the start of the regular expression

---

- ^ denotes that we want this regular expression to be found at the very beginning of the string we are searching.
- **.+** the dot symbol is used to stand in for **any** character. The plus signifies we want to find *at least one* of those. So this is equivalent to our plain-English phrase [some letters].
- **@** this is simply a character – it has no special meaning other than to say we want to find an @ character after at least one character from the beginning of the string.
- **.+** the same as before – at least one more character after the @.
- **\\.** This is interesting. We know that the dot symbol has a special meaning in a regular expression – it means "match any character". However, here we want to find an **actual dot**. Unlike @, which has no special meaning, we have to tell JavaScript to ignore the dots special meaning. We do this by preceding it with a backslash, which tells JavaScript to treat the character immediately following it as though it has no special meaning. This is a convention you will come across many times while programming. The net result here is that we want to match a dot after a series of characters.
- **.+** and again, at least one more character after the dot.
- **$** this is the mirror of the ^ at the beginning – this matches the end of the tested string.
- / tells JavaScript we are at the end of the regular expression.
- Phew! Lots to consider here. Regular expressions are an arcane art at the best of times, so don't worry too much if the above code is indecipherable. The important thing to realise at the moment is that we can perform some quite sophisticated pattern

recognition in JavaScript without having to resort to checking each individual character of a string multiple times.

---

- The following code checks a variable to see if it looks like an email address:

```
var_1 = prompt("Your email?", "");

if ( var_1.match(/^.+@.+\..+$/) )
{
  alert("valid email address");
}
else
{
  alert("are you sure?");
}
```

- There are a few problems with this code at the moment – for example, it will pass the string "-@-.-" quite happily, which is clearly wrong. We will look at ways around this later on in the course.

## Project

- Open your previous project file, and save it under the name **chapter_18.html**.
- Clear all JavaScript code from your script tags.
- Use a prompt box to capture some user input to a variable called **check_string**.
- Use a document.write statement to output the results of each of the various string methods when applied to the user input.
- Check the user input to see if it's an email address, and alter your output accordingly to either "That's an email address" or "That doesn't look like an email address to me!"
- In the latter case, output the failed string as well so that the user can see their input and modify it next time, if appropriate.

# 19 Using Functions

## Key Points

- A **function** is a named set of JavaScript statements that perform a task and appear inside the standard **<script>** tags. The task can be simple or complex, and the name of the function is up to you, within similar constraints to the naming of variables.
- JavaScript **functions** are declared before they are used. The declaration looks like this:

```
function name_of_function( )
{
  ...your code here...
}
```

- Unlike all the JavaScript instructions we have looked at so far, the code inside a function will not be run until specifically requested. Such a request is called a function **call**.
- Functions can be called from anywhere on the page that JavaScript can live, but must be called *after* the function has been declared. For example, if you declare a function in the body of a document and then call it from the head of the document, you may find that the browser returns an error message. For this reason, most JavaScript programmers define any functions they are going to use between **<script>** tags in the head section of their pages to ensure that they are all defined before they are used.
- Functions are to object methods as variables are to object properties – they are also called in a similar manner. To run the code contained in the

**name_of_function** function above, we would use the following line of code:

```
name_of_function();
```

- Note the parentheses after the function name. This lets JavaScript know that we are dealing with a function and not a variable. The parentheses also allow us to "pass" extra information to the function, which can alter its behaviour. Consider the following function:

```
function greet_user( username )
{
  message = "Hello " + username;
  alert(message);
}
```

- Whenever the function is called, it will greet the user named. How can we pass this information through? Consider:

```
greet_user("Anisa");
```

or

```
var_1 = prompt("Name?", "");
greet_user(var_1);
```

- We should use functions in our code as often as possible. Whenever we perform an action that isn't accomplished by the use of a method or an assignment operator, we should try to build a function that can accomplish the task.

- For example, we can build a function to check email addresses:

```
function check_email( address )
{
  var_1 = false;
  if ( address.match(/^.+@.+\..+$/) )
  {
    var_1 = true;
  }
}
```

- The above function will take a string that is passed to it (often called the function's **argument**), and will alter the value of **`var_1`** depending on what it finds. However, the function is lacking an important ability – the ability to communicate its findings back out to the rest of the script.

---

- We have mentioned **return values** a few times in the notes. Now we see a situation that requires a function to **return** its findings to the rest of the code. Ideally, we'd like to be able to use the above function as follows:

```
if ( check_email(address) )
{
  ...do some email things...
}
```

- In order for this to work, the return value from check_email would have to be a Boolean value. We can arrange this quite simply:

```
function check_email( address )
{
  var_1 = false;
  if ( address.match(/^.+@.+\..+$/) )
  {
    var_1 = true;
  }
  return var_1;
}
```

- Since var_1 is either true or false, the returned value will be Boolean. We can even skip the use of the variable here and be more direct:

```
function check_email( address )
{
  if ( address.match(/^.+@.+\..+$/) )
  {
    return true;
  }
  return false;
}
```

or even better, since address.match() will return a Boolean value of its own:

```
function check_email( address )
```

```
{
  return address.match(/^.+@.+\..+$/);
}
```

- The above function may not seem like a great saving. After all, we are using four lines of code to define a function that performs only one line of code. Compare:

```
function check_email( address )
{
  return address.match(/^.+@.+\..+$);
}
```

```
if ( check_email(address) )
{
  ...do some email things...
}
```

with:

```
if ( address.match(/^.+@.+\..+$/) )
{
  ...do some email things...
}
```

- While the benefits here are not obvious, consider the case where, at some point in the future, you discover a better method of checking for email addresses. In the second case abov, you will have to search your code for each and every instance of that method, and replace it with your new method, which may not be one line of code. In the first case, you will just have to change the underlying function definition, and the "upgrade" will be effective throughout your code without you having to update each occurrence.

### Project

- Open your previous project file, and save it under the name `chapter_19.html`.
- Clear all JavaScript code from your script tags.
- Ensure that you have a script element in the head area of your document, and one in the body area.

- In the head area, define a function called **show_message**. This function should take one argument, called **message**, and should use an alert box to display the contents of the argument.
- In the body area, call the function with various messages as arguments.

---

- Now use a variable in the body area to store the return value of a prompt asking the user for a message. Use this variable as the argument to a single instance of **`show_message`**.
- Define a new function in the head area called **`get_message`**. It should take no argument, but should replicate the function of your prompt in the body area and ask the user for a message via a prompt box.
- Make sure that **`get_message`** **return**s a sensible value. We are aiming to replace our prompt statement in the body area with the following code:

  ```
  message = get_message();
  ```

  so consider what you will have to return to enable this to work.
- Once you are happy with your **`get_message`** definition, try replacing your prompt code in the body area with the statement above.
- To demonstrate the power of functions, change the action of **`show_message`** to write the message to the page without changing any code in the body area of the page.

# 20 Logical Operators

## Key Points

- In our discussion of conditionals, we saw how to check the veracity of a single condition via a comparator:

```
if ( x > some_value )
{
  ...expressions...
}
```

- We have also seen the limitations of such an approach. Let us say we wanted to discover if **x** lay *between* two values, say **val_1** and **val_2**. There are a number of ways we could achieve this. In our example on student grades, we learned that we could use an **if...else** pair to achieve this effect:

```
if ( x > val_1 )
{
  ...do something...
}
else
if ( x > val_2 )
{
  ...do something else...
}
```

- The above code achieves what we want – for the second branch, x must lie between **val_2** and **val_1** (assuming **val_1** is greater than **val_2**, of course). However, it's rather unwieldy, and does not scale elegantly to checking three conditions (say we wanted to check if **x** was an even number as well), or in fact to ten conditions.

- Enter **Logical Operators**. These operators are used to join together conditional checks and return true or false depending on whether **all** or **any** of the checks are true.

---

- In English, we refer to these operators by using the words "AND" and "OR".
- For example, say we wanted to do something each Tuesday at 8pm. We would want to check whether the current day was Tuesday, **and** whether the time was 8pm.
- Another example: Let's say we wanted to do something on the first Tuesday of each month, and also on the 3rd of the month as well. We would have to check whether the current day was the first Tuesday of the month, **or** whether it was the 3rd day of the month.
- Note in the last example, if **both** conditions were true, then we would be on Tuesday the 3rd and would perform the action. In other words, an **or** condition allows for either one, or the other, *or both* conditions to be true.

- In JavaScript, we use the following syntax to check multiple conditions:

  ```
  ( 100 > 10 && 5 < 8 )
  ```

  translates as "if 100 is greater than 10 and 5 is less than 8". In this case, the result is **true**.

  ```
  ( 100 > 200 && 4 < 9 )
  ```

  in this case, the result is **false**. Note here that only the first condition is actually checked. Since **and** requires both comparisons to be true, as soon as it finds a false one it stops checking. This can be useful.

  ```
  ( 100 > 10 || 9 < 8 )
  ```

  translates as "if 100 is greater than 10 or 9 is less than 8". In this case, the result is **true**, since at least one of the conditions is met.

  ```
  ( 100 > 200 || 4 > 9 )
  ```

  in this case, the result is **false** since neither of the comparisons are true. Finally:

  ```
  ( 100 > 200 || 5 < 2 || 3 > 2 )
  ```

  in this case, the result is **true**. Any one of the three being true will provide this result.

- As we can see from the last example, this method of checking *scales* to any number of conditions. We can also mix and match the operators. For example:

  ( ( 100 > 200 && 100 > 300 ) || 100 > 2 )

  in this case, the **and** condition evaluates to **false**, but since either that **or** the last condition has to be true to return **true**, the overall condition returns **true** as 100 is indeed greater than 2.

- This sort of complex logic can take a while to comprehend, and will not form a set part of the course. However, it is useful to be aware of it.

---

## Project

- Open your previous project file, and save it under the name **`chapter_20.html`**.
- Clear all JavaScript code from your script tags.
- Ensure that you have a script element in the head area of your document, and one in the body area.
- Copy the file **`available_plugins.js`** from the network drive (your tutor will demonstrate this), and open it using NotePad's File > Open command.
- Copy and paste the entire contents of **`available_plugins.js`** into your current project file, into the script element in the head area of your page.
- Have a read through the code. Note that it defines a large, two dimensional array. The array has a list of various components that can be present in web browsers (such as Flash or Quicktime)
- Add a function to the head area script element, called **`flash_exists()`**. This function should use a **for loop** to check each of the elements of the **`available_plugins`** array and establish if Flash is present.
- Add a further function to the head area script element, called **`quicktime_exists()`**. This function should also use **a for loop** to check each element of the array, this time returning true if Quicktime is present.
- Finally, add a function to the head area script element called **`both_quicktime _and_flash_exist()`**. This function should call both of the previous functions, store their results in a variable, and produce an alert box containing the message:

- "Both Quicktime and Flash" if both functions returned true; or:
- "One of Quicktime or Flash is missing" if either of the functions return false.
- Call the final function from the body area script element.
- Check your results in your browser.

---

## 21 Using Event Handlers

### Key Points

- So far, our scripts have run as soon as the browser page has loaded. Even when we have used functions to "package" our code, those functions have run as soon as they have been called in the page, or not at all if no call was made. In other words, the only event our scripts have so far responded to has been the event of our page loading into the browser window.
- Most of the time, however, you will want your code to respond specifically to user activities. You will want to define functions, and have them spring into action only when the user does something. Enter **event handlers**.
- Every time a user interacts with the page, the browser tells JavaScript about an "event" happening. That event could be a mouse click, a mouse pointer moving over or out of a given element (such as an image or a paragraph), a user tabbing to a new part of an HTML form, the user leaving the page, the user submitting a form and so on.
- An **event handler** is a bit of JavaScript code that allows us to capture each event as it happens, and respond to it by running some JavaScript code.
- In general, we attach event handlers to specific HTML tags, so a mouse click on one element of the page might be captured by an event handler, but clicking somewhere else might do something completely different, or indeed nothing at all.
- Some common event handlers are in the table below:

| Event Handler | Occurs When… |
|---|---|
| onload | An element is loaded on the page |

| | |
|---|---|
| onunload | An element is not loaded, for example when a user leaves a page |
| onmouseover | When the mouse pointer enters the area defined by an HTML element |
| onmouseout | When the mouse pointer leaves the area defined by an HTML element |
| onclick | When the left mouse button is clicked within the area defined by an HTML element |
| onmousedown | When the left mouse button is depressed within the area defined by an HTML element |
| onmouseup | When the left mouse button is released within the area defined by an HTML element |

- The last three are related, but there are subtle differences – onclick is defined as being when **both** mousedown and mouseup events happen in the given element's area. For example, if you click on an area of the page, that registers the area's mousedown event. If you then hold the mouse down and move to another area before releasing, it will register the other area's mouseup event. The browser's click event, however, will remain unregistered.

- In theory, we can add most of these event handlers to just about any HTML tag we want. In practise, many browsers restrict what we can interact with.
- We will mostly be attaching event handlers to **<img>**, **<a>** and **<body>** tags.
- To attach an event handler to a tag, we use the following method:

```
<a href="…"
onclick="a_function();">link</a>
```

- We can use this method to attach any event handler listed above to the elements of the page. In addition to calling functions (with any optional arguments, of course), we can write JavaScript directly into our event handlers:

```
<a href="…"
onclick="alert('hello');">link</a>
```

---

- Note the potential issue with quote marks here – if you use double quotes around your event handler, you need to use single quotes within and vice versa.

## Project

- Open your previous project file, and save it under the name **chapter_21.html**.
- Clear all JavaScript code from your script tags.
- Ensure that you have a script element in the head area of your document, and none in the body area.
- Within the head area script element, define the following function:

```
function set_status( msg )
{
  window.status = msg;
}
```

- When called, this function will set the text displayed in the browser's status bar (the part of the window below the page content) to whatever is passed as an argument. For example, to set the status bar to display "Welcome", we would call:

```
set_status("Welcome");
```

- Now define the following function immediately below the last:

```
function clear_status( )
{
  set_status("");
}
```

- When called, this function will clear the status bar. Notice that we are using our previous function within the new one. This is a common programming technique that allows us to define functions of specific cases using more general functions.

- Now, add the following HTML to the body area of your page. Remember, we're adding HTML here, not JavaScript, so do not be tempted to use script tags for this part of the project:

```
<a href="#" ↵
   onmouseover="set_status('hello');" ↵
   onmouseout="clear_status();">testing</
   a>
```

---

- Load the page in your browser and observe what happens when you move your mouse over the link.
- The # value for the href attribute of the link allows us to define a "dead" link on the page. Clicking on the link will take you nowhere – try it.
- Now, alter the code to have the link point at a real website that you know of.
- Clicking on the link now will take you away from the page. Let's say we want to suppress that behaviour.
- When an event handler intercepts an event, it pauses the normal action of the event. For example, if you used an onclick handler on a link to pop up an alert box, the link would only be followed **after** the alert box had been dismissed. We can use event handlers to cancel the action if required by using their return values.
- Add a new function to the head area script element:

```
function confirm_link( )
{
  check = confirm("This will
    take you ↵ away from our
    site. Are you sure?");
  return check;
}
```

- The value of **check** will be **true** or **false**.
- Now, modify your link to contain the following event handler:

```
onclick="return confirm_link():"
```

- By using the word **return** in our event handler, the response of the function will be used to decide whether the rest of the normal action is run. In this case, if `confirm_link()` returns **false**, our link action will be cancelled.

- Load your page in your browser and view the result.

---

## 22 Working with Images

### Key Points

- In HTML, we can identify specific elements on the page using an id attribute. For example, to "name" an image, we can use the following code:

```
<img src="logo.gif" alt="" id="theLogo"
/>
```

- To refer to this element in JavaScript, we can now get to it directly by its id value:

```
document.getElementById("theLogo")
```

- This method will return an object that refers to the given element on the page. If no such element can be found, the method will return false.
- For easier use, we can assign the object found to a variable. For example, to create an object called our_logo in our scripts, we can use the following line of code:

```
our_logo =
document.getElementById("theLogo");
```

- The resultant object has a number of properties. Since, in this case, our object represents an image element, its properties include:

```
our_logo.height
our_logo.width
our_logo.src
```

- We can use JavaScript to change any of these properties, so if we wanted to change the image displayed, we could do so as follows:

```
our_logo.src = "new_logo.gif";
```

---

## Project

- Copy the folder called **`images`** from the network drive to your project folder.
- Open your previous project file, and save it under the name **`chapter_22.html`**.
- Clear all JavaScript code from your script tags.
- Ensure that you have a script element in the head area of your document, and none in the body area.
- Within the body area of your page, create an image element that loads an image from the **`images`** folder. Give the element an appropriate **`id`** attribute.
- In the head area script element, define a function called describe_image() that will pop up an alert box containing the following information about your image:

  the image file used
  the image width
  the image height

- To have each bit of text appear on a separate line, you can add the following character to your alert text:

  **`\n`**

  for example

  ```
  alert("line one\nLine two");
  ```

- Load your page in the browser and view the results.

## 23 Simple Image Rollovers

### Key Points

- A simple image rollover is an effect which happens when the mouse appears over an image (usually a linked button) on the page. The original image is replaced by another of equal size, usually giving the effect that the button is highlighted in some way.
- With what we have learned so far, we already have the ability to create a simple image rollover effect. All that remains is to clarify the particulars of the process:
- The page is loaded and the original image appears on the page as specified by the **`<img>`** tag's **`src`** attribute.
- The mouse moves offer the image and the alternative image is loaded into place.
- The mouse leaves the image and the original image is loaded back.
- As you may have realised, we are going to use JavaScript to alter the **`src`** attribute of the image tag. The best way to think of this is to picture the **`<img>`** tag as simply a space on the page into which an image file can be loaded. The **`src`** attribute tells the browser *which* image to load into the space, and so if we change that value, the image will be changed.
- In other words, the **`id`** attribute of the **`<img>`** tag is naming the "space", not the image.

- Now, in order to alter the src attribute with JavaScript, we need to tell JavaScript which image "space" we want to alter. We use the id attribute along with the getElementById() method from the last chapter to do this:

```
button_img = ↵
   document.getElementById("button");

button_img.src = "new_image.jpg";
```

- We can directly insert this code into the image's event handler:

```
<img src="old.jpg" id="button" ↵
   onmouseover=↵
   "document.getElementById('button').sr
   c ↵
    = 'new.jpg';">
```

- Note that this code is suddenly very convoluted. There are two immediate potential solutions. The first is to define a function:

```
function swap_image( id, new_image )
{
  img = document.getElementById(id);
  img.src = new_image;
}

...

<img src="old.jpg" id="button" ↵
   onmouseover= ↵
   "swap_image('button', 'new.jpg');">
```

- This is a much cleaner solution, and more importantly we can use this for any images on the page, simply by changing the arguments of our function call. We can also use the function to achieve the “swap back” functionality:

...

```
<img src="old.jpg" id="button" ↵
   onmouseover= ↵
   "swap_image('button', 'new.jpg');" ↵
   onmouseout= ↵
   "swap_image('button', 'old.jpg');">
```

- We can go even further in "cleaning up" our code, though. Because the event handler is being used to alter the object which is experiencing the event (ie, the mouse is moving over the image tag that we are trying to change), we can use the "automagic" JavaScript object **this** to perform the operation:

```
function swap_image( img, new_image )
{
  img.src = new_image;
}

...

<img src="old.jpg" id="button" ↵
    onmouseover= ↵
    "swap_image(this, 'new.jpg');">
```

- Note a couple of things. Firstly, **this** has no quotes around it – we are using it like a variable name. Secondly, our function now uses the first argument directly, instead of using it to get the relevant object from the page. We can do that because **this** is actually an object – it's an object that takes on the properties and methods of whatever object it is called from, in this case, it becomes equivalent to **document.getElementById('button' )**, although is obviously much shorter!

- Using **this** has some limitations. For example, if we wanted to change the **src** attribute of any other image on the page when the mouse moved over "**button**", we would be unable to use this, and hence would have to define another function that could take an id as its argument and get the relevant object that way.

### Project

- Copy the folder called **`buttons`** from the network drive to your project folder.
- Open your previous project file, and save it under the name **`chapter_23.html`**.
- Clear all JavaScript code from your script tags.
- Ensure that you have a script element in the head area of your document, and none in the body area.

---

- Within the body area of your page, create a paragraph containing six image elements. Set the **src** attributes of the images to load the following files in your copied **buttons** folder, and give each a sensible **id**:
- **contacts.jpg**
- **home.jpg**
- **people.jpg**
- **products.jpg**
- **quotes.jpg**
- **whatsnew.jpg**
- Create a JavaScript function in the head area script element that takes two arguments – an **id** and a file name. It should alter the src property of the appropriate image object to the file name given.
- Use this function to swap the **src** attribute of the contacts button to **contactsover.jpg** when the mouse moves over the image.
- Once you have this working, update the remaining five images with event handlers to swap their **src** attributes to their appropriate "over" image.
- Add event handlers to all six images to ensure that they return to their original state when the mouse is moved away from them. Check your work in your browser
- Add a new paragraph above the previous one, and add an **<img>** tag to it to containing the file **rocollogo.jpg** from the images folder.
- Add a text link to a new paragraph between the two paragraphs. The link should be a "dummy" link (ie use "**#**" as its **href** attribute value), but when the

mouse moves over it, the image above it should change to show **`rocollogo.gif`**.

- Moving the mouse away from the text link should return the logo to its previous state.
- Check your work in your browser.

---

## 24 Object Instantiation and Better Rollovers

### Key Points

- So far we have seen a very simple example of an image rollover. It is functional and works as desired, but it is lacking in a few finer details.
- Specifically, when we use JavaScript to change the src attribute of an <img> tag, the browser has to load this image from scratch. On our local machine, this will not cause an appreciable delay, but when dealing with a remote server (as we will be on the Internet), this delay can lead to a noticeable "lag", which can destroy the feeling of a dynamic interface.
- Ideally, we would like to instruct the browser to load any alternate images when it loads the page. This will allow us to ensure that the new images are sitting on the user's computer, ready to be swapped in and out instantly.
- To do this, we need to look at **object variables** and **object instantiation** (or *creation*). In particular, we need to look at the Image object.
- Each `<img>` tag on the page has a corresponding Image object in JavaScript. We have looked at ways of manipulating this directly, and have an idea of some of the properties an Image object can have.
- However, we can create Image objects directly in JavaScript, without the need for a corresponding `<img>` tag on the page. When we create such an object, and set its src property, the browser will load

the appropriate file into memory, but will not display the image on the page.

---

- In other words, we can create “virtual” images that exist within JavaScript, and use these Image objects to store the alternate images for our “real” images.
- To create an Image object (in fact, to create *any* object), we need to use the following code:

```
virtual_image = new Image();
```

- We have seen this sort of syntax before – the use of the **new** keyword when we created our Arrays. **new** tells JavaScript that we are creating a new object. The **virtual_image** part of the assignment is just a variable name. In this case, the variable is an **Object Variable**, since it contains an object.
- To use this variable to preload our images, we take advantage of the fact that it has the same properties and methods as any other image:

```
virtual_image.src = "contactsover.jpg";
```

- The browser will now preload our image, ready to be swapped in at a later time.

## Project

- Open your previous project file, and save it under the name **chapter_24.html**.
- Starting with your previous code, create a new function called preload_images in the head area script element of your page.
- Use this function to create seven new image objects, and use each objects corresponding object variable to preload your “over” image variations.
- Check your work in your browser to ensure that the image swapping still works as expected.

- Add your preload_images function to the body tag of your page to ensure that it runs when the page has finished loading. Use the following syntax:

```
<body onload="preload_images();">
```

---

- Once you have verified that the image swapping still works as expected, expand your preload_images function to define an array of images to preload, and then use a for loop to move through the array and assign each image to the src property of an object variable. ***Hint***: an object variable can be anything that can store information – for example an array element.
- Check your work in your browser.

## 25 Working with Browser Windows

### Key Points

- Using standard HTML links, we can open new browser windows:

```
<a href="#" target="_new">link</a>
```

- The amount of control this method affords us over the resultant image, however, is nil. We cannot control the size, shape, location on the screen or anything else about that window with this method.
- JavaScript allows us much finer control, as we may expect:

```
window.open( page_url, name, parameters
);
```

- As we can see from the above prototype, there are only three arguments that this method can take. However, the **parameters** argument is actually more complex than we might assume:

```
"param1,param2,param3,param4..."
```

  since we can use it to add many parameters to the method. Note there are no spaces in the parameter list.

- **name** is used to give the window an HTML name – so we can use that name to open links into the new window using the "**target**" method above.

- The return value from the **open** method is an object variable referring to the newly opened window. In other words, if we open a new window like so:

  ```
  win = window.open("page.html", "", "");
  ```

  we can use the object variable **win** to alter the new window through JavaScript.

- A practical example – let's say we want to open a new window 300 pixels high by 400 pixels wide, and display the BBC news page in it. The following code would suffice:

```
window.open("http://news.bbc.co.uk/", ↵
    "bbc", "width=300,height=300");
```

- Some available parameters are given in the table below:

| **Parameter** | **Value** | **Function** |
|---|---|---|
| location | Yes/no | Specifies whether or not the location (address) bar is displayed |
| menubar | Yes/no | Specifies whether the menu bar is displayed |
| status | Yes/no | Specifies whether the status bar is displayed |
| width | Pixels | Specifies the width of the new window |
| height | Pixels | Specifies the height of the new window |

| resizable | Yes/no | Allow or disallow window resizing |
|---|---|---|
| scrollbars | Yes/no | Allow or disallow window scrolling |

- If no parameters are set, then the value of each parameter is set to “yes” where appropriate. For example:

```
window.open("http://www.bbc.c
    o.uk/", ↵ "bbc", "");
```

is equivalent to:

```
<a href="http://www.bbc.co.uk/"
target="bbc">
```

- However, if **any** parameter is set, all others default to "no". So if you wanted to have a scrollbar but nothing else, the following would suffice:

```
window.open("http://www.bbc.c
    o.uk/", ↵ "bbc",
    "scrollbars=yes");
```

### Project

- Open your previous project file, and save it under the name **chapter_25.html**.
- Remove all functions and HTML from your previous file, leaving only the logo image and the link.
- Create a function in the head area script element called **view_new_logo**. This function should:
  - Open a new window 200 pixels square.
  - Load the image **rocollogo.jpg** from the images folder.
  - Be called **RocolLogo**
  - Be stored in an object variable called **objNewLogo**.
  - Have no scrollbars, be of a fixed size, and have no other features where possible.
- Remove all event handlers from the link, and add a new one to run the function above when the link is clicked.
- Once you have verified that a window pops up as required when the link is clicked, test each parameter from the table above in the function.

## 26 Positioning Browser Windows

### Key Points

- The **screen** object provides you with access to properties of the user's computer display screen within your JavaScript applications.
- Some of the available properties are:

| **Property** | **Description** |
|---|---|
| availHeight | The pixel height of the user's screen minus the toolbar and any other permanent objects (eg the Windows Taskbar) |
| availWidth | As availHeight, but dealing with horizontal space |
| colorDepth | The maximum number of colours the user's screen can display (in bit format, eg 24 bit, 16 bit etc) |
| height | The true pixel height of the user's display |
| width | The true pixel width of the user's display |

- The **`left`** and **`top`** parameters of the **`open()`** method enable you to specify the position of a window on screen by specifying the number of pixels from the left and top of the screen respectively.

- If you need to use a variable to specify the value of a parameter in the **open()** method, you would do so as follows:

```
window.open("index.html",
    "window_name", ↵
    "width=200,height=200,left="+va
    r_left+ ↵ "top="+var_top);
```

Where **var_left** and **var_top** are the appropriate variables.

---

- Note the use of the + operator to ensure that the third parameter in the **open()** method remains as one string when variables are added.
- In order to centre the window on the user's screen, a little simple geometry is required. The centre of the screen is obviously the point found when we take the width of the screen divided by two, and take the height of the screen divided by two. However, if we set the window's top and left values to these coordinates, the top left **corner** of the window will be centred, not the window itself.
- In order to centre the window, we need to subtract half of the window's height from our top value, and half of the window's width from our left value. A simple script to accomplish this is as follows:

```
win_width = 200;
win_height = 200;

win_left = (screen.availWidth/2) ↵
    - (win_width/2);
win_top = (screen.availHeight/2) ↵
    - (win_height/2);
```

- By using this script, the values of win_left and win_top will be set correctly for any window using win_width and win_height appropriately to be centred on the screen.

## Project

- Open your previous project file, and save it under the name **chapter_26.html**.
- Modify your existing code to ensure that the logo appears centred on the user's screen. If possible, do not modify your original function by doing anything more than two new functions – **get_win_left( width )** and **get_win_top( height )**.

## 27 Focus and Blur

### Key Points

- The **focus()** method of the **window** object gives focus to a particular window. In other words, it ensures that the window is placed on top of any other windows, and is made active by the computer. For example, if we have created a new window and stored the result in an object variable called **new_window**, we could ensure that the window was brought back to the front at any point after it had been opened by using the following code:

  ```
  new_window.focus();
  ```

- Conversely, we can use the **blur()** method to remove focus from the specified window – returning focus to the previously selected one as appropriate. Its use is similar to the **focus()** method.

- Both these events have associated event handlers: **onblur** and **onfocus**. However, since they do not have associated HTML tags, how can we attach event handlers to the object?

- It turns out that, within JavaScript, each object has an individual property for each event handler it can have applied to it. For example, if we wanted to add an event handler to an image tag on the page, we could apply either of the following methods to do that:

  ```
  <img src="..." id="test_img" ↵
  onclick="do_something();" />
  ```

```
<script>
document.getElementById("test_img")
    .onclick=↵ do_something();
</script>
```

- So, to attach a function to a window's **`focus`** event, we could use:

  ```
  new_window.onfocus = some_function();
  ```

## Project

- Open your previous project file, and save it under the name **`chapter_27.html`**.
- Modify your function to open another window as well as the original one, with the following features:
  - ⑨ The second window should be called **`oldRocolLogo`**, should be assigned to the object variable **`objOldLogo`**, and display the old logo from the file **`images/rocollogo.gif`**.
  - ⑩ When opened, the windows should be positioned so that both can be clearly seen.
- Test your modifications at this point.
- Observe the function's action when the windows are opened, then the original window is placed in front of them and the function is invoked again.
- Add a new statement to the function which uses the **`focus()`** method to ensure that when the function is called, both new windows are moved to the top of the "stack" of windows.
- Observe which logo appears "on top" when the function is called. Use the **`focus()`** method again to alter this.

## 28 Dynamically Created Content

### Key Points

- It's quite easy to create a new page on demand using JavaScript. In this context, we are talking about creating a completely new page in a window without loading any file into that window.
- To do this, invoke the **open()** method of the **window** object, leaving the location parameter empty:

```
new_win = window.open("",
    "newWin", ↵ "params...");
```

- Next, remember that you can write HTML code to a page using the window's **document.write()** method. Up until now, we have used only the current window's **document** object. However, we can specify *which* window's **document** we want to manipulate as follows:

```
document.write(); // write to
current window
new_win.document.write(); // or new
window
```

For example:

```
new_win.document.write("<html><head>");
new_win.document.write("<title>demo<
/title>"):
new_win.document.write("</head><body
>");
```

```
new_win.document.write("<h1>Hello!</
h1>");
new_win.document.write("</body></htm
l>");
```

### Project

- Open your previous project file, and save it under the name **`chapter_28.html`**.

---

- Modify your existing script to create a third window with the following properties:
  - The window should be called **`newHTML`**, and be assigned to the object variable **`objNewHTML`**.
  - It should be 400 pixels square.
  - It should not load any page when it is created. It should display the word "Welcome" as an **`H1`** header.
  - It should contain a paragraph with the text "Please decide which logo you would like to choose."
  - The third window should carry the title "Rocol Art"
  - When all windows have been opened, the third window should be **`focus`**sed.
- Check your work in the browser.

## 29 Working with Multiple Windows

### Key Points

- The window object's **`close()`** method enables you to close a window. If you have an object variable in the current window referring to the window you wish to close, you can simply use:

  ```
  new_window.close();
  ```

  to close the window.

- Things are a little more complicated when you wish to close a window from a window other than the one which opened the new window. In order to tackle this, we need to think about **window scope**.

- When we write JavaScript into our code, all functions and variables within that script are available for us to use **within that window**. For example, if we have a function called **`say_hello()`** in our main window, we can easily call that function. However, if we want to call the function from a newly opened window, we cannot call it directly from the new window, as our functions and variables are "tied" to the windows in which they were first defined.

- This is why, when we want to write to any window other than the one containing our JavaScript code, we must access the **`document`** object *of that window* in order to put content in the right place,

- But how about in the other direction? Let's say we use a function in our main window (call it **window**

**1**) to open a new window (**window 2**). If we store **window 2** as an object variable, we can access all properties of **window 2** from **window 1** by using that object. The question is, how do we access any properties of **window 1** from **window 2**?

---

- The key is that **window 2** and **window 1** have a special relationship – a "parent/child" relationship. We can access any property of **window 1** from **window 2** by using the special object called **`opener`**. This is an object created within any window that has been opened by JavaScript, and it always refers to the window that opened the new window.
- To illustrate this, let's consider our previous project. We have three new windows, and one "parent" window. If we wanted to use an event handler on one of the new windows to close on of the other new windows, we would need to first access the parent window, and then access the object variable within the parent window that pointed to the window we wanted to close.
- Let's say we wanted to close window_2 from a link in window_1. We would have to create an event handler in the link with the following code:

```
onclick="opener.window_2.close();"
```

## Project

- Open your previous project file, and save it under the name **`chapter_29.html`**.
- Modify your existing script to achieve the following:
  - Add two new paragraphs to the third window's content containing the following text:

    The Old

    Logo The

    New Logo

- ☹ Each line should be contained in a hyperlink whose event handler accesses the parent window's object variable pointing to the appropriate new window. Its **`close()`** method should then be invoked.

- Check your work in the browser.

---

## 30 Using an External Script File

### Key Points

- JavaScript can easily save us from having to type lots of HTML. As we have seen, we can use JavaScript to generate large form elements and tables using a small amount of code. This is good news for us, as it makes our work easier. It is also good news for our visitors, as they only have to download a small amount of code for a relatively large amount of content.
- However, we can do better. As it is, if we have one function that will generate a year drop down menu for a form's date of birth section, we need to include that function in every page that requires it. This means that our visitors are downloading identical content multiple times. In addition, if we change or improve our function, we have to ensure that we update that function in every page that has it included.
- HTML allows us to solve this problem by providing a mechanism to load an external text file into the HTML page and treat its contents as JavaScript code. Since it is a separate file, once it has been downloaded once, the browser will not download further copies of the file if it is requested by another page. In other words, we can load all our JavaScript code into one file, and any changes there will instantly be reflected across the entire site.
- To use code in an external file, we still use the `<script>` tag

– but with a new attribute, the **src** attribute. This is very similar to loading an image file on to a page:

```
<script
   language="JavaScript" ↵
   type="text/JavaScript" ↵
   src="s/script_file.js"></
   script>
```

- Note three things:

---

- ⑩ The language and type attributes are essential here.
- ⑩ The script tag still has a closing **`</script>`** tag.
- ⑩ We cannot add any further JavaScript between the tags when we are using the tags to load an external file. To add JavaScript to the current page only, we have to use a second set of **`<script>`** tags.

### Project

- Open your previous project file, and save it under the name **`chapter_30.html`**.
- Move all your JavaScript function definitions, and any other code in the head section script element to a new file called **`script.js`**.
- Modify your head section script element to load code from the new file.
- Check that your page still works as expected.
- **NOTE**: the **`.js`** file extension is just a naming convention. **`<script>`** tags will load JavaScript from any text file (hence the need to include the type and language attributes). However, it is a widely used convention, and it is worth sticking to in order to keep your code easily understood by anyone who may work on your code in the future.

## 31 Javascript and Forms

### Key Points

- Without JavaScript, the server handles all validating and processing of information submitted via a form. Using JavaScript on the client side of the equation saves time for the user and creates a more efficient process.
- Some processing can be handled by JavaScript (for example, mathematical computations) and JavaScript can ensure that only correct data is sent to the server for processing.
- JavaScript is used in conjunction with server-side processing – it is not a substitute for it.
- To access information in a form we use the document object's **getElementById()** method, as we have previously to access other objects on the page. For example, if we have a form on the page like so:

```
<form id="testForm" … >

</form>
```

we would access it in JavaScript by using:

```
document.getElementById('testForm');
```

- The resultant object is actually a multi-dimensional array. Each of its elements is itself an array containing information about the elements of the form (text boxes, buttons etc). By properly naming each of the form's elements in the appropriate <INPUT> tags, you can access information relating to each of the form's elements.

---

- To access the data stored in a text box called **Name** which is included in the form with the id **Enquiry** you use the value property like so:

```
objForm =
document.getElementById('Enquiry');

strValue = objForm.Name.value
```

- There are two ways of sending form data to the server. Using the **method** attribute, you can specify either the GET or the POST methods:

```
<form id ="enquiryform" method="GET"...
```

or

```
<form id ="enquiryform" method="POST"...
```

- In general, you should use the POST method if you want to send a lot of data (eg files, large amounts of text) from your form. You should use GET if you want to process search forms etc, as a GET form will be transmitted just like a URL, and is hence "savable" as a bookmark or link.

- In general, you will send your form to a server side script, specified by the form's action attribute:

```
<form id="enquiryform" method="GET"
  • action="process.php"...
```

- When the user clicks on a form's Submit button, without JavaScript intervention, the form's data is sent straight to the server for processing. But you can intercept the data (so you can process it with JavaScript) before it is sent, by including the **onsubmit** event handler in the **<form>** tag. This enables you to run a JavaScript function before the data is sent:

```
<form id="enquiryform" method="GET"
    • action="process.php"
    • onsubmit="functionName()">
```

- In the above example, when the user clicks on the Submit button, the function **functionName()** is run first, then the data is sent to the server.

---

- When the submit event is triggered by the form's submission, the browser waits to discover what is *returned* from the event handler. By default, the event handler will return **`true`**.
  However, if the event handler returns a **`false`** value, the form's submission will be aborted, and the page will not be submitted to the server.

- By returning a value of either true or false from your function (**`functionName()`** in the above example), and ensuring that this is also the return value of the **`onsubmit`** event handler, you can decide whether or not the form's data is actually sent to the server.

- You specify that the return value of the function is also the return value of the **`onsubmit`** event handler in the following way:

  ```
  onsubmit="return functionName();"
  ```

### Project

- Open your previous project file, and save it under the name **`chapter_31.html`**.

- Clear any content from the body element of the page, and ensure that the head area script element has no code in it.

- Save a copy of this page as **`processing_31.html`**, and put an **<h1>** element in the body area saying "**success**!".

- Now, close your **`processing_31.html`** page and create a form on your original **`chapter_31.html`** page using HTML – if you have difficulty with this, the tutor will provide an example to duplicate. Your form should:

- have an id of **jsCourseForm**.
- have a single input box with an name value of **name**.
- have a submit button.
- use the GET method of submission.
- have **processing_31.html** as its **action** attribute.

---

⑩ have an onsubmit event handler that returns the value of the (as yet non-existent) **`check_form()`** function.

- Now, create a function in the head area script element called check_form(). This function should:

  ⊛ use the document's getElementById() method to store a reference to the form's object in an object variable.

  ⊛ store the value of the form's **`name`** element in another variable.

  ⊛ if the value of the name element is not "**Bugs Bunny**", an alert box should appear stating:

```
Sorry chum!
Either you misspelled your name...
Or you haven't got what it takes...
Try again.
```

  ⑩ in addition, the form should be prevented from submitting.

- If the user enters the correct name, however, the form should submit without interruption.

- Check your work in your browser.

## 32 Form Methods and Event Handlers

### Key Points

- Each form object (e.g. text, button etc) has a set of properties associated with it. This is different for each form element. The **`value`** property is common to most form elements and is one of the most useful properties.
- You can assign the data stored in a text box called **`Name`** which is included in the form with id **`Enquiry`**, to a **`variable`** like so:

  ```
  variable =
  document.getElementById('Enquiry').
  • Name.value
  ```

- Form objects also have methods associated with them. The set of available methods is different for each form object.
- Below is a list of commonly used methods for the text object:

| Method | Description |
|---|---|
| blur() | Removes the focus from the text box |
| focus() | Gives the focus to the text box |
| select() | Selects the text box |

- Below is a list of commonly used methods for the button object:

| Method | Description |
|---|---|
| blur() | Removes the focus from the button |
| focus() | Gives the focus to the button |

| | |
|---|---|
| click() | Call's the button's onclick event handler |

- Form objects also have event handlers associated with them. The set of available event handlers is different for each form object.
- Below is a list of commonly used event handlers for the text object:

| Event handler | Runs JavaScript code when... |
|---|---|
| onblur | The text box loses the focus. |
| onfocus | The text box receives the focus. |
| onselect | The user selects some of the text within the text box.. |
| onchange | The text box loses the focus and has had its text modified. |

- Below is a list of commonly used event handlers for the button object:

| Event handler | Runs JavaScript code when... |
|---|---|
| onBlur | The button loses the focus |
| onFocus | The button receives the focus |
| onClick | The user clicks the button |

- Finally if you are sending data to the server, a submit button is not the only way. You could use the submit() method in a function which is invoked by an event handler. This operates as if the Submit button was clicked:

```
document.getElementById('Enquiry').submi
t();
```

## Project

- Open your previous project file, and save it under the name **chapter_32.html**.
- Modify your form in the following way:
  - Remove the submit button
  - Replace the submit button with a standard form button.

- Add an event handler to this button to invoke the function in the head area script element.
- Remove the **onsubmit** event handler from the form element.

---

- Now, modify the **`check_form()`** function in the following way:

  ◎ If the user types in the name "Bugs Bunny", the function submits the form using the form's submit() method.

  ◎ If the user types anything else, the previous alert box warning is displayed and the form is not submitted, but also:

    The words "please try again" are displayed in the text box.

    The text box is given focus.

    The text in the text box is selected.

- Check your work in your browser.

# 33 JavaScript and Maths

## Key Points

- The **Math** object is a pre-defined JavaScript object containing properties and methods which you can use for mathematical computation.
- Below is a selection of some useful **Math** methods:

| Method | Returns |
|---|---|
| Math.cell() | The smallest integer greater than or equal to a number.<br>That is, it rounds up any number to the next integer.<br>**Math.cell(2.6)** returns 3 and so does **Math.cell(2.2).** |
| Math.floor() | The largest integer greater than or equal to a number.<br>That is, it rounds down any number to the next integer.<br>**Math.floor(2.2)** returns 2 and so does **Math.floor(2.6).** |
| Math.max(n1,n2) | The larger of the two arguments. |
| Math.min(n1,n2) | The smaller of the two arguments. |
| Math.random() | A random number between 0 and 1. |
| Math.round() | The number rounded to its nearest integer. |
| Math.sqrt() | The square root of a number. |

- You don't need to include a Submit button in a form and you don't need to send form data to the server. You could use event handlers to invoke JavaScript code which merely processes the data on the form (e.g. you may just perform some mathematical computations on some user data).

---

- If you are not sending the data to the server, there is no need to include either the Action or Method attributes in the <FORM> tag, though by default the Action will usually submit to the current page, and the Method will be set to "get".

## Project

- Open your previous project file, and save it under the name **`chapter_33.html`**.
- Remove all content from the body section of the page.
- Copy the file **`max_wins.html`** from the network, and open it using NotePad's File > Open command.
- Copy and paste the entire contents of **`max_wins.html`** into your current project file, into the body element of the page.
- Remove all JavaScript code from the script element in the head section of the page.
- Take some time to open your project file in a browser, and study the code. This project will enable the page to:
    - Generate two random numbers when the button is pressed.
    - Display the random numbers in the text boxes marked **player 1** and **player 2**.
    - Compare the two random numbers and display the name of the player whose number is higher in the text box marked **winner**.
- When studying the code, note that the form has no valid action or method attributes. It also has no "submit" button. We are not going to allow the form to submit to the server at all, but are going to use JavaScript to do all our processing on the form.

- Now, modify the HTML code on the page to add an event handler to invoke a new function defined in the head area script element. The function should perform the following operations when the form button is clicked:
  - Place two separate random integers between 0 and 100 in each of the Player text boxes.

---

⑩ Find a way to use a Math method to compare the two entered integers. Once compared, the function should then place the appropriate value of **Player 1**, **Player 2**, or **Draw** in the Winner text box.

- Check your work in your browser.

## 34 Object Variables – A Refresher

### Key Points

- Referring to objects can be a lengthy process. Consider the Player 1 text box in the previous example. You refer to it in full as follows:

  ```
  document.getElementById("MaxWins").Playe
  r1
  ```

- This notation although precise, is tedious, time consuming and can be prone to error. Luckily, there are some shortcuts which can save time and reduce typing errors.

- We can use an object variable to simplify our work whenever we are in situations where certain objects need to be referred to repetitively. To use an object variable, you begin by simply assigning it a specific object:

  ```
  oPlayer1 =
  • document.getElementById("MaxWins").Pla
    yer1
  ```

- Once assigned, you can use the object variable in any situation where you would use the specific object itself. Using the object variables from the previous paragraph:

  ```
  oPlayer1.value
  ```

  is the same as:

```
document.getElementById("MaxWins").Playe
r1.value
```

---

- Bear in mind that you assign objects to object variables. You would assign a text box or a button or an image etc to an object variable and then refer to that object's properties as shown above **(oPlayer1.value)**. You don't assign text or string values to object variables. So:

  ```
  oPlayer1 =
  • document.getElementById("MaxWins").Pla
    yer1.value
  ```

  would merely assign the *value* stored in **Player1** to the variable **oPlayer1**.

- Hopefully it is obvious that you don't need to include the 'o' at the beginning of the object variable's name. It's just a convention to help distinguish between the different types of variables.

### Project

- Open your previous project file, and save it under the name **chapter_34.html**.
- Modify the function in the head area script element in the following way:
  - All specific object which are referred to more than once are each assigned their own object variable at the start of the function.
  - References to specific objects in the code are replaced by the appropriate object variables.
- Test your work in your browser to ensure that it functions as before.

## 35 Actions From Menu Items

### Key Points

- The HTML **<select>** form tag enables you to create a menu (select box) of options from which the user can choose:

```
<form id="menu">

<select name="Product">
  <option value="one">Image
  one</option> <option
  value="two">Image two</option>
  <option Value="three">Image
  three</option>
</select>

</form>
```

- Ordinarily, selecting an option from a select box merely specifies the value of the select box. This is then used for further processing – either by JavaScript or by the server.
- You can use JavaScript to invoke actions based on the current value of a select box (the selected option). These actions might be directly loading another page or performing some other type of processing.
- Another name for this type of action is a “jump menu”.
- In order to do this, you need to know that each select box on a form has a select object associated with it. Using the above example, you can therefore access

the current value of the Product select box (ie the value of its currently selected option) which is located on the ProductMenu form, in the following way:

```
document.getElementById("menu").Product.
value
```

---

- As you would expect, the select option has methods and event handlers associated with it:

  ☸ The focus() method gives the focus to a select box.

  ☸ The blur() method removes the focus from the select box.

- The available event handlers for the select object are given below:

| Event handler | Runs JavaScript code when.... |
|---|---|
| onblur | The select box loses the focus |
| onfocus | The select box receives the focus |
| onchange | The select box has had its value modified |

- The way to invoke action(s) when the user selects an option from a select box is to prepare a JavaScript function which will be invoked using the select object's **onchange** event handler:

```
<select name="name"
onchange="functionname()">
```

## Project

- Open your previous project file, and save it under the name **chapter_35.html**.

- Clear the head section script element of JavaScript, and remove all content from the body area of the page.

- Create a form in the body area of the page. Give the form an id of **jumpMenu**.

- In the form, place a select element. Give the select element the following values and labels eg:

```
<select name="menu">
  <option value="value">label</option>
  ...
```

</select>

| Value | Label |
|---|---|
| http://www.bbc.co.uk/ | The BBC |
| http://www.google.com/ | Google |
| http://www.hotmail.com/ | Hotmail |

| | |
|---|---|
| http://www.ed.ac.uk/ | The University of Edinburgh |
| http://www.apple.com/ | Apple Computer |
| http://www.microsoft.com/ | Microsoft Corporation |

- Finally, add an option element to the beginning of your menu like so:

```
<option value="">Select a destination</option>
```

- We are now going to use the menu's **onchange** event handler to invoke a function we are about to define. The function is to be called **jump_to_page()**.
- Define such a function in the head area script element. The function should:
  - Create an object variable referencing the form element that represents the menu.
  - Get the value of the menu at that moment.
  - If the value is not equal to "" (ie, if a valid selection has been made), the function should use the use JavaScript to load the selected page into the browser.
- Check your work in your browser.

## 36 Requiring Form Values or Selections

### Key Points

- Form data may be invalid if it is sent to the server without certain information – for example, if the user has omitted to select an item from a menu. Better not to bother processing, than to waste the time of the user and server by trying to process the invalid information.
- In the case of a selection box, one way of validating is to include a null value for the default option. In the previous project, the default value of the selection box (always the first option unless specified otherwise) was “”. If the user doesn’t actively make another selection, then you can check the value of the selection box before sending it to the server.
- Another example is the case of a set of radio buttons. Imagine that for an imaginery company, an order form contained two form elements – a selection box to specify which product was being ordered and two radio buttons to specify whether it was being ordered as a photographic print or as a slide.
- Let’s say the id of the order form is **`OrderForm`** and the name of each radio button is **`Format`**. (Remember that in HTML, radio buttons in a set are related to each other by their name that must be the same for each related radio button).

- The radio object is an array where each element of the array stores information relating to each of the radio button objects (remember, counting starts at 0).

---

- As the name is identical for each radio button in the set, you can't access an individual radio button by using its name. But you can access it using the standard array notation:

  **oOrderForm.Format[i]**

  where in this case, I is an integer between 0 and 1, and **oOrderForm** is an object variable pointing to the form element.

- Radio buttons in a set each have a checked property that stores a Boolean value specifying whether or not a radio button is checked. Obviously, you can access this value in the following way:

  **oOrderForm.Format[i].checked**

- So, to verify that in a set of radio buttons, at least one of them is checked, all you have to do is loop through each of the radio buttons using the array's length property to specify the number of iterations of the loop:

```
FormatSelected = false;
oOrderForm =
• document.getElementById("OrderForm");
for ( i=0; i < oOrderForm.Format.length;
i++ )
{
   if ( oOrderForm.Format[i].checked )
   {
      FormatSelected = true;
   }
}
```

- In our order form example, one of the products might only be available as a slide. You could use the **onchange** event handler of the **select** object to invoke a function which automatically sets the value of the relevant radio object's checked property:

```
function SetFormat ()
{
    oOrderForm =
    • document.getElementById("Orde
    rForm"); if (
    oOrderForm.Product.value ==
    • "Greek Boat" )
    {
        oOrderForm.Format[0].checked =
        true;
    }
}
```

where **Product** is the name of the select box, **Format** is the name of the group of radio buttons and the value of the first ratio button is Slide.

- Finally, to reset all form objects to their initial state, use the reset() method:

```
oFormObject.reset()
```

## Project

- Open your previous project file, and save it under the name **chapter_36.html**.
- Remove all content from the body section of the page.
- Copy the file **order_form.html** from the network, and open it using NotePad's File > Open command.

- Copy and paste the entire contents of **`order_form.html`** into your current project file, into the body element of the page.
- Remove all JavaScript code from the script element in the head section of the page.
- Take some time to open your project file in a browser, and study the code.

---

- Add an event handler to the form element on your page that will invoke a function called **`check_form()`** when the form is submitted. This function will return **`true`** or **`false`** depending on whether the form passes a number of tests as described below. Remember to precede the event handler's function call with **`return`** to ensure that the form awaits confirmation from the function before proceeding.
- Create the **`check_form()`** function in the head area script element. The function should perform the following steps:

  - If the current value of the selection menu is "":

    Display an alert with the message "**please select a product**"

    Give focus to the menu

    Return **`false`**

  - If no radio buttons are selected:

    Display an alter with the message "**please specify a format**"

    Return **`false`**

  - Otherwise, return **`true`**

- Check your work in your browser.
- The **Greek Fishing Boat** is only available in **Slide** format. Add an event handler to the select element which will run a function called **`set_format()`** when its value is changed.
- Create the function **`set_format()`** in the head area script element. The function should check first what the value of the menu is. If it is the **Greek**

**Fishing Boat**, it should then check to see if the **Slide** radio button is checked. If it is not, then the function should correct this.

- Check your work in your browser.
- Modify your check_form() function to check that, if the value of the menu is Greek Fishing Boat, then the Slide radio button is checked. If not, it should report the error as before.

---

- Finally, note that your **check_form()** function is currently not very efficient, in that it will only report one error at a time. This can be tedious for an error prone user, and it is much better practise to observe a form for *all* errors simultaneously.
- Create a variable at the beginning of the function called **error**. Set the value of this variable to "".
- Instead of using an alert box each time an error is found, add the error message to the end of the variable, eg

  ```
  error += "error message\n";
  ```

  (note the new line code at the end of each message)
- After all checks have been made, if we have caught any errors, the value of **error** will no longer be "". Thus, we can use the following code to report all errors at once:

```
if ( error != "" )
{
alert("The following errors were found: \n\n"
            • error
        ); return
            false;
}
else
{
    return true;
}
```

- Modify your function to be more efficient.

## 37 Working with Dates

### Key Points

- The date object stores all aspects of a date and time from year to milliseconds.
- To use a new date object, you must create it and assign it to an object variable simultaneously. The following code creates a new date object which stores the current date and time and assigns it to the variable **dtNow**

```
dtNow = new Date();
```

- You can specify your own parameters for the date object when you create it:

```
theDate = new Date(
   year, month, day, hours,
   minutes, seconds, mseconds
);
```

- Note that months are represented by the numbers 0 to 11 (January to December). Days are represented by 1 to 31, hours by 0 to 23, minutes and seconds by 0 to 59 and milliseconds by 0 to 999.
- The following code stores 17th July 2004 at 9:15:30pm in the variable **theDate**:

```
theDate = new
Date(2004,6,17,21,15,30,0);
```

- The first three parameters are mandatory, while the rest are optional:

```
theDate = new Date(2004,6,17);
```

gives you midnight of the date above.

---

- You can assign a date to a variable using a string in the following way:

```
theDate =
  new Date("Sun, 10 Oct 2000 21:15:00 -
  0500);
```

- Everything from the hours onwards is optional, and in practical terms the day is not necessary either. For example:

```
theDate = new Date("10 Oct 2000");
```

is a valid date.

## Project

- Open your previous project file, and save it under the name **`chapter_37.html`**.
- Remove all content from the body section of the page.
- Create a function in a head section script element that displays an alert box containing the current date and time. Have this function called from a body section script element.
- Now modify your script so that it also writes the date and time 17th July 1955 1:00am to the page in standard date and time format. Do this by entering the appropriate parameters into the **`new Date()`** constructor.
- Now, using parameters once again, add a new line to your script that will display midnight on 17th July 2004 on a separate line under the existing date.
- Finally, using the string approach in the date object, add a new line to your script which will display midnight on 31st December 1999 on a separate line under the existing information and in standard date and time format.

## 38 Retrieving Information from Date Objects

### Key Points

- Below is a selection of some useful methods which enable you to retrieve some useful information from date objects:

| Method | Returns |
|---|---|
| getDate() | The day of the month (1-31) |
| getDay() | The day of the week (0 = Sunday, 6 = Saturday) |
| getFullYear() | The year as four digits |
| getHours() | The hour (0-23) |
| getMilliseconds() | The milliseconds (0-999) |
| getMinutes() | The minutes (0-59) |
| getMonth() | The month (0-11) |
| getSeconds() | The seconds (0-59) |
| getTime() | The date and time in milliseconds – also called Unix Time |

- JavaScript stores date and time information internally as the number of milliseconds from 1st January 1970. This is common to most programming languages, and is actually the way most computer systems store time information.

---

- For example:

```
dtNow = new Date();
document.write(dtNow.getTime());
```

  writes the number of milliseconds that have passed since 1st January 1970.

- Being aware that there are 1000 milliseconds in a second, 60 seconds in a minute, 60 minutes in an hour and 24 hours in a day, you can establish the number of days (or hours or minutes etc) between two dates by subtracting on date in millisecond format from the other in millisecond format. To achieve the units you require, perform the appropriate division (so for the number of minutes, divide the result of the subtraction first by 1000, then by 60), and then use Math.floor() on the result to round the number down as required.

**Project**

- Open your previous project file, and save it under the name **`chapter_38.html`**.
- Clear any JavaScript from the page's script elements.
- Create a function in the head section script element that performs the following:
  - Create two arrays, one storing the days of the week ("Sunday", "Monday" etc), the other storing the months of the year ("January", "February" etc)
  - Use a new date object, along with the arrays and the appropriate date methods to write today's date to the page in the following format:

    Today it is: dayName, month,

    dayNumber. for example:

Today it is Tuesday, October 17.

---

⑩ Below the date, write the time in the following

format: It is currently hh:mm am (or pm)

***Note:*** *to convert from the 24hr clock, subtract 12 from any value over 12, and replace a zero value with 12. Anything greater than or equal to twelve should receive a "pm" suffix.*

⑩ Below the time, write the number of days since the start of the millennium in the following format:

It is n days since the start of the millennium.

- Finally, call your function from the body area script element on your page, and check your work in your browser.

# 39 Creating a JavaScript Clock

## Key Points

- **`setTimeout()`** is a method of the window object. In its common form, it enables you to run any JavaScript function after an allotted time (in milliseconds) has passed. For example:

  ```
  window.setTimeout("functionName()",
  1000)
  ```

  will run **`functionName()`** after one second. Note the quote marks!

- You can have any number of "timed out" methods running at any one time. To identify each "timeout", it is a good idea to assign the return value of each one you create to an object variable:

  ```
  firstTimeout =
    window.setTimeout("functionName()",
    1000)
  ```

- The most common reason to track timeouts is to be able to cancel them if necessary – for example, you may wish a window to close after 5 seconds unless a button is clicked:

  ```
  firstTimeout =
     window.setTimeout("window.close()",
     5000);
  ```

  adding the following code to the button's **`onclick`** event handler:

```
window.clearTimeout(firstTimeout);
```

will do the trick.

---

- Ordinarily, it is a bad idea to "recurse" a function – to have a function call itself. For example, imagine the annoyance of the following:

```
function annoy_me( )
{
    window.alert("BOO!");
    annoy_me();
}
```

  This will potentially keep popping up alert boxes, and perhaps even lock up the user's computer!

- However, you may wish a function to use a **setTimeout** method to call itself periodically. Imagine a function that calls itself every second to check on the time, and then displays the result in the same place. In effect, this could be seen as a digital clock.

- If you want to clear the clock's timeout – which in this case would stop the clock – the timeout must already be in operation. You can't clear a timeout that doesn't yet exist. So, you have to check first whether a timeout is in operation. One way of doing this is to set a Boolean variable to true whenever the clock is started. By checking this variable before you attempt to clear the timeout, you know whether or not the clock is running and therefore can be stopped.

- To show an am/pm clock you obviously need to carry out the conversion you created in the previous chapter's project.

- But, so as the display doesn't show a "moving" effect at different times, you need to consider the situation where either the minutes or seconds on the clock are fewer than 10. For example, consider:

```
10:59:59 am
```

changing to:

```
11:0:0 am
```

---

- In this situation, we need to concatenate an extra "0" on to the front of the actual value to produce:

  **`11:00:00 am`**

  as we might expect.

- We can use a shortened form of the if conditional to make this simple. For example:

  s = theDate.getSeconds;
  s = ( s < 10 ) ? "0" + s : s;

- What is happening here? First, we get the current value of the seconds and store that in a variable called "s". Next, we reset the value of s depending on the condition in the brackets. The prototype of this form of the if conditional is:

```
var = ( condition )
    ? value if true
    : value if false;
```

  in other words, we can think of the ? as being like the opening brace { of an if conditional, the : as being the } else {, and the ; as being the closing brace. The result of the conditional test is then stored in var.

  Note that this has been split over three lines to aid reading. In practice (see above) we can place this on one line for ease of use.

## Project

- Open your previous project file, and save it under the name **`chapter_39.html`**.
- Remove all content from the body section of the page.
- In the body section, create a form input element with the id **`clockBox`**, and two form input buttons labelled Start and Stop.

- In the head section scrip element, create two empty functions – **`start_clock()`** and **`stop_clock()`**.
- Before the two function definitions, as the first statement of the script element, create a variable called **`timer`**, and assign it a value of **`null`**.

---

- Immediately below that statement, create a variable called timer_running. Assign it a value of false.
- We will use these variables to track the clock's status.
- Now, add statements to the start_clock() function that will:
  - Get the current time.
  - Format the current time as hh:mm:ss am/pm (as appropriate).
  - Display the formatted time in the text field on the page.
  - Create a timeout which will run the **`start_clock()`** function again in half a second, and assign that timeout's return object to the **`timer`** object variable.
  - Set the **`timer_running`** variable to **`true`**.
- Add statements to the **`stop_clock()`** function that will:
  - Check to see if the clock is running.
  - If it is, clear the timer timeout and set **`timer_running`** to **`false`**.
- Finally, add event handlers to the two form buttons to ensure that the one labelled Stop calls the function **`stop_clock()`** when clicked, and the one labelled Start calls the function **`start_clock()`** when clicked.
- While this should work (test your code!), you'll notice that the output is a little ugly. Displaying the time in a text field is not the most unobtrusive way to show a clock on a page.

- Luckily, we can modify our code very slightly to achieve something much more professional.
- Replace your input field with the following:

```
<span id="clockBox"></span>
```

- **<span>** is an HTML tag that allows you to mark areas of content without any semantic meaning – eg, the clock is not a paragraph or a header, so we don’t want to label it as such.

---

- With JavaScript, we can control the content of just about any element on the page. In our previous example, we used **`getElementById`** (hopefully!) to obtain a reference to the input field, and then altered its **`value`** property to show our clock.

- Since we are using the same id value here, we do not have to alter our function too much. However, the **`getElementById`** method now returns a different type of object – one that has no **`value`** property.

- However, all content tags in HTML (like **<p>**, **<h1>**, **<div>** etc) have a special property when they are returned as JavaScript objects which refers to their text content – the property is **`innerHTML`**.

- We can use this to alter the content of the tags. For example, if our previous input-field solution had the following code:

```
clk =
document.getElementById
("clockBox"); clk.value
= formatted_time;
```

where **formatted_time** is a variable containing the formatted time as required, then replacing it with this code:

```
clk =
document.getElementById
("clockBox");
clk.innerHTML =
formatted_time;
```

will allow us to use the modified **<span>** element in place of the **<input>** element.

- Try adapting your code to use this method of displaying content on the page.

# Chapter 40

# History and evolution of JavaScript

## Contents

## 3.1 How JavaScript was created

JavaScript was created in May 1995, in 10 days, by Brendan Eich. Eich worked at Netscape and implemented JavaScript for their web browser, *Netscape Navigator*.

The idea was that major interactive parts of the client-side web were to be implemented in Java. JavaScript was supposed to be a glue language for those parts and to also make HTML slightly more interactive. Given its role of assisting Java, JavaScript had to look like Java. That ruled out existing solutions such as Perl, Python, TCL and others.

Initially, JavaScript's name changed several times:

- Its code name was *Mocha*.
- In the Netscape Navigator 2.0 betas (September 1995), it was called *LiveScript*.
- In Netscape Navigator 2.0 beta 3 (December 1995), it got its final name, *JavaScript*.

## 3.2 Standardizing JavaScript

There are two standards for JavaScript:

- ECMA-262 is hosted by Ecma International. It is the primary standard.
- ISO/IEC 16262 is hosted by the International Organization for Standardization (ISO) and the International Electrotechnical Commission (IEC). This is a secondary standard.

The language described by these standards is called *ECMAScript*, not *JavaScript*. A differ-ent name was chosen, because Sun (now Oracle) had a trademark for the latter name. The “ECMA” in “ECMAScript” comes from the organization that hosts the primary standard.

The original name of that organization was *ECMA*, an acronym for *European Computer Manufacturers Association*. It was later changed to *Ecma International* (with “Ecma” being a proper name, not an acronym), because the organization’s activities had expanded be-yond Europe. The initial all-caps acronym explains the spelling of ECMAScript.

In principle, JavaScript and ECMAScript mean the same thing. Sometimes, the following distinction is made:

- The term *JavaScript* refers to the language and its implementations.
- The term *ECMAScript* refers to the language standard and language versions.

Therefore, *ECMAScript 6* is a version of the language (its 6th edition).

## 3.3 Timeline of ECMAScript versions

This is a brief timeline of ECMAScript versions:

- ECMAScript 1 (June 1997): First version of the standard.
- ECMAScript 2 (June 1998): Small update, to keep ECMA-262 in sync with the ISO standard.
- ECMAScript 3 (December 1999): Adds many core features – "[...] regular expres-sions, better string handling, new control statements [do-while, switch], try/catch exception handling, [...]"
- ECMAScript 4 (abandoned in July 2008): Would have been a massive upgrade (with static typing, modules, namespaces and more), but ended up being too am-bitious and dividing the language's stewards. Therefore, it was abandoned.
- ECMAScript 5 (December 2009): Brought minor improvements – a few standard library features and *strict mode*.
- ECMAScript 5.1 (June 2011): Another small update to keep Ecma and ISO stan-dards in sync.
- ECMAScript 6 (June 2015): A large update that fulfilled many of the promises of ECMAScript 4. This version is the first one whose official name – *ECMAScript 2015*
  – is based on the year of publication.
- ECMAScript 2016 (June 2016): First yearly release. The shorter release life cycle resulted in fewer new features – compared to the large ES6.
- ECMAScript 2017 (June 2017). Second yearly release.

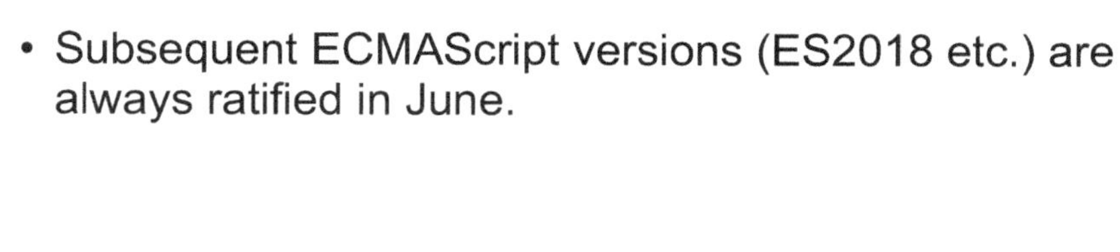

- Subsequent ECMAScript versions (ES2018 etc.) are always ratified in June.

## 3.4 Ecma Technical Committee 39 (TC39)

TC39 is the committee that evolves JavaScript. Its member are, strictly speaking, com-panies: Adobe, Apple, Facebook, Google, Microsoft, Mozilla, Opera, Twitter, and others. That is, companies that are usually fierce competitors are working together for the good of the language.

Every two months, TC39 has meetings that are attended

by member-appointed delegates and invited experts.

The minutes of those meetings are public, in a GitHub

repository.

## 3.5 The TC39 process

With ECMAScript 6, two issues with the release process used at that time became obvious:

- If too much time passes between releases then features that are ready early, have to wait a long time until they can be released. And features that are ready late, risk being rushed to make the deadline.
- Features were often designed long before they were implemented and used. De-sign deficiencies related to implementation and use were therefore discovered too late.

In response to these issues, TC39 instituted the new *TC39 process*:

- ECMAScript features are designed independently and go through stages, starting at 0 (“strawman”), ending at 4 (“finished”).
- Especially the later stages require prototype implementations and real-world test-ing, leading to feedback loops between designs and implementations.
- ECMAScript versions are released once per year and include all features that have reached stage 4 prior to a release deadline.

The result: smaller, incremental releases, whose features have already been field-tested.

Fig. 3.1 illustrates the TC39 process.

ES2016 was the first ECMAScript version that was designed according to the TC39 pro-cess.

### 3.5.1 Tip: think in individual features and stages, not ECMAScript ver-sions

Up to and including ES6, it was most common to think about JavaScript in terms of ECMAScript versions. For example: “Does this browser support ES6, yet?”

Starting with ES2016, it’s better to think in individual features: Once a feature reaches stage 4, you can safely use it (if it’s supported by the JavaScript engines you are targeting). You don’t have to wait until the next ECMAScript release.

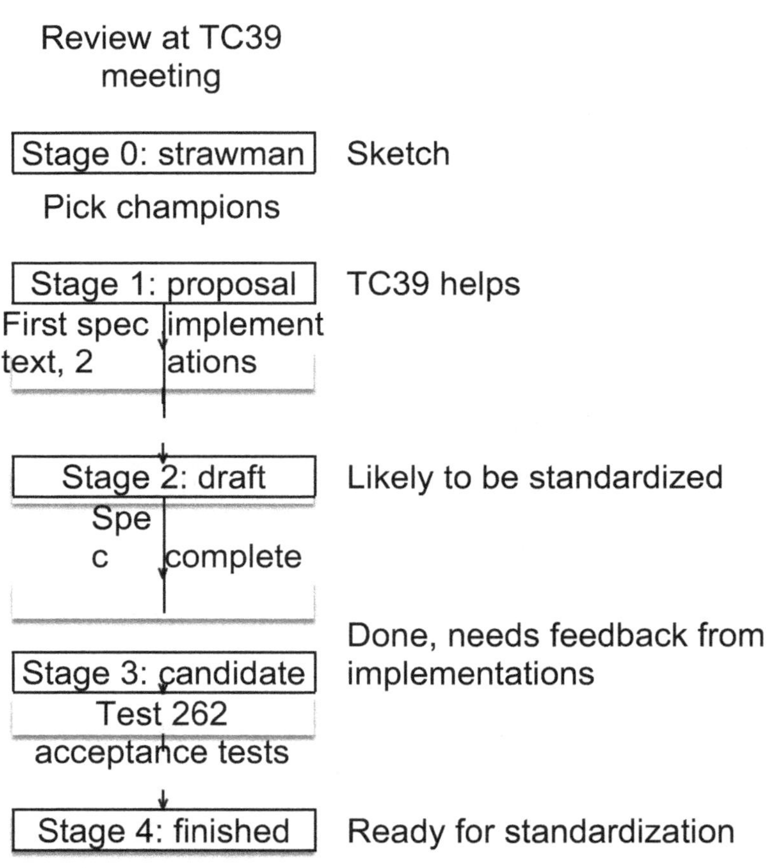


Figure 3.1: Each ECMAScript feature proposal goes through stages that are numbered from 0 to 4.

*Champions* are TC39 members that support the authors of a feature. Test 262 is a suite of tests that checks JavaScript engines for compliance with the language specification.

## 3.6 FAQ: TC39 process

### 3.6.1 How is [my favorite proposed feature] doing?

If you are wondering what stages various proposed features are in, consult the GitHub repository `proposals`.

### 3.6.2 Is there an official list of ECMAScript features?

Yes, the TC39 repo lists finished proposals and mentions in which ECMAScript versions they were introduced.

## 3.7 Evolving JavaScript: don't break the web

One idea that occasionally comes up, is to clean up JavaScript, by removing old features and quirks. While the appeal of that idea is obvious, it has significant downsides.

Let's assume we create a new version of JavaScript that is not backward compatible and fixes all of its flaws. As a result, we'd encounter the following problems:

- JavaScript engines become bloated: they need to support both the old and the new version. The same is true for tools such as IDEs and build tools.
- Programmers need to know, and be continually conscious of, the differences be-tween the versions.
- You can either migrate all of an existing code base to the new version (which can be a lot of work). Or you can mix versions and refactoring becomes

harder, because you can't move code between versions without changing it.

- You somehow have to specify per piece of code – be it a file or code embedded in a web page – what version it is written in. Every conceivable solution has pros and cons. For example, *strict mode* is a slightly cleaner version of ES5. One of the reasons why it wasn't as popular as it should have been: it was a hassle to opt in via a directive at the beginning of a file or a function.

So what is the solution? Can we have our cake and eat it? The approach that was chosen for ES6 is called "One JavaScript":

- New versions are always completely backward compatible (but there may occa-sionally be minor, hardly noticeable clean-ups).
- Old features aren't removed or fixed. Instead, better versions of them are intro-duced. One example is declaring variables via `let` – which is an improved version of `var`.
- If aspects of the language are changed, it is done so inside new syntactic constructs. That is, you opt in implicitly. For example, `yield` is only a keyword inside gener-ators (which were introduced in ES6). And all code inside modules and classes (both introduced in ES6) is implicitly in strict mode.

See quiz app.

## Chapter 41

# FAQ: JavaScript

## Contents



## 4.1 What are good references for JavaScript?

Please consult §5.3 "JavaScript references".

## 4.2 How do I find out what JavaScript features are sup-ported where?

This book usually mentions if a feature is part of ECMAScript 5 (as required by older browsers) or a newer version. For more detailed information (incl. pre-ES5 versions), there are several good compatibility tables available online:

- ECMAScript compatibility tables for various engines (by kangax, webbedspace, zloirock)
- Node.js compatibility tables (by William Kapke)
- Mozilla's MDN web docs have tables for each feature that describe relevant ECMA-Script versions and browser support.
- "Can I use…" documents what features (including JavaScript language features) are supported by web browsers.

## 4.3 Where can I look up what features are planned for JavaScript?

Please consult the following sources:

- §3.5 "The TC39 process" describes how upcoming features are planned.
- §3.6 "FAQ: TC39 process" answers various questions regarding upcoming features.

## 4.4 Why does JavaScript fail silently so often?

JavaScript often fails silently. Let's look at two examples.

First example: If the operands of an operator don't have the appropriate types, they are converted as necessary.

```
> '3' * '5'
15
```

Second example: If an arithmetic computation fails, you get an error value, not an excep-tion.

```
> 1 / 0
Infinity
```

The reason for the silent failures is historical: JavaScript did not have exceptions until ECMAScript 3. Since then, its designers have tried to avoid silent failures.

## 4.5 Why can't we clean up JavaScript, by removing quirks and outdated features?

This question is answered in §3.7 "Evolving JavaScript: don't break the web".

## 4.6 How can I quickly try out a piece of JavaScript code?

§7.1 "Trying out JavaScript code" explains how to do that.

## Part II

## First steps

# Chapter 42

# The big picture

## Contents

In this chapter, I'd like to paint the big picture: What are you learning in this book and how does it fit into the overall landscape of web development?

## 5.1 What are you learning in this book?

This book teaches the JavaScript language. It focuses on just the language, but offers occasional glimpses at two platforms where JavaScript can be used:

- Web browser
- Node.js

Node.js is important for web development in three ways:

- You can use it to write server-side software in JavaScript.
- You can also use it to write software for the command line (think Unix shell, Win-dows PowerShell, etc.). Many JavaScript-related tools are based on (and executed via) Node.js.
- Node's software registry, npm, has become the dominant way of installing tools (such as compilers and build tools) and libraries – even for client-side development.

## 5.2 The structure of browsers and Node.js

The structures of the two JavaScript platforms *web browser* and *Node.js* are similar (fig. 5.1):

- The foundational layer consists of the JavaScript engine and platform-specific "core" functionality.

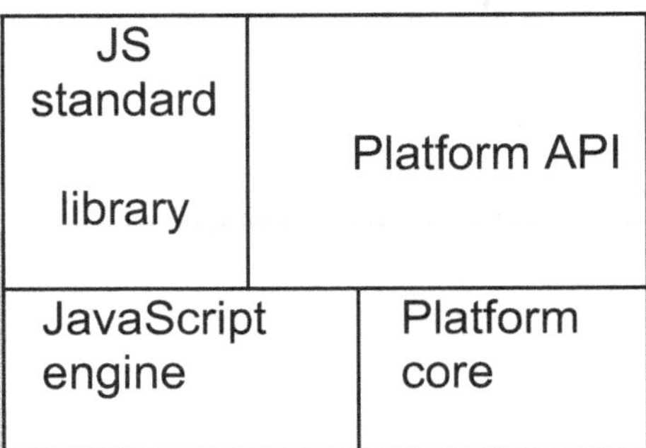


Figure 5.1: The structure of the two JavaScript platforms *web browser* and *Node.js*. The APIs “standard library” and “platform API” are hosted on top of a foundational layer with a JavaScript engine and a platform-specific “core”.

- Two APIs are hosted on top of this foundation:
  - The JavaScript standard library is part of JavaScript proper and runs on top of the engine.
  - The platform API are also available from JavaScript – it provides access to platform-specific functionality. For example:
    - In browsers, you need to use the platform-specific API if you want to do anything related to the user interface: react to mouse clicks, play sounds, etc.
    - In Node.js, the platform-specific API lets you read and write files, down-load data via HTTP, etc.

## 5.3 JavaScript references

When you have a question about a JavaScript, a web search usually helps. I can recom-mend the following online sources:

- MDN web docs: cover various web technologies such as CSS, HTML, JavaScript and more. An excellent reference.
- Node.js Docs: document the Node.js API.
- ExploringJS.com: My other books on JavaScript go into greater detail than this book and are free to read online. You can look up features by ECMAScript version:
  - ES1–ES5: "Speaking JavaScript"
  - ES6: "Exploring ES6"
  - ES2016–ES2017: "Exploring ES2016 and ES2017"
  - Etc.

## 5.4 Further reading

- A bonus chapter provides a more comprehensive look at web development.

## Chapter 43

# Syntax

## Contents

---

## 6.1 An overview of JavaScript's syntax

### 6.1.1 Basic syntax

Comments:

```
// single-line comment

/*
Comment with
multiple lines
*/
```

*Primitive* (atomic) values:

```
// Booleans
true
false
```

```
• Numbers (JavaScript only has a
single type for numbers) -123
1.141
```

```
• Strings (JavaScript has no type for
  characters)
'abc'
"abc"
```

An *assertion* describes what the result of a computation is expected to look like and throws an exception if those expectations aren't correct. For example, the following assertion states that the result of the computation 7 plus 1 must be 8:

```
assert.equal(7 + 1, 8);
```

`assert.equal()` is a method call (the object is `assert`, the method is `.equal()`) with two arguments: the actual result and the expected result. It is part of a Node.js assertion API that is explained later in this book.

Logging to the console of a browser or Node.js:

```
• Printing a value to standard
out (another method call)
console.log('Hello!');

• Printing error information to standard
  error
console.error('Something went wrong!');
```

Operators:

```
// Operators for booleans
assert.equal(true && false, false); //
And
```

```
assert.equal(true || false, true); // Or

• Operators
for numbers
assert.equal(
3 + 4, 7);
assert.equal(
5 - 1, 4);
assert.equal(
3 * 4, 12);
assert.equal(
9 / 3, 3);

• Operators for
strings
assert.equal('a'
+ 'b', 'ab');
assert.equal('I see ' + 3 + ' monkeys', 'I
see 3 monkeys');

• Comparison operators
assert.equal(3 < 4, true);
assert.equal(3 <= 4, true);
assert.equal('abc' === 'abc', true);
assert.equal('abc' !== 'def', true);
```

Declaring variables:

```
let x; // declaring x (mutable)
x = 3 * 5; // assign a value to x

let y = 3 * 5; // declaring and assigning
```

```
const z = 8; // declaring z (immutable)
```

Control flow statements:

```
// Conditional statement
if (x < 0) { // is x less than zero?
 x = -x;
}
```

Ordinary function declarations:

```
// add1() has the parameters a and b
function add1(a, b) {
 return a + b;
}
• Calling

function add1()

assert.equal(ad

d1(5, 2), 7);
```

Arrow function expressions (used especially as arguments of function calls and method calls):

```
const add2 = (a, b) => { return a + b };
• Calling

function add2()

assert.equal(ad

d2(5, 2), 7);

• Equivalent to add2:
const add3 = (a, b) => a + b;
```

The previous code contains the following two arrow functions (the terms *expression* and *statement* are explained later in this chapter):

```
• An arrow function whose
body is a code block (a,
b) => { return a + b }

• An arrow function whose
body is an expression (a,
b) => a + b
```

Objects:

```
// Creating a plain object
via an object literal const
obj = {
  first: 'Jane', // property
  last: 'Doe', // property
  getFullName() { // property (method)
   return this.first + ' ' + this.last;
  },
};

• Getting a
property value
assert.equal(obj.f
irst, 'Jane');
• Setting a property value
obj.first = 'Janey';
```

```
// Calling the method
assert.equal(obj.getFullName(), 'Janey
Doe');
```

Arrays (Arrays are also objects):

```
// Creating an Array
via an Array literal
const arr = ['a', 'b',
'c'];

• Getting an
Array element
assert.equal(ar
r[1], 'b');
• Setting an
Array element
arr[1] = 'β';
```

### 6.1.2Modules

Each module is a single file. Consider, for example, the following two files with modules in them:

```
file-tools.mjs
main.mjs
```

The module in `file-tools.mjs` exports its function `isTextFilePath()`:

```
export function isTextFilePath(filePath)
{
 return filePath.endsWith('.txt');
}
```

The module in `main.mjs` imports the whole module `path` and the function `is-`

`TextFilePath()`:

```
// Import whole module as
namespace object `path`
import * as path from
'path';
// Import a single export of

module file-tools.mjs import

{isTextFilePath} from

'./file-tools.mjs';
```

### 6.1.3 Legal variable and property names

The grammatical category of variable names and property names is called *identifier*.

Identifiers are allowed to have the following characters:

- Unicode letters: `A–Z`, `a–z` (etc.)
- `$`, `_`
- Unicode digits: `0–9` (etc.)
  - Variable names can't start with a digit

Some words have special meaning in JavaScript and are called *reserved*. Examples include:

`if`, `true`, `const`.

Reserved words can't be used as variable names:

```
const if = 123;
  // SyntaxError: Unexpected token if
```

But they are allowed as names of properties:

- `const obj = { if: 123 };`

- `obj.if`

```
123
```

### 6.1.4 Casing styles

Common casing styles for concatenating words are:

- Camel case: `threeConcatenatedWords`
- Underscore case (also called *snake case*): `three_concatenated_words`
- Dash case (also called *kebab case*): `three-concatenated-words`

### 6.1.5 Capitalization of names

In general, JavaScript uses camel case, except for constants.

Lowercase:

- Functions, variables: `myFunction`
- Methods: `obj.myMethod`
- CSS:
  - CSS entity: `special-class`
  - Corresponding JavaScript variable: `specialClass`

Uppercase:

- Classes: `MyClass`
- Constants: `MY_CONSTANT`
  - Constants are also often written in camel case: `myConstant`

### 6.1.6 More naming conventions

The following naming conventions are popular in JavaScript.

If the name of a parameter starting with an underscore (or is an underscore) means that this parameter is not used. For example:

```
arr.map((_x, i) => i)
```

If the name of a property of an object starts with an underscore then that property is considered private:

```
class ValueWrapper {
 constructor(value) {
  this._value = value;
 }
}
```

### 6.1.7 Where to put semicolons?

At the end of a statement:

```
const x = 123;
func();
```

But not if that statement ends with a curly brace:

```
while (false) {
```

```
  // ...
} // no semicolon

function func() {
  // ...
} // no semicolon
```

However, adding a semicolon after such a statement is not a syntax error – it is interpreted as an empty statement:

```
// Function declaration followed by
empty statement:
function func() {
  // ...
};
```

> **Quiz: basic**
>
> See quiz app.

## 6.2 (Advanced)

All remaining sections of this chapter are advanced.

## 6.3 Identifiers

### 6.3.1 Valid identifiers (variable names etc.)

First character:

- Unicode letter (including accented characters such as `é` and `ü` and characters from non-latin alphabets, such as α)
- `$`
- `_`

Subsequent characters:

Legal first characters
Unicode digits (including Eastern Arabic numerals)
Some other Unicode marks and punctuations

Examples:

```
const ε = 0.0001;
const строка = '';
let _tmp = 0;
const $foo2 = true;
```

### 6.3.2 Reserved words

Reserved words can't be variable names, but they can be property names.

All JavaScript *keywords* are reserved words:

```
await break case catch class const
continue debugger default delete do
else export extends finally for
function if import in instanceof let
```

```
new return static super switch this
throw try typeof var void while with
yield
```

The following tokens are also keywords, but currently not used in the language:

```
enum implements package protected
interface private public
```

The following literals are reserved words:

```
true false null
```

Technically, these words are not reserved, but you should avoid them, too, because they effectively are keywords:

```
Infinity NaN undefined async
```

You shouldn’t use the names of global variables (`String`, `Math`, etc.) for your own vari-ables and parameters, either.

## 6.4 Statement vs. expression

In this section, we explore how JavaScript distinguishes two kinds of syntactic constructs: *statements* and *expressions*. Afterwards, we'll see that that can cause problems, because the same syntax can mean different things, depending on where it is used.

> **We pretend there are only statements and expressions**
> For the sake of simplicity, we pretend that there are only statements and expressions in JavaScript.

### 6.4.1 Statements

A *statement* is a piece of code that can be executed and performs some kind of action. For example, `if` is a statement:

```
let myStr;
if (myBool) {
 myStr = 'Yes';
} else {
 myStr =
 'No';
}
```

One more example of a statement: a function declaration.

```
function twice(x) {
```

```
  return x + x;
}
```

### 6.4.2 Expressions

An *expression* is a piece of code that can be *evaluated* to produce a value. For example, the code between the parentheses is an expression:

```
let myStr = (myBool ? 'Yes' : 'No');
```

The operator `_?_:_` used between the parentheses is called the *ternary operator*. It is the expression version of the `if` statement.

Let's look at more examples of expressions. We enter expressions and the REPL evaluates them for us:

```
> 'ab' + 'cd'
'abcd'
> Number('123')
123
> true || false
true
```

### 6.4.3 What is allowed where?

The current location within JavaScript source code determines which kind of syntactic constructs you are allowed to use:

- The body of a function must be a sequence of statements:

```
function max(x, y) {
 if (x > y) {
  return x;
 } else {
  return y;
 }
}
```

- The arguments of a function call or a method call must be expressions:

```
console.log('ab' + 'cd',
Number('123'));
```

However, expressions can be used as statements. Then they are called *expression state-ments*. The opposite is not true: when the context requires an expression, you can't use a statement.

The following code demonstrates that any expression `bar()` can be either expression or statement – it depends on the context:

```
function f() {
 console.log(bar()); // bar() is
 expression
```

```
  bar(); // bar(); is (expression)
  statement
}
```

## 6.5 Ambiguous syntax

JavaScript has several programming constructs that are syntactically ambiguous: The same syntax is interpreted differently, depending on whether it is used in statement con-text or in expression context. This section explores the phenomenon and the pitfalls it causes.

### 6.5.1 Same syntax: function declaration and function expression

A *function declaration* is a statement:

```
function id(x) {
  return x;
}
```

A *function expression* is an expression (right-hand side of =):

```
const id = function me(x) {
  return x;
};
```

### 6.5.2 Same syntax: object literal and block

In the following code, `{}` is an *object literal*: an expression that creates an empty object.

```
const obj = {};
```

This is an empty code block (a statement):

```
{
}
```

### 6.5.3 Disambiguation

The ambiguities are only a problem in statement context: If the JavaScript parser encoun-ters ambiguous syntax, it doesn't know if it's a plain statement or an expression statement. For example:

- If a statement starts with `function`: Is it a function declaration or a function expres-sion?
- If a statement starts with `{`: Is it an object literal or a code block?

To resolve the ambiguity, statements starting with `function` or `{` are never interpreted as expressions. If you want an expression statement to start with either one of these tokens, you must wrap it in parentheses:

```
(function (x) { console.log(x)
})('abc');

Output:
'abc'
```

In this code:

1. We first create a function, via a function expression:

```
function (x) { console.log(x) }
```

2. Then we invoke that function: `('abc')`

#1 is only interpreted as an expression, because we wrap it in parentheses. If we didn't, we would get a syntax error, because then JavaScript expects a function declaration and complains about the missing function name. Additionally, you can't put a function call immediately after a function declaration.

Later in this book, we'll see more examples of pitfalls caused by syntactic ambiguity:

- Assigning via object destructuring
- Returning an object literal from an arrow function

## 6.6 Semicolons

### 6.6.1 Rule of thumb for semicolons

Each statement is terminated by a semicolon.

```
const x = 3;
someFunction('abc');
i++;
```

Except: statements ending with blocks.

```
function foo() {
  // ···
}
if (y > 0) {
  // ···
}
```

The following case is slightly tricky:

```
const func = () => {}; // semicolon!
```

The whole `const` declaration (a statement) ends with a semicolon, but inside it, there is an arrow function expression. That is: It's not the statement per se that ends with a curly brace; it's the embedded arrow function expression. That's why there is a semicolon at the end.

### 6.6.2Semicolons: control statements

The body of a control statement is itself a statement. For example, this is the syntax of the `while` loop:

```
while (condition)
  statement
```

The body can be a single statement:

```
while (a > 0) a--;
```

But blocks are also statements and therefore legal bodies of control statements:

```
while (a > 0) {
```

```
  a--;
}
```

If you want a loop to have an empty body, your first option is an empty statement (which is just a semicolon):

```
while (processNextItem() > 0);
```

Your second option is an empty block:

```
while (processNextItem() > 0) {}
```

## 6.7 Automatic semicolon insertion (ASI)

While I recommend to always write semicolons, most of them are optional in JavaScript. The mechanism that makes this possible is called *automatic semicolon insertion* (ASI). In a way, it corrects syntax errors.

ASI works as follows. Parsing of a statement continues until there is either:

A semicolon

A line terminator followed by an illegal token

In other words, ASI can be seen as inserting semicolons at line breaks. The next subsec-tions cover the pitfalls of ASI.

### 6.7.1 ASI triggered unexpectedly

The good news about ASI is that – if you don't rely on it and always write semicolons

– there is only one pitfall that you need to be aware of. It is that JavaScript forbids line breaks after some tokens. If you do insert a line break, a semicolon will be inserted, too.

The token where this is most practically relevant is `return`. Consider, for example, the following code:

```
return
{
 first: 'jane'
};
```

This code is parsed as:

```
return;
{
 first: 'jane';
}
;
```

That is, an empty return statement, followed by a code block, followed by an empty statement.

Why does JavaScript do this? It protects against accidentally returning a value in a line after a `return`.

### 6.7.2 ASI unexpectedly not triggered

In some cases, ASI is *not* triggered when you think it should be. That makes life more complicated for people who don't like semicolons, because they need to be aware of those cases. The following are three examples. There are more.

**Example 1:** Unintended function call.

```
a = b + c
(d + e).print()
```

Parsed as:

```
a = b + c(d + e).print();
```

**Example 2:** Unintended division.

```
a = b
/hi/g.exec(c).map(d)
```

Parsed as:

```
a = b / hi / g.exec(c).map(d);
```

**Example 3:** Unintended property access.

```
someFunction()
['ul', 'ol'].map(x => x + x)
```

Executed as:

```
const propKey =
('ul','ol'); // comma
operator
assert.equal(propKey,
'ol');

someFunction()[propKey].map(x => x + x);
```

## 6.8 Semicolons: best practices

I recommend that you always write semicolons:

- I like the visual structure it gives code – you clearly see when a statement ends.
- There are less rules to keep in mind.
- The majority of JavaScript programmers use semicolons.

However, there are also many people who don't like the added visual clutter of semi-colons. If you are one of them: code without them *is* legal. I recommend that you use tools to help you avoid mistakes. The following are two examples:

- The automatic code formatter Prettier can be configured to not use semicolons. It then automatically fixes problems. For example, if it encounters a line that starts with a square bracket, it prefixes that line with a semicolon.

The static checker ESLint has a rule that you tell your preferred style (always semi-colons or as few semicolons as possible) and that warns you about critical issues.

## 6.9 Strict mode vs. sloppy mode

Starting with ECMAScript 5, JavaScript has two *modes* in which JavaScript can be exe-cuted:

Normal "sloppy" mode: is the default in scripts (code fragments that are a precur-sor to modules and supported by browsers).

Strict mode: is the default in modules and classes, and can be switched on in scripts (how, is explained later). In this mode, several pitfalls of normal mode are removed and more exceptions are thrown.

You'll rarely encounter sloppy mode in modern JavaScript code, which is almost always located in modules. In this book, I assume that strict mode is always switched on.

### 6.9.1 Switching on strict mode

In script files and CommonJS modules, you switch on strict mode for a complete file, by putting the following code in the first line:

```
'use strict';
```

The neat thing about this “directive” is that ECMAScript versions before 5 simply ignore it: it’s an expression statement that does nothing.

You can also switch on strict mode for just a single function:

```
function functionInStrictMode() {
  'use strict';
}
```

### 6.9.2Improvements in strict mode

Let’s look at three things that strict mode does better than sloppy mode. Just in this one section, all code fragments are executed in sloppy mode.

#### 6.9.2.1 Sloppy mode pitfall: changing an undeclared variable creates a global vari-able

In non-strict mode, changing an undeclared variable creates a global variable.

```
function
sloppyFunc() {
undeclaredVar1 =
123;
}
sloppyFunc();
  Created global variable
`undeclaredVar1`:
```

```
assert.equal(undeclaredV
ar1, 123);
```

Strict mode does it better and throws a ReferenceError. That makes it easier to detect typos.

```
function strictFunc() {
  'use strict';
  undeclaredVar2 = 123;
}
assert.throws(
  () => strictFunc(),
  {
    name: 'ReferenceError',
    message:
  'undeclaredVar2 is not
  defined', });
```

The assert.throws() states that its first argument, a function, throws a ReferenceError when it is called.

#### 6.9.2.2 Function declarations are block-scoped in strict mode, function-scoped in sloppy mode

In strict mode, a variable created via a function declaration only exists within the inner-most enclosing block:

```
function strictFunc() {
  'use strict';
```

```
  {
    function foo() { return 123 }
  }
  return foo(); // ReferenceError
}
assert.throws(
  () => strictFunc(),
  {
    name: 'ReferenceError',
    message: 'foo is not defined',
  });
```

In sloppy mode, function declarations are function-scoped:

```
function sloppyFunc() {
  {
    function foo() { return 123 }
  }
  return foo(); // works
}
assert.equal(sloppyFunc(), 123);
```

#### 6.9.2.3 Sloppy mode doesn't throw exceptions when changing immutable data

In strict mode, you get an exception if you try to change immutable data:

```
function strictFunc() {
  'use strict';
  true.prop = 1; // TypeError
}
assert.throws(
```

```
  () => strictFunc(),
  {
   name: 'TypeError',
   message: "Cannot create property
  'prop' on boolean 'true'", });
```

In sloppy mode, the assignment fails silently:

```
function sloppyFunc() {
  true.prop = 1; // fails silently
  return true.prop;
}
assert.equal(sloppyFunc(), undefined);
```

> **Further reading: sloppy mode**
>
> For more information on how sloppy mode differs from strict mode, see MDN.

### Quiz: advanced

See quiz app.

# Chapter 44

# Consoles: interactive JavaScript command lines

## Contents



## 7.1 Trying out JavaScript code

You have many options for quickly running pieces of JavaScript code. The following subsections describe a few of them.

### 7.1.1 Browser consoles

Web browsers have so-called *consoles*: Interactive command lines to which you can print text via `console.log()` and where you can run pieces of code. How to open the console differs from browser to browser. Fig. 7.1 shows the console of Google Chrome.

To find out how to open the console in your web browser, you can do a web search for "console «name-of-your-browser»". These are pages for a few commonly used web browsers:

- Apple Safari
- Google Chrome
- Microsoft Edge
- Mozilla Firefox

### 7.1.2 The Node.js REPL

*REPL* stands for *read-eval-print loop* and basically means *command line*. To use it, you must first start Node.js from an operating system command line, via the command `node`. Then an interaction with it looks as depicted in fig. 7.2: The text after > is input from the user; everything else is output from Node.js.

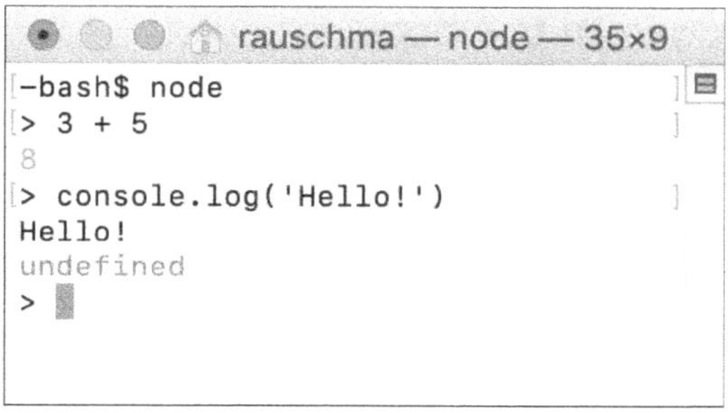

```
rauschma — node — 35×9
-bash$ node
> 3 + 5
8
> console.log('Hello!')
Hello!
undefined
>
```

Figure 7.2: Starting and using the Node.js REPL (interactive command line).

> **Reading: REPL interactions**
>
> I occasionally demonstrate JavaScript via REPL interactions. Then I also use greater-than symbols (>) to mark input. For example:
>
> ```
> > 3 + 5
> 8
> ```

### 7.1.3 Other options

Other options include:

There are many web apps that let you experiment with JavaScript in web browsers. For example, Babel's REPL.

There are also native apps and IDE plugins for running JavaScript.

> ⚠ **Consoles often run in non-strict mode**
> In modern JavaScript, most code (e.g. modules) is executed in strict mode. However, consoles often run in non-strict mode. Therefore, you may occasionally get slightly different results when using a console to execute code from this book.

## 7.2 The `console.*` API: printing data and more

In browsers, the console is something you can bring up that is normally hidden. For Node.js, the console is the terminal that Node.js is currently running in.

The full `console.*` API is documented on MDN web docs and on the Node.js website. It is not part of the JavaScript language standard, but much functionality is supported by both browsers and Node.js.

In this chapter, we only look at the following two methods for printing data. “Printing” means displaying in the console.

```
console.log()
console.error()
```

### 7.2.1 Printing values: `console.log()` (stdout)

There are two variants of this operation:

```
console.log(...values: any[]): void
console.log(pattern: string, ...values: any[]): void
```

#### 7.2.1.1 Printing multiple values

The first variant prints (text representations of) values on the console:

```
console.log('abc', 123, true);
  Output:
  abc 123 true
```

At the end, `console.log()` always prints a newline.

Therefore, if you call it with zero arguments, it just prints a newline.

#### 7.2.1.2 Printing a string with substitutions

The second variant performs string substitution:

```
console.log('Test: %s %j', 123, 'abc');
  Output:
  Test: 123 "abc"
```

These are some of the directives you can use for substitutions:

- `%s` converts the corresponding value to a string and inserts it.

  ```
  console.log('%s %s', 'abc', 123);
    Output:
    abc 123
  ```

  `%o` inserts a string representation of an object.

  ```
  console.log('%o', {foo: 123, bar:
  'abc'});
    Output:
    { foo: 123, bar: 'abc' }
  ```

  `%j` converts a value to a JSON string and inserts it.

  ```
  console.log('%j', {foo: 123, bar:
  'abc'});
    Output:
    {"foo":123,"bar":"abc"}
  ```

- `%%` inserts a single `%`.

```
console.log('%s%%', 99);
  Output:
  99%
```

### 7.2.2 Printing error information: `console.error()` (stderr)

`console.error()` works the same as `console.log()`, but what it logs is considered error information. For Node.js, that means that the output goes to stderr instead of stdout on Unix.

### 7.2.3 Printing nested objects via `JSON.stringify()`

`JSON.stringify()` is occasionally useful for printing nested objects:

```
console.log(JSON.stringify({first: 'Jane',
last: 'Doe'}, null, 2));
```

Output:

```
{
 "first": "Jane",
 "last": "Doe"
}
```

# Chapter 8

# Assertion API

## Contents



## 8.1 Assertions in software development

In software development, *assertions* state facts about values or pieces of code that must be true. If they aren't, an exception is thrown. Node.js supports assertions via its built-in module `assert`. For example:

```
import {strict as assert} from 'assert';
assert.equal(3 + 5, 8);
```

This assertion states that the expected result of 3 plus 5 is 8. The import statement uses the recommended `strict` version of `assert`.

## 8.2 How assertions are used in this book

In this book, assertions are used in two ways: to document results in code examples and to implement test-driven exercises.

51

### 8.2.1 Documenting results in code examples via assertions

In code examples, assertions express expected results.

Take, for example, the following function:

```
function id(x) {
 return x;
}
```

`id()` returns its parameter. We can show it in action via an assertion:

```
assert.equal(id('abc'), 'abc');
```

In the examples, I usually omit the statement for importing `assert`.

The motivation behind using assertions is:

You can specify precisely what is expected.

Code examples can be tested automatically, which ensures that they really work.

### 8.2.2 Implementing test-driven exercises via assertions

The exercises for this book are test-driven, via the test framework AVA. Checks inside the tests are made via methods of `assert`.

The following is an example of such a test:

```
  For the exercise, you must implement
  the function hello().
  The test checks if you have done it
  properly.
test('First exercise', t => {
```

```
  assert.equal(hello('world'), 'Hello
  world!');
  assert.equal(hello('Jane'), 'Hello
  Jane!');
  assert.equal(hello('John'), 'Hello
  John!');
  assert.equal(hello(''), 'Hello !');
});
```

For more information, consult §9 “Getting started with quizzes and exercises”.

## 8.3 Normal comparison vs. deep comparison

The strict `equal()` uses === to compare values. Therefore, an object is only equal to itself – even if another object has the same content (because === does not compare the contents of objects, only their identities):

```
assert.notEqual({foo: 1}, {foo: 1});
```

`deepEqual()` is a better choice for comparing objects:

```
assert.deepEqual({foo: 1}, {foo: 1});
```

This method works for Arrays, too:

```
assert.notEqual(['a', 'b',
'c'], ['a', 'b', 'c']);
assert.deepEqual(['a', 'b',
'c'], ['a', 'b', 'c']);
```

## 8.4 Quick reference: module `assert`

For the full documentation, see the Node.js docs.

### 8.4.1 Normal equality

`function equal(actual: any, expected: any, message?: string): void` `actual === expected` must be `true`. If not, an `AssertionError` is thrown.

```
assert.equal(3+3, 6);
```

`function notEqual(actual: any, expected: any, message?: string): void` `actual !== expected` must be `true`. If not, an `AssertionError` is thrown.

```
assert.notEqual(3+3, 22);
```

The optional last parameter `message` can be used to explain what is asserted. If the asser-tion fails, the message is used to set up the `AssertionError` that is thrown.

```
let e;
try {
 const x = 3;
 assert.equal(x, 8, 'x must be equal to 8')
} catch (err) {
 assert.equal(String(err), 'AssertionError
 [ERR_ASSERTION]: x must be equal to 8');
```

```
}
```

### 8.4.2 Deep equality

`function deepEqual(actual: any, expected: any, message?: string): void`

`actual` must be deeply equal to `expected`. If not, an `AssertionError` is thrown.

```
assert.deepEqual([1,2,3], [1,2,3]);
assert.deepEqual([], []);

  To .equal(), an object is

only equal to itself:

assert.notEqual([], []);
```

`function notDeepEqual(actual: any, expected: any, message?: string): void`

`actual` must not be deeply equal to `expected`. If it is, an `AssertionError` is thrown.

```
assert.notDeepEqual([1,2,3], [1,2]);
```

### 8.4.3 Expecting exceptions

If you want to (or expect to) receive an exception, you need `throws()`: This function calls its first parameter, the function `block`, and only succeeds if it throws an exception. Additional parameters can be used to specify what that exception must look like.

- `function throws(block: Function, message?: string): void`

```
assert.throws(
  () => {
   null.prop;
  }
);
```

function throws(block: Function, error: Function, message?: string): void

```
assert.throws(
  () => {
   null.prop;
  },
  TypeError
);
```

function throws(block: Function, error: RegExp, message?: string): void

```
assert.throws(
  () => {
   null.prop;
  },
/^TypeError: Cannot read property 'prop' of null$/
);
```

function throws(block: Function, error: Object, message?: string): void

```
assert.throws(
  () => {
   null.prop;
```

```
  },
  {
   name: 'TypeError',
   message: `Cannot read property
   'prop' of null`,
  }
 );
```

### 8.4.4 Another tool function

```
function fail(message: string | Error):
never
```

Always throws an `AssertionError` when it is called. That is occasionally useful for unit testing.

```
try {
  functionThatShouldThrow();
  assert.fail();
} catch (_) {
    Success
}
```

**Quiz**

See quiz app.

Chapter 45

# Getting started with quizzes and exercises

## Contents



Throughout most chapters, there are quizzes and exercises. These are a paid feature, but a comprehensive preview is available. This chapter explains how to get started with them.

## 9.1 Quizzes

Installation:

- Download and unzip `impatient-js-quiz.zip`

Running the quiz app:

- Open `impatient-js-quiz/index.html` in a web browser
- You'll see a TOC of all the quizzes.

## 9.2 Exercises

### 9.2.1 Installing the exercises

To install the exercises:

Download and unzip `impatient-js-code.zip`

Follow the instructions in `README.txt`

### 9.2.2 Running exercises

24 Exercises are referred to by path in this book.

– For example: `exercises/quizzes-exercises/first_module_test.mjs`

25 Within each file:

– The first line contains the command for running the exercise.

– The following lines describe what you have to do.

## 9.3 Unit tests in JavaScript

All exercises in this book are tests that are run via the test framework AVA. This section gives a brief introduction.

### 9.3.1 A typical test

Typical test code is split into two parts:

Part 1: the code to be tested.

Part 2: the tests for the code.

Take, for example, the following two files:

`id.mjs` (code to be tested)

`id_test.mjs` (tests)

#### 9.3.1.1 Part 1: the code

The code itself resides in `id.mjs`:

```
export function id(x) {
```

```
  return x;
}
```

The key thing here is: everything you want to test must be exported. Otherwise, the test code can't access it.

#### 9.3.1.2 Part 2: the tests

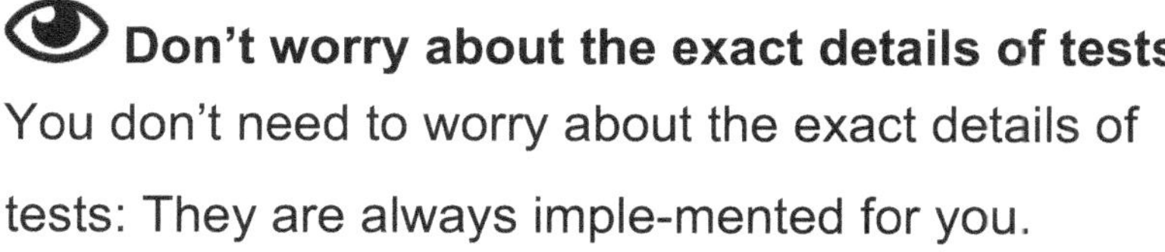

**Don't worry about the exact details of tests**

You don't need to worry about the exact details of tests: They are always imple-mented for you. Therefore, you only need to read them, but not write them.

The tests for the code reside in `id_test.mjs`:

```
import test from 'ava'; // (A)
import {strict as assert} from 'assert';
// (B)
import {id} from './id.mjs'; // (C)
```

```
test('My test', t => { // (D)
  assert.equal(id('abc'), 'abc'); // (E)
});
```

The core of this test file is line E – an assertion: `assert.equal()` specifies that the expected result of `id('abc')` is `'abc'`.

As for the other lines:

Line A: We import the test framework.

Line B: We import the assertion library. AVA has built-in assertions, but module `assert` lets us remain compatible with plain Node.js.

Line C: We import the function to test.

Line D: We define a test. This is done by calling the function `test()`:

- First parameter: the name of the test.
- Second parameter: the test code, which is provided via an arrow function. The parameter `t` gives us access to AVA's testing API (assertions etc.).

To run the test, we execute the following in a command line:

```
npm t demos/quizzes-exercises/id_test.mjs
```

The `t` is an abbreviation for `test`. That is, the long version of this command is:

```
npm test demos/quizzes-
exercises/id_test.mjs
```

**Exercise: Your first exercise**

The following exercise gives you a first taste of what exercises are like:

exercises/quizzes-exercises/first_module_test.mjs

### 9.3.2 Asynchronous tests in AVA

**Reading**

You can postpone reading this section until you get to the chapters on asynchronous programming.

Writing tests for asynchronous code requires extra work: The test receives its results later and has to signal to AVA that it isn't finished, yet, when it returns. The following subsec-tions examine three ways of doing so.

#### 9.3.2.1 Asynchronicity via callbacks

If we call `test.cb()` instead of `test()`, AVA switches to callback-based asynchronicity.
When we are done with our asynchronous work, we have to call `t.end()`:

```
test.cb('divideCallback', t => {
  divideCallback(8, 4, (error, result) => {
```

```
    if (error) {
     t.end(error);
    } else {
     assert.strictEqu
     al(result, 2);
     t.end();
    }
   });
  });
```

#### 9.3.2.2 Asynchronicity via Promises

If a test returns a Promise, AVA switches to Promise-based asynchronicity. A test is con-sidered successful if the Promise is fulfilled and failed if the Promise is rejected.

```
test('dividePromise 1',
         t => {
return dividePromise(8,
           4)
    .then(result => {
     assert.strictEqual(result, 2);
    });
  });
```

#### 9.3.2.3 Async functions as test "bodies"

Async functions always return Promises. Therefore, an async function is a convenient way of implementing an asynchronous test. The following code is equivalent to the pre-vious example.

```
test('dividePromise 2', async t => {
  const result = await dividePromise(8,
  4);
  assert.strictEqual(result, 2);
    No explicit return necessary!
});
```

You don’t need to explicitly return anything: The implicitly returned `undefined` is used to fulfill the Promise returned by this async function. And if the test code throws an exception then the async function takes care of rejecting the returned Promise.

# Part III

# Variables and values

## Chapter 10

## Variables and assignment

### Contents

---

These are JavaScript's main ways of declaring variables:

- `let` declares mutable variables.

- `const` declares *constants* (immutable variables).

Before ES6, there was also `var`. But it has several quirks, so it's best to avoid it in modern JavaScript. You can read more about it in "Speaking JavaScript".

## 10.1 `let`

Variables declared via `let` are mutable:

```
let i;
i = 0;
i = i + 1;
assert.equal(i, 1);
```

You can also declare and assign at the same time:

```
let i = 0;
```

## 10.2 `const`

Variables declared via `const` are immutable. You must always initialize immediately:

```
const i = 0; // must initialize

assert.throws(
  () => { i = i + 1 },
  {
   name: 'TypeError',
   message: 'Assignment to constant
   variable.',
  }
);
```

### 10.2.1 `const` and immutability

In JavaScript, `const` only means that the *binding* (the association between variable name and variable value) is immutable. The value itself may be mutable, like `obj` in the follow-ing example.

```
const obj = { prop: 0 };

  Allowed: changing
properties of `obj`
obj.prop = obj.prop +
1;
assert.equal(obj.prop,
1);

  Not allowed:
assigning to `obj`
assert.throws(
  () => { obj = {} },
  {
   name: 'TypeError',
   message: 'Assignment to constant
   variable.',
```

```
  }
);
```

### 10.2.2 const and loops

You can use `const` with `for-of` loops, where a fresh binding is created for each iteration:

```
const arr = ['hello', 'world'];
for (const elem of arr) {
 console.log(elem);
}
  Output:
  'hello'
  'world'
```

In plain `for` loops, you must use `let`, however:

```
const arr = ['hello', 'world'];
for (let i=0; i<arr.length; i++) {
 const elem = arr[i];
 console.log(elem);
}
```

## 10.3 Deciding between let and const

I recommend the following rules to decide between `let` and `const`:

- `const` indicates an immutable binding and that a variable never changes its value. Prefer it.
- `let` indicates that the value of a variable changes. Use it only when you can't use `const`.

**Exercise: const**

```
exercises/variables-
assignment/const_exrc.mjs
```

## 10.4 The scope of a variable

The *scope* of a variable is the region of a program where it can be accessed. Consider the following code.

```
{ // // Scope A.
 Accessible: x
 const x = 0;
 assert.equal(x,
 0);
 { // Scope B.
  Accessible: x,
  y const y = 1;
  assert.equal(x,
  0);
  assert.equal(y,
  1);
  { // Scope C. Accessible: x, y, z
```

```
      const z = 2;
      assert.equal(x, 0);
      assert.equal(y, 1);
      assert.equal(z, 2);
    }
  }
}
// Outside. Not accessible: x, y, z
assert.throws(
  () => console.log(x),
  {
    name: 'ReferenceError',
    message: 'x is not defined',
  }
);
```

- Scope A is the *(direct) scope* of `x`.
- Scopes B and C are *inner scopes* of scope A.
- Scope A is an *outer scope* of scope B and scope C.

Each variable is accessible in its direct scope and all scopes nested within that scope.

The variables declared via `const` and `let` are called *block-scoped*, because their scopes are always the innermost surrounding blocks.

### 10.4.1 Shadowing variables

You can't declare the same variable twice at the same level:

```
assert.throws(
```

```
  () => {
   eval('let x = 1; let x = 2;');
  },
  {
   name: 'SyntaxError',
   message: "Identifier 'x' has
 already been declared", });
```

> **Why `eval()`?**
>
> `eval()` delays parsing (and therefore the `SyntaxError`), until the callback of `assert.throws()` is executed. If we didn't use it, we'd already get an error when this code is parsed and `assert.throws()` wouldn't even be executed.

You can, however, nest a block and use the same variable name `x` that you used outside the block:

```
const x = 1;
assert.equal(x, 1);
{
```

```
    const x = 2;
    assert.equal(x, 2);
  }
  assert.equal(x, 1);
```

Inside the block, the inner x is the only accessible variable with that name. The inner x is said to *shadow* the outer x. Once you leave the block, you can access the old value again.

**Quiz: basic**

See quiz app.

## 10.5 (Advanced)

All remaining sections are advanced.

## 10.6 Terminology: static vs. dynamic

These two adjectives describe phenomena in programming languages:

> *Static* means that something is related to source code and can be determined with-out executing code.
>
> *Dynamic* means at runtime.

Let's look at examples for these two terms.

### 10.6.1 Static phenomenon: scopes of variables

Variable scopes are a static phenomenon. Consider the following code:

```
function
    f() {
const x =
        3;
  // ···
}
```

`x` is *statically* (or *lexically*) *scoped*. That is, its scope is fixed and doesn't change at runtime.

Variable scopes form a static tree (via static nesting).

### 10.6.2 Dynamic phenomenon: function calls

Function calls are a dynamic phenomenon. Consider the following code:

```
function g(x) {}
function h(y) {
  if (Math.random()) g(y); // (A)
}
```

Whether or not the function call in line A happens, can only be decided at runtime.

Function calls form a dynamic tree (via dynamic calls).

## 10.7 Global variables

A variable is global if it is declared in the top-level scope. Every nested scope can access such a variable. In JavaScript, there are multiple layers of global scopes (Fig. 10.1):

The outermost global scope is special: its variables can be accessed via the proper-ties of an object, the so-called *global object*. The global object is referred to by `window` and `self` in browsers. Variables in this scope are created via:

- Properties of the global object
- `var` and `function` at the top level of a *script*. (Scripts are supported by browsers. They are simple pieces of code and precursors to modules. Consult §24.2 "Before we had modules, we had scripts" for details.)

Nested in that scope is the global scope of scripts. Variables in this scope are created by `let`, `const` and `class` at the top level of a script.

Nested in that scope are the scopes of modules. Each module has its own global scope. Variables in that scope are created by declarations at the top level of the module.

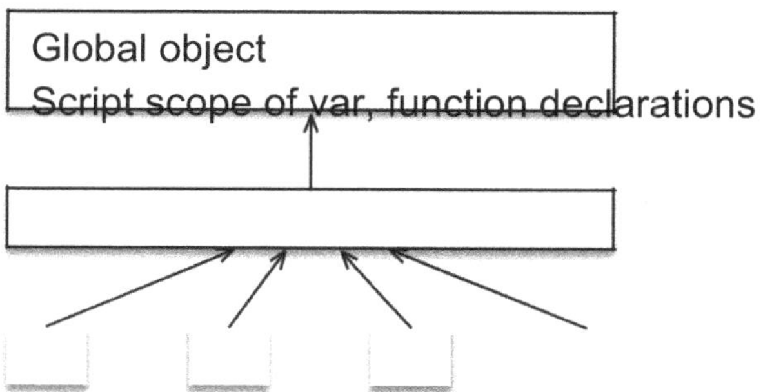

Script scope of let, const, class declarations

M1 M2 M3 ...

Module scopes (one per module)

Figure 10.1: JavaScript has multiple global scopes.

### 10.7.1 The global object

The global object lets you access the outermost global scope via an object. The two are always in sync:

- If you create a variable in the outermost global scope, the global object gets a new property. If you change such a global variable, the property changes.
- If you create or delete a property of the global object, the corresponding global variable is created or deleted. If you change a property of the global object, the corresponding global variable changes.

The global object is available via special variables:

- `window`: is the classic way of referring to the global object. But it only works in normal browser code, not in Node.js and not in *Web Workers* (processes running concurrently to normal browser code; consult $full for details).
- `self`: is available everywhere in browsers, including in Web Workers. But it isn't supported by Node.js.
- `global`: is only available in Node.js.

Let's examine how `window` works:

```
// At the top level of a script
var myGlobalVariable = 123;
assert.equal('myGlobalVariable' in window,
true);

delete window.myGlobalVariable;
assert.throws(() =>
console.log(myGlobalVariable),
ReferenceError);

// Create a global variable anywhere:
if (true) {
 window.anotherGlobalVariable = 'abc';
}
assert.equal(anotherGlobalVariable,
'abc');
```

### 10.7.2 Avoid the global object!

Brendan Eich called the global object one of his biggest regrets about JavaScript. It is best not to put variables into its scope:

In general, variables that are global to all scripts on a web page, risk name clashes.

Via the global object, you can create and delete global variables anywhere. Doing so makes code unpredictable, because it's normally not possible to make this kind of change in nested scopes.

You occasionally see `window.globalVariable` in tutorials on the web, but the prefix "`window.`" is not necessary. I prefer to omit it:

```
window.encodeURIComponent(str); // no
encodeURIComponent(str); // yes
```

## 10.8 Declarations: scope and activation

These are two key aspects of declarations:

Scope: Where can a declared entity be seen? This is a static trait.

Activation: When can I access an entity? This is a dynamic trait. Some entities can be accessed as soon as we enter their scopes. For others, we have to wait until execution reaches their declarations.

Tbl. 10.1 summarizes how various declarations handle these aspects.

Table 10.1: Aspects of declarations. "Duplicates" describes if a declara-tion can be used twice with the same same (per scope). "Global prop." describes if a declaration adds a property to the global object, when it is executed in the global scope of a script. *TDZ* means *temporal dead zone* (which is explained later). (*) Function declarations are normally block-scoped, but function-scoped in sloppy mode.

| | Scope | Activation | Duplicates | Global prop. |
|---|---|---|---|---|
| `const` | Block | decl. (TDZ) | ✘ | ✘ |
| `let` | Block | decl. (TDZ) | ✘ | ✘ |
| `function` | Block (*) | start | ✔ | ✔ |
| `class` | Block | decl. (TDZ) | ✘ | ✘ |
| `import` | Module | same as export | ✘ | ✘ |
| `var` | Function | start, partially | ✔ | ✔ |

`import` is described in §24.4 "ECMAScript modules".

The following sections describe the other constructs in more detail.

### 10.8.1 `const` and `let`: temporal dead zone

For JavaScript, TC39 needed to decide what happens if you access a constant in its direct scope, before its declaration:

```
{
  console.log(x); // What happens here?
  const x;
}
```

Some possible approaches are:

The name is resolved in the scope surrounding the current scope.

You get `undefined`.

There is an error.

was rejected, because there is no precedent in the language for this approach. It would therefore not be intuitive to JavaScript programmers.

was rejected, because then `x` wouldn't be a constant – it would have different values before and after its declaration.

`let` uses the same approach (3) as `const`, so that both work similarly and it's easy to switch between them.

The time between entering the scope of a variable and executing its declaration is called the *temporal dead zone* (TDZ) of that variable:

During this time, the variable is considered to be uninitialized (as if that were a special value it has).

If you access an uninitialized variable, you get a `ReferenceError`.

Once you reach a variable declaration, the variable is set to either the value of the initializer (specified via the assignment symbol) or `undefined` – if there is no ini-tializer.

The following code illustrates the temporal dead zone:

```
if (true) { // entering
 scope of `tmp`, TDZ starts
 // `tmp` is uninitialized:
 assert.throws(() => (tmp =

 'abc'), ReferenceError);

 assert.throws(() =>

 console.log(tmp),

 ReferenceError);

 let tmp; // TDZ ends
 assert.equal(tmp, undefined);
}
```

The next example shows that the temporal dead zone is truly *temporal* (related to time):

```
if (true) { // entering scope
 of `myVar`, TDZ starts const
 func = () => {
  console.log(myVar); // executed later
 };

  We are within the TDZ:
```

```
    Accessing `myVar` causes
    `ReferenceError`

  let myVar = 3; // TDZ ends
  func(); // OK, called outside TDZ
}
```

Even though `func()` is located before the declaration of `myVar` and uses that variable, we can call `func()`. But we have to wait until the temporal dead zone of `myVar` is over.

### 10.8.2 Function declarations and early activation

>  **More information on functions**
>
> In this section, we are using functions – before we had a chance to learn them prop-erly. Hopefully, everything still makes sense. Whenever it doesn't, please see §23 "Callable values".

A function declaration is always executed when entering its scope, regardless of where it is located within that scope. That enables you to call a function `foo()` before it is declared:

```
assert.equal(foo(), 123); // OK
function foo() { return 123; }
```

The early activation of `foo()` means that the previous code is equivalent to:

```
function foo() { return 123; }
assert.equal(foo(), 123);
```

If you declare a function via `const` or `let`, then it is not activated early: In the following example, you can only use `bar()` after its declaration.

```
assert.throws(
  () => bar(), // before declaration
  ReferenceError);

const bar = () => { return 123; };

assert.equal(bar(), 123); // after
declaration
```

#### 10.8.2.1 Calling ahead without early activation

Even if a function `g()` is not activated early, it can be called by a preceding function `f()` (in the same scope) – if we adhere to the following rule: `f()` must be invoked after the declaration of `g()`.

```
const f = () => g();
const g = () => 123;

  We call f() after
g() was declared:
assert.equal(f(),
123);
```

The functions of a module are usually invoked after its complete body was executed.

Therefore, in modules, you rarely need to worry about the order of functions.

Lastly, note how early activation automatically keeps the aforementioned rule: When entering a scope, all function declarations are executed first, before any calls are made.

#### 10.8.2.2 A pitfall of early activation

If you rely on early activation to call a function before its declaration, then you need to be careful that it doesn't access data that isn't activated early.

```
funcDecl();

const MY_STR = 'abc';
function funcDecl() {
 assert.throws(
  () => MY_STR,
  ReferenceError);
}
```

The problem goes away if you make the call to `funcDecl()` after the declaration of `MY_-STR`.

#### 10.8.2.3 The pros and cons of early activation

We have seen that early activation has a pitfall and that you can get most of its benefits without using it. Therefore, it is better to avoid early activation. But I don't feel strongly about this and, as mentioned before, often use function declarations, because I like their syntax.

### 10.8.3 Class declarations are not activated early

Even though they are similar to function declarations in some ways, class declarations are not activated early:

```
assert.throws(
  () => new MyClass(),
  ReferenceError);

class MyClass {}

assert.equal(new MyClass() instanceof
MyClass, true);
```

Why is that? Consider the following class declaration:

```
class MyClass extends Object {}
```

The operand of `extends` is an expression. Therefore, you can do things like this:

```
const identity = x => x;
class MyClass extends identity(Object) {}
```

Evaluating such an expression must be done at the location where it is mentioned. Any-thing else would be confusing. That explains why class declarations are not activated early.

### 10.8.4 `var`: hoisting (partial early activation)

`var` is an older way of declaring variables that predates `const` and `let` (which are pre-ferred now). Consider the following `var` declaration.

```
var x = 123;
```

This declaration has two parts:

Declaration `var x`: The scope of a `var`-declared variable is the innermost surround-ing function and not the innermost surrounding block, as for most other declara-tions. Such a variable is already active at the beginning of its scope and initialized with `undefined`.

Assignment `x = 123`: The assignment is always executed in place.

The following code demonstrates the effects of `var`:

```
function f() {
   Partial early
  activation:
  assert.equal(x,
  undefined);
  if (true) {
   var x = 123;
     The assignment is
   executed in place:
   assert.equal(x, 123);
  }
   Scope is
  function, not
  block:
  assert.equal(x,
  123);
}
```

## 10.9 Closures

Before we can explore closures, we need to learn about bound variables and free vari-ables.

### 10.9.1 Bound variables vs. free variables

Per scope, there is a set of variables that are mentioned. Among these variables we dis-tinguish:

*Bound variables* are declared within the scope. They are parameters and local vari-ables.

*Free variables* are declared externally. They are also called *non-local variables*.

Consider the following code:

```
function func(x)
        {
   const y = 123;
   console.log(z);
  }
```

In the body of `func()`, `x` and `y` are bound variables. `z` is a free variable.

### 10.9.2 What is a closure?

What is a closure, then?

A *closure* is a function plus a connection to the variables that exist at its "birth place".

What is the point of keeping this connection? It provides the values for the free variables of the function. For example:

```
function funcFactory(value) {
  return () => {
    return value;
  };
}

const func = funcFactory('abc');
assert.equal(func(), 'abc'); // (A)
```

`funcFactory` returns a closure that is assigned to `func`. Because `func` has the connection to the variables at its birth place, it can still access the free variable `value` when it is called in line A (even though it "escaped" its scope).

> **All functions in JavaScript are closures**
> Static scoping is supported via closures in JavaScript. Therefore, every function is a closure.

### 10.9.3 Example: A factory for incrementors

The following function returns *incrementors* (a name that I just made up). An incrementor is a function that internally stores a number. When it is called, it updates that number by adding the argument to it and returns the new value.

```
function createInc(startValue) {
  return (step) => { // (A)
    startValue += step;
    return startValue;
  };
}
const inc = createInc(5);
assert.equal(inc(2), 7);
```

We can see that the function created in line A keeps its internal number in the free variable `startValue`. This time, we don't just read from the birth scope, we use it to store data that we change and that persists across function calls.

We can create more storage slots in the birth scope, via local variables:

```
function createInc(startValue) {
  let index = -1;
  return (step) => {
    startValue += step;
    index++;
    return [index, startValue];
  };
}
```

```
const inc = createInc(5);
assert.deepEqual(inc(2), [0, 7]);
assert.deepEqual(inc(2), [1, 9]);
assert.deepEqual(inc(2), [2, 11]);
```

### 10.9.4 Use cases for closures

What are closures good for?

- For starters, they are simply an implementation of static scoping. As such, they provide context data for callbacks.
- They can also be used by functions to store state that persists across function calls. `createInc()` is an example of that.
- And they can provide private data for objects (produced via literals or classes). The details of how that works are explained in "Exploring ES6".

> **Quiz: advanced**
>
> See quiz app.

## 10.10 Further reading

For more information on how variables are handled under the hood (as described in the ECMAScript specification), consult $full.

# Chapter 11

# Values

## Contents

---

In this chapter, we'll examine what kinds of values JavaScript has.

 **Supporting tool: ===**

In this chapter, we'll occasionally use the strict equality operator. `a === b` evaluates to `true` if `a` and `b` are equal. What exactly that means is explained in §12.4.2 "Strict equality (=== and !==)".

### 11.1 What's a type?

For this chapter, I consider types to be sets of values. For example, the type `boolean` is the set { `false`, `true` }.

## 11.2 JavaScript's type hierarchy

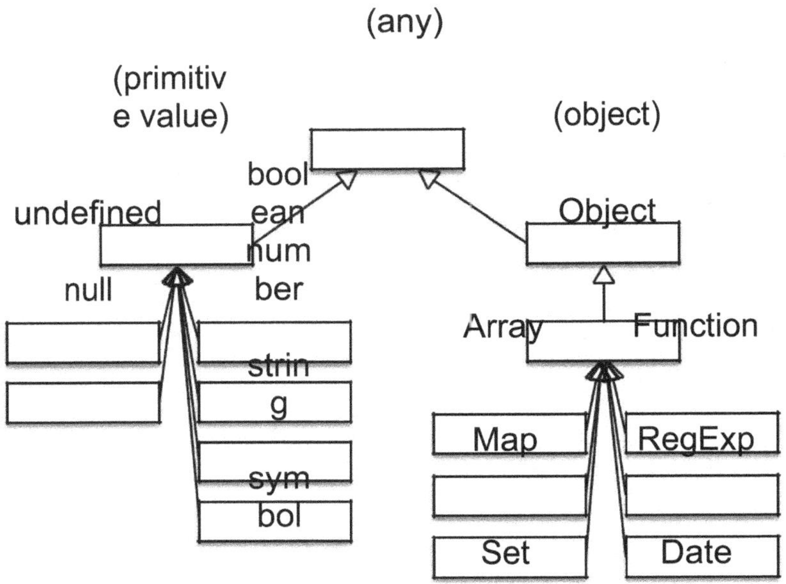


Figure 11.1: A partial hierarchy of JavaScript's types. Missing are the classes for errors, the classes associated with primitive types, and more. The diagram hints at the fact that not all objects are instances of `Object`.

Fig. 11.1 shows JavaScript's type hierarchy. What do we learn from that diagram?

JavaScript distinguishes two kinds of values: primitive values and objects. We'll see soon what the difference is.

The diagram differentiates objects and instances of class `Object`. Each instance of `Object` is also an object, but not vice versa. However, virtually all objects that you'll encounter in practice are instances of `Object`. For example, objects created via object literals, are. More details on this topic are explained in §26.4.3.4 "Objects that aren't instances of `Object`".

## 11.3 The types of the language specification

The ECMAScript specification only knows a total of 7 types. The names of those types are (I'm using TypeScript's names, not the spec's names):

- `undefined`: with the only element `undefined`.
- `null`: with the only element `null`.
- `boolean`: with the elements `false` and `true`.
- `number`: the type of all numbers (e.g. `-123`, `3.141`).
- `string`: the type of all strings (e.g. `'abc'`).
- `symbol`: the type of all symbols (e.g. `Symbol('My Symbol')`).
- `object`: the type of all objects (different from `Object`, the type of all instances of class `Object` and its subclasses).

## 11.4 Primitive values vs. objects

The specification makes an important distinction between values:

- *Primitive values* are the elements of the types `undefined`, `null`, `boolean`, `number`, `string`, `symbol`.
- All other values are *objects*.

In contrast to Java (that inspired JavaScript here), primitive values are not second-class citizens. The difference between them and objects is more subtle. In a nutshell, it is:

Primitive values: are atomic building blocks of data in JavaScript.

- They are *passed by value*: When primitive values are assigned to variables or passed to functions, their contents are copied.
- They are *compared by value*: When comparing two primitive values, their con-tents are compared.

Objects: are compound pieces of data.

- They are *passed by identity* (my term): When objects are assigned to variables or passed to functions, their *identities* (think pointers) are copied.
- They are *compared by identity* (my term): When comparing two objects, their identities are compared.

Other than that, primitive values and objects are quite similar: They both have *properties* (key-value entries) and can be used in the same locations.

Next, we'll look at primitive values and objects in more depth.

### 11.4.1 Primitive values (short: primitives)

#### 11.4.1.1 Primitives are immutable

You can't change, add or remove properties of primitives:

```
let str = 'abc';
assert.equal(str.length, 3);
assert.throws(
  () => { str.length = 1 },
  /^TypeError: Cannot assign to read only
  property 'length'/
);
```

#### 11.4.1.2 Primitives are *passed by value*

Primitives are *passed by value*: Variables (including parameters) store the contents of the primitives. When assigning a primitive value to a variable or passing it as an argument to a function, its content is copied.

```
let x = 123;
let y = x;
assert.equal(y, 123);
```

#### 11.4.1.3 Primitives are *compared by value*

Primitives are *compared by value*: When comparing two primitive values, we compare their contents.

```
assert.equal(123 === 123, true);
assert.equal('abc' === 'abc', true);
```

To see what's so special about this way of comparing, read on and find out how objects are compared.

### 11.4.2 Objects

Objects are covered in detail in §25 "Single objects" and the following chapter. Here, we mainly focus on how they differ from primitive values.

Let's first explore two common ways of creating objects:

- Object literal:

  ```
  const obj = {
    first: 'Jane',
    last: 'Doe',
  };
  ```

  The object literal starts and ends with curly braces `{}`. It creates an object with two properties. The first property has the key `'first'` (a string) and the value `'Jane'`. The second property has the key `'last'` and the value `'Doe'`. For more information on object literals, consult §25.2.1 "Object literals: properties".

- Array literal:

  ```
  const arr = ['foo', 'bar'];
  ```

The Array literal starts and ends with square brackets `[]`. It creates an Array with two *elements*: `'foo'` and `'bar'`. For more information on Array literals, consult $full.

### 11.4.2.1 Objects are mutable by default

By default, you can freely change, add and remove the properties of objects:

```
const obj = {};

obj.foo = 'abc'; // add a property
assert.equal(obj.foo, 'abc');

obj.foo = 'def'; // change a property
assert.equal(obj.foo, 'def');
```

### 11.4.2.2 Objects are *passed by identity*

Objects are *passed by identity* (my term): Variables (including parameters) store the *identi-ties* of objects.

The identity of an object is like a pointer (or a transparent reference) to the object's actual data on the *heap* (think shared main memory of a JavaScript engine).

When assigning an object to a variable or passing it as an argument to a function, its identity is copied. Each object literal creates a fresh object on the heap and returns its identity.

```
const a = {}; // fresh empty object
// Pass the identity in `a` to `b`:
const b = a;

  Now `a` and `b` point to the same object
  (they "share" that object):
assert.equal(a === b, true);

  Changing `a`
also changes `b`:
a.foo = 123;
assert.equal(b.foo
, 123);
```

JavaScript uses *garbage collection* to automatically manage memory:

```
let obj = { prop: 'value' };
obj = {};
```

Now the old value `{ prop: 'value' }` of `obj` is *garbage* (not used anymore). JavaScript will automatically *garbage-collect* it (remove it from memory), at some point in time (pos-sibly never if there is enough free memory).

> **Details: passing by identity**
>
> "Passing by identity" means that the identity of an object (a transparent reference) is passed by value. This approach is also called "passing by sharing".

#### 11.4.2.3 Objects are *compared by identity*

Objects are *compared by identity* (my term): Two variables are only equal if they contain the same object identity. They are not equal if they refer to different objects with the same content.

```
const obj = {}; // fresh empty object
assert.equal(obj === obj, true); // same identity
assert.equal({} === {}, false); // different identities, same content
```

## 11.5 The operators `typeof` and `instanceof`: what's the type of a value?

The two operators `typeof` and `instanceof` let you determine what type a given value `x` has:

```
if (typeof x === 'string') ···
if (x instanceof Array) ···
```

How do they differ?

`typeof` distinguishes the 7 types of the specification (minus one omission, plus one addition).

`instanceof` tests which class created a given value.

> **Rule of thumb: `typeof` is for primitive values, `instanceof` is for objects**

### 11.5.1 `typeof`

Table 11.1: The results of the `typeof` operator.

| x | typeof x |
|---|---|
| undefined | 'undefined' |
| null | 'object' |
| Boolean | 'boolean' |
| Number | 'number' |
| String | 'string' |
| Symbol | 'symbol' |
| Function | 'funct |

| | |
|---|---|
| | ion' |
| All other objects | 'object' |

Tbl. 11.1 lists all results of `typeof`. They roughly correspond to the 7 types of the language specification. Alas, there are two differences and they are language quirks:

- `typeof null` returns `'object'` and not `'null'`. That's a bug. Unfortunately, it can't be fixed. TC39 tried to do that, but it broke too much code on the web.
- `typeof` of a function should be `'object'` (functions are objects). Introducing a separate category for functions is confusing.

> **Exercises: Two exercises on `typeof`**
>
> - `exercises/values/typeof_exrc.mjs`
> - Bonus: `exercises/values/is_object_test.mjs`

### 11.5.2 `instanceof`

This operator answers the question: has a value `x` been created by a class `C`?

```
x instanceof C
```

For example:

```
> (function() {}) instanceof Function
true
> ({}) instanceof Object
true
> [] instanceof Array
true
```

Primitive values are not instances of anything:

```
> 123 instanceof Number
false
> '' instanceof String
false
> '' instanceof Object
false
```

> **Exercise: `instanceof`**
>
> `exercises/values/instanceof_exrc.mjs`

## 11.6 Classes and constructor functions

JavaScript's original factories for objects are *constructor functions*: ordinary functions that return "instances" of themselves if you invoke them via the `new` operator.

ES6 introduced *classes*, which are mainly better syntax for constructor functions.

In this book, I'm using the terms *constructor function* and *class* interchangeably.

Classes can be seen as partitioning the single type `object` of the specification into sub-types – they give us more types than the limited 7 ones of the specification.

Each class is the type of the objects that were created by it.

### 11.6.1 Constructor functions associated with primitive types

Each primitive type (except for the spec-internal types for `undefined` and `null`) has an associated *constructor function* (think class):

The constructor function `Boolean` is associated with booleans.

The constructor function `Number` is associated with numbers.

The constructor function `String` is associated with strings.

The constructor function `Symbol` is associated with symbols.

Each of these functions plays several roles. For example, `Number`:

- You can use it as a function and convert values to numbers:

```
assert.equal(Number('123'), 123);
```

- `Number.prototype` provides the properties for numbers. For example, method `.toString()`:

```
assert.equal((123).toString,
Number.prototype.toString);
```

`Number` is a namespace/container object for tool functions for numbers. For exam-ple:

```
assert.equal(Number.isInteger(123),
true);
```

Lastly, you can also use `Number` as a class and create number objects. These objects are different from real numbers and should be avoided.

```
assert.notEqual(new Number(123),
123);
assert.equal(new
Number(123).valueOf(), 123);
```

#### 11.6.1.1 Wrapping primitive values

The constructor functions related to primitive types are also called *wrapper types*, because they provide the canonical way of converting primitive values to objects. In the process, primitive values are “wrapped” in objects.

```
const prim = true;
assert.equal(typeof prim, 'boolean');
assert.equal(prim instanceof Boolean,
false);

const wrapped = Object(prim);
assert.equal(typeof wrapped, 'object');
assert.equal(wrapped instanceof Boolean,
true);
```

```
assert.equal(wrapped.valueOf(), prim);
// unwrap
```

Wrapping rarely matters in practice, but it is used internally in the language specification, to give primitives properties.

## 11.7 Converting between types

There are two ways in which values are converted to other types in JavaScript:

- Explicit conversion: via functions such as `String()`.
- *Coercion* (automatic conversion): happens when an operation receives operands/-parameters that it can't work with.

### 11.7.1 Explicit conversion between types

The function associated with a primitive type explicitly converts values to that type:

```
> Boolean(0)
false
> Number('123')
123
> String(123)
'123'
```

You can also use `Object()` to convert values to objects:

```
> typeof Object(123)
'object'
```

#### 11.7.2 Coercion (automatic conversion between types)

For many operations, JavaScript automatically converts the operands/parameters if their types don't fit. This kind of automatic conversion is called *coercion*.

For example, the multiplication operator coerces its operands to numbers:

```
> '7' * '3'
21
```

Many built-in functions coerce, too. For example, `parseInt()` coerces its parameter to string (parsing stops at the first character that is not a digit):

```
> parseInt(123.45)
123
```

> **Exercise: Converting values to primitives**
>
> `exercises/values/conversion_exrc.mjs`

>  **Quiz**
>
> See quiz app.

86
*Values*

*11*

# Chapter 12

# Operators

## Contents

---

## 12.1 Making sense of operators

JavaScript's operators may seem quirky. With the following two rules, they are easier to understand:

Operators coerce their operands to appropriate types
Most operators only work with primitive values

87

### 12.1.1 Operators coerce their operands to appropriate types

If an operator gets operands that don't have the proper types, it rarely throws an excep-tion. Instead, it *coerces* (automatically converts) the operands so that it can work with them. Let's look at two examples.

First, the multiplication operator can only work with numbers. Therefore, it converts strings to numbers before computing its result.

```
> '7' * '3'
21
```

Second, the square brackets operator (`[ ]`) for accessing the properties of an object can only handle strings and symbols. All other values are coerced to string:

```
const obj = {};
obj['true'] = 123;

  Coerce true to the

string 'true'

assert.equal(obj[tr

ue], 123);
```

### 12.1.2 Most operators only work with primitive values

As mentioned before, most operators only work with primitive values. If an operand is an object, it is usually coerced to a primitive value. For example:

```
> [1,2,3] + [4,5,6]
'1,2,34,5,6'
```

Why? The plus operator first coerces its operands to primitive values:

```
> String([1,2,3])
'1,2,3'
> String([4,5,6])
'4,5,6'
```

Next, it concatenates the two strings:

```
> '1,2,3' + '4,5,6'
'1,2,34,5,6'
```

## 12.2 The plus operator (+)

The plus operator works as follows in JavaScript:

First, it converts both operands to primitive values.

Then it switches to one of two modes:

- String mode: If one of the two primitive values is a string, then it converts the other one to a string, concatenates both strings and returns the result.
- Number mode: Otherwise, it converts both operands to numbers, adds them and returns the result.

String mode lets us use + to assemble strings:

```
> 'There are ' + 3 + ' items'
'There are 3 items'
```

Number mode means that if neither operand is a string (or an object that becomes a string)

then everything is coerced to numbers:

```
> 4 + true
5
```

`Number(true)` is `1`.

## 12.3 Assignment operators

### 12.3.1 The plain assignment operator

The plain assignment operator is used to change storage locations:

```
x = value; // assign to a
previously declared variable
obj.propKey = value; // assign
to a property arr[index] =
value; // assign to an Array
element
```

Initializers in variable declarations can also be viewed as a form of assignment:

```
const x = value;
let y = value;
```

### 12.3.2 Compound assignment operators

Given an operator `op`, the following two ways of assigning are equivalent:

```
myvar op= value
```

```
myvar = myvar op value
```

If, for example, `op` is `+` then we get the operator `+=` that works as follows.

```
let str = '';
str += '<b>';
str += 'Hello!';
str += '</b>';

assert.equal(str, '<b>Hello!</b>');
```

### 12.3.3 A list of all compound assignment operators

- Arithmetic operators:

  ```
  += -= *= /= %= **=
  ```

  `+=` also works for string concatenation

- Bitwise operators:

  ```
  <<= >>= >>>= &= ^= |=
  ```

## 12.4 Equality: == vs. ===

JavaScript has two kinds of equality operators: loose equality (==) and strict equality (===). The recommendation is to always use the latter.

> **Other names for == and ===**
>
> == is also called *double equals*. Its official name in the language specification is *abstract equality comparison*.
>
> === is also called *triple equals*.

### 12.4.1 Loose equality (== and !=)

Loose equality is one of JavaScript's quirks. It often coerces operands. Some of those coercions make sense:

```
> '123' == 123
true
> false == 0
true
```

Others less so:

```
> '' == 0
true
```

Objects are coerced to primitives if (and only if!) the other operand is primitive:

```
> [1, 2, 3] == '1,2,3'
true
```

```
> ['1', '2', '3'] == '1,2,3'
true
```

If both operands are objects, they are only equal if they are the same object:

```
> [1, 2, 3] == ['1', '2', '3']
false
> [1, 2, 3] == [1, 2, 3]
false

 const arr = [1, 2, 3];
 arr == arr
true
```

Lastly, `==` considers `undefined` and `null` to be equal:

```
> undefined == null
true
```

### 12.4.2 Strict equality (=== and !==)

Strict equality never coerces. Two values are only equal if they have the same type. Let's revisit our previous interaction with the == operator and see what the === operator does:

```
> false === 0
false
> '123' === 123
false
```

An object is only equal to another value if that value is the same object:

```
> [1, 2, 3] === '1,2,3'
false
> ['1', '2', '3'] === '1,2,3'
false

> [1, 2, 3] === ['1', '2', '3']
false
> [1, 2, 3] === [1, 2, 3]
false

 const arr = [1, 2, 3];
 arr === arr
true
```

The === operator does not consider `undefined` and `null` to be equal:

```
> undefined === null
false
```

### 12.4.3 Recommendation: always use strict equality

I recommend to always use ===. It makes your code easier to understand and spares you from having to think about the quirks of ==.

Let's look at two use cases for == and what I recommend to do instead.

#### 12.4.3.1 Use case for ==: comparing with a number or a string

lets you check if a value x is a number or that number as a string – with a single comparison:

```
if (x == 123) {
  // x is either 123 or '123'
}
```

I prefer either of the following two alternatives:

```
if (x === 123 || x === '123') ···
if (Number(x) === 123) ···
```

You can also convert x to a number when you first encounter it.

#### 12.4.3.2 Use case for ==: comparing with `undefined` or `null`

Another use case for `==` is to check if a value `x` is either `undefined` or `null`:

```
if (x == null) {
  // x is either null or undefined
}
```

The problem with this code is that you can't be sure if someone meant to write it that way or if they made a typo and meant `=== null`.

I prefer either of the following two alternatives:

```
if (x === undefined || x === null) ···
if (!x) ···
```

The second alternative is even more sloppy than using `==`, but it is a well-established pattern in JavaScript (to be explained in detail in §14.2 "Falsy and truthy values").

The following three conditions are also roughly equivalent:

```
if (x != null) ···
if (x !== undefined && x !== null) ···
if (x) ···
```

### 12.4.4 Even stricter than ===: `Object.is()`

Method `Object.is()` compares two values:

```
> Object.is(123, 123)
true
> Object.is(123, '123')
```

```
false
```

It is even stricter than ===. For example, it considers NaN, the error value for computations involving numbers, to be equal to itself:

```
> Object.is(NaN, NaN)
true
> NaN === NaN
false
```

That is occasionally useful. For example, you can use it to implement an improved ver-sion of the Array method .indexOf():

```
const myIndexOf = (arr, elem) => {
  return arr.findIndex(x => Object.is(x,
  elem));
};
```

myIndexOf() finds NaN in an Array, while .indexOf() doesn't:

```
> myIndexOf([0,NaN,2], NaN)
1
> [0,NaN,2].indexOf(NaN)
-1
```

The result `-1` means that `.indexOf()` couldn't find its argument in the Array.

## 12.5 Ordering operators

Table 12.1: JavaScript's ordering operators.

| Operator | name |
|---|---|
| | less than |
| <= | Less than or equal |
| | Greater than |
| >= | Greater than or equal |

JavaScript's ordering operators (tbl. 12.1) work for both numbers and strings:

```
> 5 >= 2
true
> 'bar' < 'foo'
true
```

`<=` and `>=` are based on strict equality.

> ⚠ **The ordering operators don't work well for human languages**
>
> The ordering operators don't work well for comparing text in a human language, e.g. when capitalization or accents are involved. The details are explained in §18.5 "Comparing strings".

## 12.6 Various other operators

Operators for booleans, strings, numbers, objects: are covered elsewhere in this book.

The next two subsections discuss two operators that are rarely used.

### 12.6.1 Comma operator

The comma operator has two operands, evaluates both of them and returns the second one:

```
> 'a', 'b'
'b'
```

For more information on this operator, see "Speaking JavaScript".

### 12.6.2 `void` operator

The `void` operator evaluates its operand and returns `undefined`:

```
> void (3 + 2)
undefined
```

For more information on this operator, see “Speaking JavaScript”.

See quiz app.

# Part IV

## Primitive values

# Chapter 13

## The non-values `undefined` and `null`

### Contents



Many programming languages have one "non-value" called `null`. It indicates that a vari-able does not currently point to an object. For example, when it hasn't been initialized, yet.

In contrast, JavaScript has two of them: `undefined` and `null`.

## 13.1 `undefined` vs. `null`

Both values are very similar and often used interchangeably. How they differ is therefore subtle. The language itself makes the following distinction:

- `undefined` means "not initialized" (e.g. a variable) or "not existing" (e.g. a property of an object).
- `null` means "the intentional absence of any object value" (a quote from the lan-guage specification).

Programmers may make the following distinction:

- `undefined` is the non-value used by the language (when something is uninitialized etc.).

97

> `null` means “explicitly switched off”. That is, it helps implement a type that com-prises both meaningful values and a meta-value that stands for “no meaningful value”. Such a type is called *option type* or *maybe type* in functional programming.

## 13.2 Occurrences of `undefined` and `null`

The following subsections describe where `undefined` and `null` appear in the language.

We’ll encounter several mechanisms that are explained in more detail later in this book.

### 13.2.1 Occurrences of `undefined`

Uninitialized variable `myVar`:

```
let myVar;
assert.equal(myVar, undefined);
```

Parameter `x` is not provided:

```
function func(x) {
 return x;
}
assert.equal(func(), undefined);
```

Property `.unknownProp` is missing:

```
const obj = {};
assert.equal(obj.unknownProp,
undefined);
```

If you don't explicitly specify the result of a function via a `return` statement, JavaScript returns `undefined` for you:

```
function func() {}
assert.equal(func(), undefined);
```

### 13.2.2 Occurrences of `null`

The prototype of an object is either an object or, at the end of a chain of prototypes, `null`.

`Object.prototype` does not have a prototype:

```
>
Object.getPrototypeOf(Object.prototype)
null
```

If you match a regular expression (such as `/a/`) against a string (such as `'x'`), you either get an object with matching data (if matching was successful) or `null` (if matching failed):

```
> /a/.exec('x')
null
```

The JSON data format does not support `undefined`, only `null`:

```
> JSON.stringify({a: undefined, b:
null})
'{"b":null}'
```

## 13.3 Checking for `undefined` or `null`

Checking for either:

```
if (x === null) ···
if (x === undefined) ···
```

Does `x` have a value?

```
if (x !== undefined && x !== null) {
  // ···
}
if (x) { // truthy?
  // x is neither: undefined, null, false,
  0, NaN, ''
}
```

Is `x` either `undefined` or `null`?

```
if (x === undefined || x === null) {
  // ···
}
if (!x) { // falsy?
  // x is: undefined, null, false, 0, NaN,
  ''
}
```

*Truthy* means "is `true` if coerced to boolean". *Falsy* means "is `false` if coerced to boolean".

Both concepts are explained properly in §14.2 "Falsy and truthy values".

## 13.4 `undefined` and `null` don't have properties

`undefined` and `null` are the two only JavaScript values where you get an exception if you try to read a property. To explore this phenomenon, let's use the following function, which reads ("gets") property `.foo` and returns the result.

```
function getFoo(x) {
  return x.foo;
}
```

If we apply `getFoo()` to various value, we can see that it only fails for `undefined` and `null`:

```
> getFoo(undefined)
TypeError: Cannot read property 'foo' of
undefined
> getFoo(null)
TypeError: Cannot read property 'foo' of
null

> getFoo(true)
undefined
> getFoo({})
undefined
```

## 13.5 The history of `undefined` and `null`

In Java (which inspired many aspects of JavaScript), initialization values depend on the static type of a variable:

- Variables with object types are initialized with `null`.
- Each primitive type has its own initialization value. For example, `int` variables are initialized with `0`.

In JavaScript, each variable can hold both object values and primitive values. Therefore, if `null` means "not an object", JavaScript also needs an initialization value that means "neither an object nor a primitive value". That initialization value is `undefined`.

> **Quiz**
>
> See quiz app.

# Chapter 14

# Booleans

## Contents

The primitive type *boolean* comprises two values – `false` and `true`:

```
> typeof false
'boolean'
> typeof true
'boolean'
```

## 14.1 Converting to boolean

These are three ways in which you can convert an arbitrary value `x` to a boolean.

`Boolean(x)`
Most descriptive; recommended.

`x ? true : false`
Uses the conditional operator (explained later in this chapter).

101

`!!x`
Uses the logical Not operator (`!`). This operator coerces its operand to boolean. It is applied a second time to get a non-negated result.

Tbl. 14.1 describes how various values are converted to boolean.

Table 14.1: Converting values to booleans.

| | `Boolean(x)` |
|---|---|
| `undefined` | `false` |
| `null` | `false` |
| boolean value | `x` (no change) |
| number value | `0` → `false`, `NaN` → `false`<br>other numbers → `true` |
| string value | `''` → `false`<br>other strings → `true` |
| object value | always `true` |

## 14.2 Falsy and truthy values

In JavaScript, if you read something that doesn't exist (e.g. a missing parameter or a missing property), you usually get `undefined` as a result. In these cases, an existence check amounts to comparing a value with undefined. For example, the following code checks if object obj has the property .prop:

```
if (obj.prop !==
  undefined) {
 // obj has property .prop
}
```

To simplify this check, we can use the fact that the if statement always converts its con-ditional value to boolean:

```
if ('abc') { // true, if converted to
boolean
 console.log('Yes!');
}
```

Therefore, we can use the following code to check if obj.prop exists. That is less precise than comparing with undefined, but also shorter:

```
if (obj.prop) {
 // obj has property .prop
}
```

This simplified check is so popular that the following two names were introduced:

A value is called *truthy* if it is true when converted to boolean.

A value is called *falsy* if it is false when converted to boolean.

Consulting tbl. 14.1, we can make an exhaustive list of falsy values:

undefined, null

Booleans: `false`

Numbers: `0`, `NaN`

Strings: `''`

All other values (incl. *all* objects) are truthy:

```
> Boolean('abc')
true
> Boolean([])
true
> Boolean({})
true
```

### 14.2.1 Pitfall: truthiness checks are imprecise

Truthiness checks have one pitfall: they are not very precise. Consider this previous example:

```
if (obj.prop) {
  // obj has property .prop
}
```

The body of the `if` statement is skipped if:

`obj.prop` is missing (in which case, JavaScript returns `undefined`). However, it is also skipped if:

`obj.prop` is `undefined`.

`obj.prop` is any other falsy value (`null`, `0`, `''`, etc.).

In practice, this rarely causes problems, but you have to be aware of this pitfall.

### 14.2.2 Checking for truthiness or falsiness

```
if (x) {
 // x is truthy
}

if (!x) {
 // x is falsy
}

if (x) {
   x is
truthy }
else {
   x is falsy
}

const result = x ? 'truthy' : 'falsy';
```

The conditional operator that is used in the last line, is explained later in this chapter.

### 14.2.3 Use case: was a parameter provided?

A truthiness check is often used to determine if the caller of a function provided a param-eter:

```
function func(x) {
  if (!x) {
    throw new Error('Missing parameter
    x');
  }
  // ···
}
```

On the plus side, this pattern is established and short. It correctly throws errors for `un-defined` and `null`. On the minus side, there is the previously mentioned pitfall: the code also throws errors for all other falsy values.

An alternative is to check for `undefined`:

```
if (x === undefined) {
  throw new Error('Missing parameter x');
}
```

### 14.2.4 Use case: does a property exist?

Truthiness checks are also often used to determine if a property exists:

```
function readFile(fileDesc) {
  if (!fileDesc.path) {
    throw new Error('Missing property:
    .path');
  }
```

```
  // ···
}
readFile({ path: 'foo.txt' }); // no
error
```

This pattern is also established and has the usual caveat: it not only throws if the property is missing, but also if it exists and has any of the falsy values.

If you truly want to check if the property exists, you have to use the `in` operator:

```
if (! ('path' in fileDesc)) {
  throw new Error('Missing property:
  .path');
}
```

> **Exercise: Truthiness**
>
> `exercises/booleans/truthiness_exrc.mjs`

### 14.3 Conditional operator (? :)

The conditional operator is the expression version of the `if` statement. Its syntax is:

```
«condition» ? «thenExpression» : «elseExpression»
```

It is evaluated as follows:

> If `condition` is truthy, evaluate and return `thenExpression`.
>
> Otherwise, evaluate and return `elseExpression`.

The conditional operator is also called *ternary operator*, because it has three operands.

Examples:

```
> true ? 'yes' : 'no'
'yes'
> false ? 'yes' : 'no'
'no'
> '' ? 'yes' : 'no'
'no'
```

The following code demonstrates that, whichever of the two branches "then" and "else" is chosen via the condition – only that branch is evaluated. The other branch isn't.

```
const x = (true ? console.log('then') : console.log('else'));

  Output:
  'then'
```

## 14.4 Binary logical operators: And (x && y), Or (x || y)

The operators `&&` and `||` are *value-preserving* and *short-circuiting*. What does that mean?

*Value-preservation* means that operands are interpreted as booleans, but returned unchanged:

```
> 12 || 'hello'
12
> 0 || 'hello'
'hello'
```

*Short-circuiting* means: If the first operand already determines the result, then the second operand is not evaluated. The only other operator that delays evaluating its operands is the conditional operator: Usually, all operands are evaluated before performing an operation.

For example, logical And (`&&`) does not evaluate its second operand if the first one is falsy:

```
const x = false && console.log('hello');
// No output
```

If the first operand is truthy, `console.log()` is executed:

```
const x = true && console.log('hello');

  Output:
  'hello'
```

### 14.4.1 Logical And (`x && y`)

The expression `a && b` ("`a` And `b`") is evaluated as follows:

Evaluate `a`.

Is the result falsy? Return it.
Otherwise, evaluate `b` and return the result.

In other words, the following two expressions are roughly equivalent:

```
a && b
!a ? a : b
```

Examples:

```
> false && true
false
> false && 'abc'
false

> true && false
false
> true && 'abc'
'abc'

> '' && 'abc'
''
```

### 14.4.2 Logical Or (`||`)

The expression `a || b` ("`a` Or `b`") is evaluated as follows:

Evaluate `a`.

Is the result truthy? Return it.

Otherwise, evaluate `b` and return the result.

In other words, the following two expressions are roughly equivalent:

```
a || b
a ? a : b
```

Examples:

```
> true || false
true
> true || 'abc'
true

> false || true
true
> false || 'abc'
'abc'
```

```
> 'abc' || 'def'
'abc'
```

### 14.4.3 Default values via logical Or (||)

Sometimes you receive a value and only want to use it if it isn't either `null` or `undefined`. Otherwise, you'd like to use a default value, as a fallback. You can do that via the `||` operator:

```
const valueToUse = valueReceived ||
defaultValue;
```

The following code shows a real-world example:

```
function countMatches(regex, str) {
 const matchResult =
 str.match(regex); // null or
 Array return (matchResult ||
 []).length;
}
```

If there are one or more matches for `regex` inside `str` then `.match()` returns an Array. If there are no matches, it unfortunately returns `null` (and not the empty Array). We fix that via the `||` operator.

> **Exercise: Default values via the Or operator (||)**
>
> `exercises/booleans/default_via_or_exrc.mjs`

## 14.5 Logical Not (!)

The expression `!x` ("Not `x`") is evaluated as follows:

Evaluate `x`.

Is it truthy? Return `false`.

Otherwise, return `true`.

Examples:

```
> !false
true
> !true
false

> !0
true
> !123
false

> !''
true
> !'abc'
false
```

See quiz app.

# Chapter 15

# Numbers

## Contents

---

This chapter covers JavaScript's single type for numbers, `number`.

## 15.1 JavaScript only has floating point numbers

You can express both integers and floating point numbers in JavaScript:

```
98
123.45
```

However, there is only a single type for all numbers: They are all *doubles*, 64-bit floating point numbers implemented according to the IEEE Standard for Floating-Point Arith-metic (IEEE 754).

Integers are simply floating point numbers without a decimal fraction:

```
> 98 === 98.0
true
```

Note that, under the hood, most JavaScript engines are often able to use real integers, with all associated performance and storage size benefits.

## 15.2 Number literals

Let's examine literals for numbers.

### 15.2.1 Integer literals

Several *integer literals* let you express integers with various bases:

```
Binary
(base 2)
assert.equal
(0b11, 3);

Octal
(base 8)
assert.equal
(0o10, 8);

Decimal
(base 10):
assert.equa
l(35, 35);

Hexadecimal
(base 16)
```

```
assert.equal(
0xE7, 231);
```

### 15.2.2 Floating point literals

Floating point numbers can only be expressed in base 10.

Fractions:

```
> 35.0
35
```

Exponent: `eN` means ×$10^N$

```
> 3e2
300
> 3e-2
0.03
> 0.3e2
30
```

### 15.2.3 Syntactic pitfall: properties of integer literals

Accessing a property of an integer literal entails a pitfall:

If the integer literal is immedi-ately followed by a dot then

that dot is interpreted as a decimal dot:

```
7.toString(); // syntax error
```

There are four ways to work around this pitfall:

```
7.0.toString()
(7).toString()
7..toString()
7 .toString()   // space before dot
```

## 15.3 Arithmetic operators

### 15.3.1 Binary arithmetic operators

Tbl. 15.1 lists JavaScript's binary arithmetic operators.

Table 15.1: Binary arithmetic operators.

| Operator | Name | | Example |
|---|---|---|---|
| n + m | Addition | ES1 | 3+ 4 → 7 |
| n - m | Subtraction | ES1 | 9- 1 → 8 |
| n * m | Multiplication | ES1 | * 2.25 3→ 6.75 |
| n / m | Division | ES1 | 5.6 / 5 → 25 1.125 |
| n % m | Remainder | ES1 | % 85 → 3 -8 % 5 → -3 |
| n ** m | Exponentiation | ES2016 | ** 42 → 16 |

Note that % is a remainder operator (not a modulo operator) – its result has the sign of the first operand:

```
> 3 % 2
1
> -3 % 2
-1
```

### 15.3.2 Unary plus (+) and negation (-)

Tbl. 15.2 summarizes the two operators *unary plus* (+) and *negation* (-).

Table 15.2: The operators unary plus (+) and negation (-).

| Operator | Name | | Example |
|---|---|---|---|
| +n | Unary plus | ES1 | +(-7) → -7 |
| -n | Unary negation | ES1 | -(-7) → 7 |

Both operators coerce their operands to numbers:

```
> +'5'
5
> +'-12'
-12
> -'9'
-9
```

Thus, unary plus lets us convert arbitrary values to numbers.

### 15.3.3 Incrementing (++) and decrementing (--)

The incrementation operator ++ exists in a prefix version and a suffix version. In both versions, it destructively adds one to its operand. Therefore, its operand must be a storage location that can be changed.

The decrementation operator -- works the same, but subtracts one from its operand. The next two examples explain the difference between the prefix and the suffix version.

Tbl. 15.3 summarizes the incrementation and decrementation operators.

Table 15.3: Incrementation operators and decrementation operators.

| Operator | Name | | Example |
|---|---|---|---|
| `v++` | Increment | ES1 | `let v=0; [v++, v] → [0, 1]` |
| `++v` | Increment | ES1 | `let v=0; [++v, v] → [1, 1]` |
| `v--` | Decrement | ES1 | `let v=1; [v--, v] → [1, 0]` |
| `--v` | Decrement | ES1 | `let v=1; [--v, v] → [0, 0]` |

Next, we'll look at examples of these operators in use.

Prefix ++ and prefix -- change their operands and then return them.

```
let foo = 3;
assert.equal(++foo, 4);
assert.equal(foo, 4);

let bar = 3;
assert.equal(--bar, 2);
assert.equal(bar, 2);
```

Suffix ++ and suffix -- return their operands and then change them.

```
let foo = 3;
assert.equal(foo++, 3);
assert.equal(foo, 4);

let bar = 3;
assert.equal(bar--, 3);
assert.equal(bar, 2);
```

#### 15.3.3.1 Operands: not just variables

You can also apply these operators to property values:

```
const obj = { a: 1 };
++obj.a;
assert.equal(obj.a, 2);
```

And to Array elements:

```
const arr = [ 4 ];
arr[0]++;
assert.deepEqual(arr, [5]);
```

> **Exercise: Number operators**
>
> `exercises/numbers-math/is_odd_test.mjs`

## 15.4 Converting to number

These are three ways of converting values to numbers:

- `Number(value)`
- `+value`
- `parseFloat(value)` (avoid; different than the other two!)

Recommendation: use the descriptive `Number()`. Tbl. 15.4 summarizes how it works.

Table 15.4: Converting values to numbers.

| | `Number(x)` |
|---|---|
| `undefined` | `NaN` |
| `null` | `0` |
| boolean | `false → 0`, `true → 1` |
| number | `x` (no change) |
| string | `''` → `0`<br>other → parsed number, ignoring leading/trailing whitespace |
| object | configurable (e.g. via `.valueOf()`) |

Examples:

```
assert.equal(Number(123.45), 123.45);

assert.equal(Number(''), 0);
assert.equal(Number('\n 123.45 \t'), 123.45);
assert.equal(Number('xyz'), NaN);
```

How objects are converted to numbers can be configured. For example, by overriding `.valueOf()`:

```
> Number({ valueOf() { return 123 } })
123
```

**Exercise: Converting to number**

exercises/numbers-math/parse_number_test.mjs

## 15.5 Error values

Two number values are returned when errors happen:

```
NaN
Infinity
```

## 15.6 Error value: NaN

`NaN` is an abbreviation of “not a number”. Ironically, JavaScript considers it to be a num-ber:

```
> typeof NaN
'number'
```

When is `NaN` returned?

`NaN` is returned if a number can’t be parsed:

```
> Number('$$$')
NaN
> Number(undefined)
NaN
```

`NaN` is returned if an operation can't be performed:

```
> Math.log(-1)
NaN
> Math.sqrt(-1)
NaN
```

`NaN` is returned if an operand or argument is `NaN` (to propagate errors):

```
> NaN - 3
NaN
> 7 ** NaN
NaN
```

### 15.6.1 Checking for NaN

`NaN` is the only JavaScript value that is not strictly equal to itself:

```
const n = NaN;
assert.equal(n === n, false);
```

These are several ways of checking if a value `x` is `NaN`:

```
const x = NaN;

assert.equal(Number.isNaN(x
), true); // preferred
assert.equal(Object.is(x,
NaN), true); assert.equal(x
!== x, true);
```

In the last line, we use the comparison quirk to detect `NaN`.

### 15.6.2 Finding `NaN` in Arrays

Some Array methods can't find `NaN`:

```
> [NaN].indexOf(NaN)
-1
```

Others can:

```
> [NaN].includes(NaN)
true
> [NaN].findIndex(x => Number.isNaN(x))
0
> [NaN].find(x => Number.isNaN(x))
NaN
```

Alas, there is no simple rule of thumb, you have to check for each method, how it handles `NaN`.

## 15.7 Error value: `Infinity`

When is the error value `Infinity` returned?

Infinity is returned if a number is too large:

```
> Math.pow(2, 1023)
8.98846567431158e+307
> Math.pow(2, 1024)
Infinity
```

Infinity is returned if there is a division by zero:

```
> 5 / 0
Infinity
> -5 / 0
-Infinity
```

### 15.7.1 `Infinity` as a default value

`Infinity` is larger than all other numbers (except `NaN`), making it a good default value:

```
function findMinimum(numbers) {
  let min = Infinity;
  for (const n of numbers) {
    if (n < min) min = n;
  }
  return min;
}

assert.equal(findMinimu

m([5, -1, 2]), -1);
```

```
assert.equal(findMinimu
m([]), Infinity);
```

### 15.7.2 Checking for `Infinity`

These are two common ways of checking if a value `x` is `Infinity`:

```
const x = Infinity;
assert.equal(x ===
Infinity, true);
assert.equal(Number.is
Finite(x), false);
```

> **Exercise: Comparing numbers**
>
> `exercises/numbers-math/find_max_test.mjs`

## 15.8 The precision of numbers: careful with decimal frac-tions

Internally, JavaScript floating point numbers are represented with base 2 (according to the IEEE 754 standard). That means that decimal fractions (base 10) can't always be rep-resented precisely:

```
> 0.1 + 0.2
0.30000000000000004
> 1.3 * 3
3.9000000000000004
> 1.4 * 100000000000000
139999999999999.98
```

You therefore need to take rounding errors into consideration when performing arith-metic in JavaScript. Read on for an explanation of this phenomenon.

> **Quiz: basic**
>
> See quiz app.

## 15.9 (Advanced)

All remaining sections of this chapter are advanced.

## 15.10 Background: floating point precision

In JavaScript, computations with numbers don't always produce correct results. For ex-ample:

```
> 0.1 + 0.2
0.30000000000000004
```

To understand why, we need to explore how JavaScript represents floating point numbers internally. It uses three integers to do so, which take up a total of 64 bits of storage (double precision):

| Component | Size | Integer range |
|---|---|---|
| Sign | 1 bit | [0, 1] |
| Fraction | 52 bits | [0, $2^{52}-1$] |
| Exponent | 11 bits | [−1023, 1024] |

The floating point number represented by these integers is computed as follows:

$(-1)^{\text{sign}} \times \text{0b1.fraction} \times 2^{\text{exponent}}$

This representation can't encode a zero, because its second component (involving the fraction) always has a leading 1. Therefore, a zero is encoded via the special exponent −1023 and a fraction 0.

### 15.10.1 A simplified representation of floating point numbers

To make further discussions easier, we simplify the previous representation:

Instead of base 2 (binary), we use base 10 (decimal), because that's what most peo-ple are more familiar with.

The *fraction* is a natural number that is interpreted as a fraction (digits after a point). We switch to a *mantissa*, an integer that is interpreted as itself. As a consequence, the exponent is used differently, but its fundamental role doesn't change.

As the mantissa is an integer (with its own sign), we don't need a separate sign, anymore.

The new representation works like this:

$\text{mantissa} \times 10^{\text{exponent}}$

Let's try out this representation for a few floating point numbers.

- For the integer −123, we mainly need the mantissa:

```
> -123 * (10 ** 0)
-123
```

For the number 1.5, we imagine there being a point after the mantissa. We use a negative exponent to move that point one digit to the left:

```
> 15 * (10 ** -1)
1.5
```

- For the number 0.25, we move the point two digits to the left:

```
> 25 * (10 ** -2)
0.25
```

Representations with negative exponents can also be written as fractions with positive exponents in the denominators:

```
> 15 * (10 ** -1) === 15 / (10 ** 1)
true
> 25 * (10 ** -2) === 25 / (10 ** 2)
true
```

These fractions help with understanding why there are numbers that our encoding can-not represent:

`1/10` can be represented. It already has the required format: a power of 10 in the denominator.

`1/2` can be represented as `5/10`. We turned the 2 in the denominator into a power of 10, by multiplying numerator and denominator with 5.

- `1/4` can be represented as `25/100`. We turned the 4 in the denominator into a power of 10, by multiplying numerator and denominator with 25.
- `1/3` cannot be represented. There is no way to turn the denominator into a power of 10. (The prime factors of 10 are 2 and 5. Therefore, any denominator that only has these prime factors can be converted to a power of 10, by multiplying both numerator and denominator with enough twos and fives. If a denominator has a different prime factor, then there's nothing we can do.)

To conclude our excursion, we switch back to base 2:

- `0.5 = 1/2` can be represented with base 2, because the denominator is already a power of 2.
- `0.25 = 1/4` can be represented with base 2, because the denominator is already a power of 2.
- `0.1 = 1/10` cannot be represented, because the denominator cannot be converted to a power of 2.
- `0.2 = 2/10` cannot be represented, because the denominator cannot be converted to a power of 2.

Now we can see why `0.1 + 0.2` doesn't produce a correct result: Internally, neither of the two operands can be represented precisely.

The only way to compute precisely with decimal fractions is by internally switching to base 10. For many programming languages, base 2 is the default and base 10 an option. For example, Java has the class `BigDecimal` and Python has the module `decimal`. There are tentative plans to add something similar to

JavaScript: The ECMAScript proposal "Decimal" is currently at stage 0.

## 15.11 Integers in JavaScript

JavaScript doesn't have a special type for integers.

Instead, they are simply normal (float-ing point) numbers without a decimal fraction:

```
> 1 === 1.0
true
> Number.isInteger(1.0)
true
```

In this section, we'll look at a few tools for working with these pseudo-integers.

### 15.11.1 Converting to integer

The recommended way of converting numbers to integers is to use one of the rounding methods of the `Math` object:

- `Math.floor(n)`: returns the largest integer `i` ≤ `n`

  ```
  > Math.floor(2.1)
  2
  > Math.floor(2.9)
  2
  ```

- `Math.ceil(n)`: returns the smallest integer `i` ≥ `n`

```
> Math.ceil(2.1)
3
> Math.ceil(2.9)
3
```

`Math.round(n)`: returns the integer that is "closest" to `n`. 0.5 is rounded up. For example:

```
> Math.round(2.4)
2
> Math.round(2.5)
3
```

`Math.trunc(n)`: removes any decimal fraction (after the point) that `n` has, therefore turning it into an integer.

```
> Math.trunc(2.1)
2
> Math.trunc(2.9)
2
```

For more information on rounding, consult §16.3 "Rounding".

### 15.11.2 Ranges of integers in JavaScript

These are important ranges of integers in JavaScript:

**Safe integers:** can be represented "safely" by JavaScript (more on what that means in the next subsection)

- Precision: 53 bits plus sign
- Range: $(-2^{53}, 2^{53})$

**Array indices**

- Precision: 32 bits, unsigned
- Range: $[0, 2^{32}-1)$ (excluding the maximum length)
- Typed Arrays have a larger range of 53 bits (safe and unsigned)

**Bitwise operators** (bitwise Or etc.)

- Precision: 32 bits
- Range of unsigned right shift (>>>): unsigned, $[0, 2^{32})$
- Range of all other bitwise operators: signed, $[-2^{31}, 2^{31})$

### 15.11.3 Safe integers

This is the range of integers that are *safe* in JavaScript (53 bits plus a sign):

$$[-2^{53}-1, 2^{53}-1]$$

An integer is *safe* if it is represented by exactly one JavaScript number. Given that JavaScript numbers are encoded as a fraction multiplied by 2 to the power of an exponent, higher integers can also be represented, but then there are gaps between them.

For example (18014398509481984 is $2^{54}$):

```
> 18014398509481984
18014398509481984
> 18014398509481985
18014398509481984
> 18014398509481986
18014398509481984
> 18014398509481987
18014398509481988
```

The following properties of `Number` help determine if an integer is safe:

```
assert.equal(Number.MAX_SAFE_INTEGER, (2 ** 53) - 1);
assert.equal(Number.MIN_SAFE_INTEGER, -Number.MAX_SAFE_INTEGER);

assert.equal(Number.isSafeInteger(5), true);
assert.equal(Number.isSafeInteger('5'), false);
assert.equal(Number.isSafeInteger(5.1), false);
assert.equal(Number.isSafeInteger(Number.MAX_SAFE_INTEGER), true);
assert.equal(Number.isSafeInteger(Number.MAX_SAFE_INTEGER+1), false);
```

> **Exercise: Detecting safe integers**
>
> `exercises/numbers-math/is_safe_integer_test.mjs`

#### 15.11.3.1 Safe computations

Let's look at computations involving unsafe integers.

The following result is incorrect and unsafe, even though both of its operands are safe.

```
> 9007199254740990 + 3
9007199254740992
```

The following result is safe, but incorrect. The first operand is unsafe, the second operand is safe.

```
> 9007199254740995 - 10
9007199254740986
```

Therefore, the result of an expression `a op b` is correct if and only if:

```
isSafeInteger(a) && isSafeInteger(b) &&
isSafeInteger(a op b)
```

That is: both operands and the result must be safe.

## 15.12 Bitwise operators

### 15.12.1 Internally, bitwise operators work with 32-bit integers

Internally, JavaScript's bitwise operators work with 32-bit integers. They produce their results in the following steps:

Input (JavaScript numbers): The 1–2 operands are first converted to JavaScript numbers (64-bit floating point numbers) and then to 32-bit integers.

Computation (32-bit integers): The actual operation processes 32-bit integers and produces a 32-bit integer.

Output (JavaScript number): Before returning the result, it is converted back to a JavaScript number.

#### 15.12.1.1 The types of operands and results

For each bitwise operator, this book mentions the types of its operands and its result.

Each type is always one of the following two:

| Type | Description | Size | Range |
|---|---|---|---|
| Int32 | signed 32-bit integer | 32 bits incl. sign | $[-2^{31}, 2^{31})$ |
| Uint32 | unsigned 32-bit integer | 32 bits | $[0, 2^{32})$ |

Considering the previously mentioned steps, I recommend to pretend that bitwise oper-ators internally work with unsigned 32-bit integers (step “computation”). And that Int32 and Uint32 only affect how JavaScript numbers are converted to and from integers (steps “input” and “output”).

#### 15.12.1.2 Displaying JavaScript numbers as unsigned 32-bit integers

While exploring the bitwise operators, it occasionally helps to display JavaScript numbers as unsigned 32-bit integers in binary notation. That's what `b32()` does (whose implemen-tation is shown later):

```
assert.equal(
  b32(-1),
  '11111111111111111111111111111111');
assert.equal(
  b32(1),
  '00000000000000000000000000000001');
assert.equal(
  b32(2 ** 31),
  '10000000000000000000000000000000');
```

### 15.12.2 Binary bitwise operators

Table 15.7: Binary bitwise operators.

| Operation | Name | Type signature | |
|---|---|---|---|
| `num1 & num2` | Bitwise And | Int32 × Int32 → Int32 | ES1 |
| `num1 ¦ num2` | Bitwise Or | Int32 × Int32 → Int32 | ES1 |
| `num1 ^ num2` | Bitwise Xor | Int32 × Int32 → Int32 | ES1 |

The binary bitwise operators (tbl. 15.7) combine the bits of their operands to produce their results:

```
> (0b1010 &
0b0011).toString(2).padStart(4, '0')
'0010'
> (0b1010 |
0b0011).toString(2).padStart(4, '0')
'1011'
> (0b1010 ^
0b0011).toString(2).padStart(4, '0')
'1001'
```

### 15.12.3 Bitwise Not

Table 15.8: The bitwise Not operator.

| Operation | Name | Type signature | |
|---|---|---|---|
| `~num` | Bitwise Not, ones' complement | Int32 → Int32 | ES1 |

The bitwise Not operator (tbl. 15.8) inverts each binary digit of its operand:

```
> b32(~0b100)
'11111111111111111111111111111011'
```

### 15.12.4 Bitwise shift operators

Table 15.9: Bitwise shift operators.

| Operation | Name | Type signature | |
|---|---|---|---|
| `num << count` | Left shift | Int32 × Uint32 → Int32 | ES1 |
| `num count` | Signed right | Int32 × Uint32 → | E |

| | | | |
|---|---|---|---|
| `>> t` | shift | Int32 | S1 |
| `num >>> count` | Unsigned right shift | Uint32 × Uint32 → Uint32 | ES1 |

The shift operators (tbl. 15.9) move binary digits to the left or to the right:

```
> (0b10 << 1).toString(2)
'100'
```

preserves highest bit, >>> doesn't:

```
> b32(0b10000000000000000000000000000010 >> 1)
'11000000000000000000000000000001'
> b32(0b10000000000000000000000000000010 >>> 1)
'01000000000000000000000000000001'
```

### 15.12.5 `b32()`: displaying unsigned 32-bit integers in binary notation

We have now used `b32()` a few times. The following code is an implementation of it.

```
/**
  Return a string representing n as a
  32-bit unsigned integer,
  in binary notation.
*/
funct
  ionb32(n) {
   //ensures highest bit isn't
  >>>interpreted as a sign
      (n >>>
 retu0).toString(2).padStart(32
   rn, '0');
}
assert.equal(
 b32(6),
 '00000000000000000000000000000110');
```

`>>> 0` means that we are shifting `n` zero bits to the right. Therefore, in principle, the `>>>` operator does nothing, but it still coerces `n` to an unsigned 32-bit integer:

```
> 12 >>> 0
12
> -12 >>> 0
4294967284
> (2**32 + 1) >>> 0
1
```

## 15.13 Quick reference: numbers

### 15.13.1 Global functions for numbers

JavaScript has the following four global functions for numbers:

```
isFinite()
isNaN()
parseFloat()
parseInt()
```

However, it is better to use the corresponding methods of `Number` (`Number.isFinite()` etc.), which have fewer pitfalls. They were introduced with ES6 and are discussed below.

### 15.13.2 Static properties of `Number`

`.EPSILON: number` [ES6]

The difference between 1 and the next representable floating point number. In general, a machine epsilon provides an upper bound for rounding errors in floating point arithmetic.

– Approximately: 2.2204460492503130808472633361816 × $10^{-16}$

`.MAX_SAFE_INTEGER: number` [ES6]

The largest integer that JavaScript can represent unambiguously ($2^{53}-1$).

`.MAX_VALUE: number` [ES1]

The largest positive finite JavaScript number.

  - Approximately: $1.7976931348623157 \times 10^{308}$

- `.MIN_SAFE_INTEGER: number` [ES6]

  The smallest integer that JavaScript can represent unambiguously ($-2^{53}+1$).

- `.MIN_VALUE: number` [ES1]

  The smallest positive JavaScript number. Approximately $5 \times 10^{-324}$.

- `.NaN: number` [ES1]

  The same as the global variable `NaN`.

- `.NEGATIVE_INFINITY: number` [ES1]

  The same as `-Number.POSITIVE_INFINITY`.

- `.POSITIVE_INFINITY: number` [ES1]

  The same as the global variable `Infinity`.

### 15.13.3 Static methods of `Number`

- `.isFinite(num: number): boolean` [ES6]

  Returns `true` if `num` is an actual number (neither `Infinity` nor `-Infinity` nor `NaN`).

  ```
  > Number.isFinite(Infinity)
  false
  > Number.isFinite(-Infinity)
  false
  > Number.isFinite(NaN)
  false
  > Number.isFinite(123)
  true
  ```

- `.isInteger(num: number): boolean` [ES6]

  Returns `true` if `num` is a number and does not have a decimal fraction.

  ```
  > Number.isInteger(-17)
  ```

```
true
> Number.isInteger(33)
true
> Number.isInteger(33.1)
false
> Number.isInteger('33')
false
> Number.isInteger(NaN)
false
> Number.isInteger(Infinity)
false
```

- `.isNaN(num: number): boolean` [ES6]
  Returns `true` if `num` is the value `NaN`:

```
> Number.isNaN(NaN)
true
> Number.isNaN(123)
false
> Number.isNaN('abc')
false
```

- `.isSafeInteger(num: number): boolean` [ES6]

  Returns `true` if `num` is a number and unambiguously represents an integer.

- `.parseFloat(str: string): number` [ES6]

  Coerces its parameter to string and parses it as a floating point number. For con-verting strings to numbers, `Number()` (which ignores leading and trailing whites-pace) is usually a better choice than `Number.parseFloat()` (which ignores leading whitespace and illegal trailing characters and can hide problems).

  ```
  > Number.parseFloat(' 123.4#')
  123.4
  > Number(' 123.4#')
  NaN
  ```

- `.parseInt(str: string, radix=10): number` [ES6]

  Coerces its parameter to string and parses it as an integer, ignoring leading whites-pace and illegal trailing characters:

  ```
  > Number.parseInt('    123#')
  ```

```
123
```

The parameter `radix` specifies the base of number to be parsed:

```
> Number.parseInt('101', 2)
5
> Number.parseInt('FF', 16)
255
```

Do not use this method to convert numbers to integers: Coercing to string is ineffi-cient. And stopping before the first non-digit is not a good algorithm for removing the fraction of a number. Here is an example where it goes wrong:

```
> Number.parseInt(1e21, 10) // wrong
1
```

It is better to use one of the rounding functions of `Math` to convert a number to an integer:

```
> Math.trunc(1e21) // correct
1e+21
```

### 15.13.4 Methods of `Number.prototype`

(`Number.prototype` is where the methods of numbers are stored.)

- `.toExponential(fractionDigits?: number): string` [ES3]

  Returns a string that represents the number via exponential notation. With `frac-tionDigits`, you can specify, how many digits should be shown of the number that is multiplied with the exponent (the default is to show as many digits as necessary).

  Example: number too small to get a positive exponent via `.toString()`.

  ```
  > 1234..toString()
  '1234'

  > 1234..toExponential() // 3 fraction digits
  '1.234e+3'
  > 1234..toExponential(5)
  '1.23400e+3'
  > 1234..toExponential(1)
  '1.2e+3'
  ```

  Example: fraction not small enough to get a negative exponent via `.toString()`.

  ```
  > 0.003.toString()
  '0.003'
  > 0.003.toExponential()
  '3e-3'
  ```

- `.toFixed(fractionDigits=0): string` [ES3]

  Returns an exponent-free representation of the number, rounded to `fractionDig-its` digits.

```
>
0.00000012.toString()
// with exponent
'1.2e-7'

> 0.00000012.toFixed(10) // no exponent
'0.0000001200'
> 0.00000012.toFixed()
'0'
```

If the number is $10^{21}$ or greater, even `.toFixed()` uses an exponent:

```
> (10 ** 21).toFixed()
'1e+21'
```

- `.toPrecision(precision?: number): string` [ES3]

  Works like `.toString()`, but `precision` specifies how many digits should be shown. If `precision` is missing, `.toString()` is used.

```
> 1234..toPrecision(3) //
requires exponential notation
'1.23e+3'

> 1234..toPrecision(4)
'1234'
```

```
> 1234..toPrecision(5)
'1234.0'

> 1.234.toPrecision(3)
'1.23'
```

- `.toString(radix=10): string` [ES1]

  Returns a string representation of the number.

  By default, you get a base 10 numeral as a result:

  ```
  > 123.456.toString()
  '123.456'
  ```

  If you want the numeral to have a different base, you can specify it via `radix`:

  ```
  > 4..toString(2) // binary (base 2)
  '100'
  > 4.5.toString(2)
  '100.1'

  > 255..toString(16) // hexadecimal
  (base 16)
  'ff'
  > 255.66796875.toString(16)
  'ff.ab'

  > 1234567890..toString(36)
  'kf12oi'
  ```

  `parseInt()` provides the inverse operation: It converts a string that contains an integer (no fraction!) numeral with a given base, to a number.

```
> parseInt('kf12oi', 36)
1234567890
```

### 15.13.5 Sources

- Wikipedia
- TypeScript's built-in typings
- MDN web docs for JavaScript
- ECMAScript language specification

**Quiz: advanced**

See quiz app.

# Chapter 16

## Math

### Contents



`Math` is an object with data properties and methods for processing numbers. You can see it as a poor man's module: It was created long before JavaScript had modules.

### 16.1 Data properties

- `Math.E: number` [ES1]

  Euler's number, base of the natural logarithms, approximately 2.7182818284590452354.

- `Math.LN10: number` [ES1]

  The natural logarithm of 10, approximately 2.302585092994046.

- `Math.LN2: number` [ES1]

  The natural logarithm of 2, approximately 0.6931471805599453.

- `Math.LOG10E: number` [ES1]

  The logarithm of *e* to base 10, approximately 0.4342944819032518.

- `Math.LOG2E: number` [ES1]

  The logarithm of *e* to base 2, approximately 1.4426950408889634.

- `Math.PI: number` [ES1]

The mathematical constant π, ratio of a circle's circumference to its diameter, ap-proximately 3.141592653589793.

- `Math.SQRT1_2: number` [ES1]

  The square root of 1/2, approximately 0.7071067811865476.

- `Math.SQRT2: number` [ES1]

  The square root of 2, approximately 1.4142135623730951.

## 16.2 Exponents, roots, logarithms

- `Math.cbrt(x: number): number` [ES6]

  Returns the cube root of `x`.

  ```
  > Math.cbrt(8)
  2
  ```

- `Math.exp(x: number): number` [ES1]

  Returns $e^x$ (*e* being Euler's number). The inverse of `Math.log()`.

  ```
  > Math.exp(0)
  1
  > Math.exp(1) === Math.E
  true
  ```

- `Math.expm1(x: number): number` [ES6]

  Returns `Math.exp(x)-1`. The inverse of `Math.log1p()`. Very small numbers (frac-tions close to 0) are represented with a higher precision.

Therefore, this function returns more precise values whenever `.exp()` returns values close to 1.

- `Math.log(x: number): number` [ES1]

  Returns the natural logarithm of `x` (to base *e*, Euler's number). The inverse of `Math.exp()`.

  ```
  > Math.log(1)
  0
  > Math.log(Math.E)
  1
  > Math.log(Math.E ** 2)
  2
  ```

- `Math.log1p(x: number): number` [ES6]

  Returns `Math.log(1 + x)`. The inverse of `Math.expm1()`. Very small numbers (fractions close to 0) are represented with a higher precision. Therefore, you can provide this function with a more precise argument whenever the argument for `.log()` is close to 1.

- `Math.log10(x: number): number` [ES6]

Returns the logarithm of `x` to base 10. The inverse of `10 ** x`.

```
> Math.log10(1)
0
> Math.log10(10)
1
> Math.log10(100)
2
```

- `Math.log2(x: number): number` [ES6]

  Returns the logarithm of `x` to base 2. The inverse of `2 ** x`.

```
> Math.log2(1)
0
> Math.log2(2)
1
> Math.log2(4)
2
```

- `Math.pow(x: number, y: number): number` [ES1]

  Returns $x^y$, `x` to the power of `y`. The same as `x ** y`.

```
> Math.pow(2, 3)
8
> Math.pow(25, 0.5)
5
```

- `Math.sqrt(x: number): number` [ES1]

  Returns the square root of `x`. The inverse of `x ** 2`.

```
> Math.sqrt(9)
3
```

## 16.3 Rounding

Rounding means converting an arbitrary number to an integer (a number without a dec-imal fraction). The following functions implement different approaches to rounding.

- `Math.ceil(x: number): number` [ES1]

  Returns the smallest (closest to −∞) integer `i` with `x` ≤ `i`.

  ```
  > Math.ceil(2.1)
  3
  > Math.ceil(2.9)
  3
  ```

- `Math.floor(x: number): number` [ES1]

  Returns the largest (closest to +∞) integer `i` with `i` ≤ `x`.

```
> Math.floor(2.1)
2
> Math.floor(2.9)
2
```

- `Math.round(x: number): number` [ES1]

  Returns the integer that is closest to `x`. If the decimal fraction of `x` is `.5` then `.round()` rounds up (to the integer closer to positive infinity):

  ```
  > Math.round(2.4)
  2
  > Math.round(2.5)
  3
  ```

- `Math.trunc(x: number): number` [ES6]

  Removes the decimal fraction of `x` and returns the resulting integer.

  ```
  > Math.trunc(2.1)
  2
  > Math.trunc(2.9)
  2
  ```

Tbl. 16.1 shows the results of the rounding functions for a few representative inputs.

Table 16.1: Rounding functions of `Math`. Note how things change with negative numbers, because "larger" always means "closer to positive in-finity".

| -2. | -2. | -2. | 2.1 | 2.5 | 2. |
|---|---|---|---|---|---|

| | 9 | 5 | 1 | | | 9 |
|---|---|---|---|---|---|---|
| Math.f loor | -3 | -3 | -3 | 2 | 2 | 2 |
| Math.c eil | -2 | -2 | -2 | 3 | 3 | 3 |
| Math.r ound | -3 | -2 | -2 | 2 | 3 | 3 |
| Math.t runc | -2 | -2 | -2 | 2 | 2 | 2 |

## 16.4 Trigonometric Functions

All angles are specified in radians. Use the following two functions to convert between degrees and radians.

```
function degreesToRadians(degrees) {
 return degrees / 180 * Math.PI;
}
assert.equal(degreesToRadians(90),
Math.PI/2);

function radiansToDegrees(radians) {
 return radians / Math.PI * 180;
}
assert.equal(radiansToDegrees(Math.PI),
180);
```

- `Math.acos(x: number): number` [ES1]

  Returns the arc cosine (inverse cosine) of `x`.

  ```
  > Math.acos(0)
  1.5707963267948966
  > Math.acos(1)
  0
  ```

- `Math.acosh(x: number): number` [ES6]

  Returns the inverse hyperbolic cosine of `x`.

- `Math.asin(x: number): number` [ES1]

  Returns the arc sine (inverse sine) of `x`.

  ```
  > Math.asin(0)
  0
  > Math.asin(1)
  1.5707963267948966
  ```

- `Math.asinh(x: number): number` [ES6]

  Returns the inverse hyperbolic sine of `x`.

- `Math.atan(x: number): number` [ES1]

  Returns the arc tangent (inverse tangent) of `x`.

- `Math.atanh(x: number): number` [ES6]

  Returns the inverse hyperbolic tangent of `x`.

- `Math.atan2(y: number, x: number): number` [ES1]

  Returns the arc tangent of the quotient y/x.

- `Math.cos(x: number): number` [ES1]

  Returns the cosine of `x`.

  ```
  > Math.cos(0)
  1
  ```

```
> Math.cos(Math.PI)
-1
```

- `Math.cosh(x: number): number` [ES6]

  Returns the hyperbolic cosine of `x`.

- `Math.hypot(...values: number[]): number` [ES6]

  Returns the square root of the sum of the squares of `values` (Pythagoras' theorem):

  ```
  > Math.hypot(3, 4)
  5
  ```

- `Math.sin(x: number): number` [ES1]

  Returns the sine of `x`.

  ```
  > Math.sin(0)
  0
  > Math.sin(Math.PI / 2)
  1
  ```

- `Math.sinh(x: number): number` [ES6]

  Returns the hyperbolic sine of `x`.

- `Math.tan(x: number): number` [ES1]

  Returns the tangent of `x`.

  ```
  > Math.tan(0)
  0
  > Math.tan(1)
  1.5574077246549023
  ```

- `Math.tanh(x: number): number;` [ES6]

  Returns the hyperbolic tangent of `x`.

## 16.5 Various other functions

- `Math.abs(x: number): number` [ES1]

  Returns the absolute value of `x`.

  ```
  > Math.abs(3)
  3
  > Math.abs(-3)
  3
  > Math.abs(0)
  0
  ```

- `Math.clz32(x: number): number` [ES6]

Counts the leading zero bits in the 32-bit integer `x`. Used in DSP algorithms.

```
> Math.clz32(0b01000000000000000000000000000000)
1
> Math.clz32(0b00100000000000000000000000000000)
2
> Math.clz32(2)
30
> Math.clz32(1)
31
```

- `Math.max(...values: number[]): number` [ES1]

  Converts `values` to numbers and returns the largest one.

```
> Math.max(3, -5, 24)
24
```

- `Math.min(...values: number[]): number` [ES1]

  Converts `values` to numbers and returns the smallest one.

  ```
  > Math.min(3, -5, 24)
  -5
  ```

- `Math.random(): number` [ES1]

  Returns a pseudo-random number `n` where 0 ≤ `n` < 1.

  Computing a random integer `i` where 0 ≤ `i` < `max`:

  ```
  function getRandomInteger(max) {
    return Math.floor(Math.random() * max);
  }
  ```

- `Math.sign(x: number): number` [ES6]

  Returns the sign of a number:

  ```
  > Math.sign(-8)
  -1
  > Math.sign(0)
  0
  > Math.sign(3)
  1
  ```

## 16.6 Sources

- Wikipedia
- TypeScript's built-in typings
- MDN web docs for JavaScript
- ECMAScript language specification

136

*Math*

16

## Chapter 17

# Unicode – a brief introduction (advanced)

### Contents



Unicode is a standard for representing and managing text in most of the world's writing systems. Virtually all modern software that works with text, supports Unicode. The standard is maintained by the Unicode Consortium. A new version of the standard is published every year (with new Emojis etc.). Unicode version 1.0.0 was published in October 1991.

## 17.1 Code points vs. code units

Two concepts are crucial for understanding Unicode:

- *Code points* are numbers that represent Unicode characters.
- *Code units* are numbers that encode code points, to store or transmit Unicode text. One or more code units encode a single code point. Each code unit has the same size, which depends on the *encoding format* that is used. The most popular format, UTF-8, has 8-bit code units.

### 17.1.1 Code points

The first version of Unicode had 16-bit code points. Since then, the number of characters has grown considerably and the size of code points was extended to 21 bits. These 21 bits are partitioned in 17 planes, with 16 bits each:

- Plane 0: **Basic Multilingual Plane (BMP)**, 0x0000–0xFFFF
  - Contains characters for almost all modern languages (Latin characters, Asian characters, etc.) and many symbols.
- Plane 1: Supplementary Multilingual Plane (SMP), 0x10000–0x1FFFF
  - Supports historic writing systems (e.g. Egyptian hieroglyphs and cuneiform) and additional modern writing systems.
  - Supports emoji and many other symbols.
- Plane 2: Supplementary Ideographic Plane (SIP), 0x20000–0x2FFFF
  - Contains additional CJK (Chinese, Japanese, Korean) ideographs.
- Plane 3–13: Unassigned
- Plane 14: Supplementary Special-Purpose Plane (SSP), 0xE0000–0xEFFFF
  - Contains non-graphical characters such as tag characters and glyph variation selectors.
- Plane 15–16: Supplementary Private Use Area (S PUA A/B), 0x0F0000–0x10FFFF
  - Available for character assignment by parties outside the ISO and the Uni-code Consortium. Not standardized.

Planes 1-16 are called supplementary planes or **astral planes**.

Let's check the code points of a few characters:

```
> 'A'.codePointAt(0).toString(16)
'41'
> 'ü'.codePointAt(0).toString(16)
'fc'
> 'π'.codePointAt(0).toString(16)
'3c0'
> '🙂'.codePointAt(0).toString(16)
'1f642'
```

The hexadecimal numbers of the code points tell us that the first three characters reside in plane 0 (within 16 bits), while the emoji resides in plane 1.

### 17.1.2 Encoding Unicode code points: UTF-32, UTF-16, UTF-8

The main ways of encoding code points are three *Unicode Transformation Formats* (UTFs): UTF-32, UTF-16, UTF-8. The number at the end of each format indicates the size (in bits) of its code units.

#### 17.1.2.1 UTF-32 (Unicode Transformation Format 32)

UTF-32 uses 32 bits to store code units, resulting in one code unit per code point. This format is the only one with *fixed-length encoding*; all others use a varying number of code units to encode a single code point.

#### 17.1.2.2 UTF-16 (Unicode Transformation Format 16)

UTF-16 uses 16-bit code units. It encodes code points as follows:

- BMP (first 16 bits of Unicode): are stored in single code units.
- Astral planes: The BMP comprises 0x10_000 code points. Given that Unicode has a total of 0x110_000 code points, we still need to encode the remaining 0x100_000 code points (20 bits). The BMP has two ranges of unassigned code points that provide the necessary storage:
  - Most significant 10 bits (*leading surrogate*): 0xD800-0xDBFF
  - Least significant 10 bits (*trailing surrogate*): 0xDC00-0xDFFF

In other words: The two hexadecimal digits at the end contribute 8 bits. But we can only use those 8 bits if a BMP starts with one of the following 2-digit pairs:

- D8, D9, DA, DB
- DC, DD, DE, DF

Per surrogate, we have a choice between 4 pairs, which is where the remaining 2 bits come from.

As a consequence, each UTF-16 code unit is always either a leading surrogate, a trailing surrogate or encodes a BMP code point.

These are two examples of UTF-16-encoded code points:

- Code point 0x03C0 (π) is in the BMP and can therefore be represented by a single UTF-16 code unit: 0x03C0.
- Code point 0x1F642 (☺) is in an astral plane and represented by two code units: 0xD83D and 0xDE42.

#### 17.1.2.3 UTF-8 (Unicode Transformation Format 8)

UTF-8 has 8-bit code units. It uses 1–4 code units to encode a code point:

| Code points | Code units |
|---|---|
| 0000–007F | 0bbbbbbb (7 bits) |
| 0080–07FF | 110bbbbb, 10bbbbbb (5+6 bits) |
| 0800–FFFF | 1110bbbb, 10bbbbbb, 10bbbbbb (4+6+6 bits) |
| 10000–1FFFFF | 11110bbb, 10bbbbbb, 10bbbbbb, 10bbbbbb (3+6+6+6 bits) |

Notes:

- The bit prefix of each code unit tells us:
  - Is it first in a series of code units? If yes, how many code units will follow?
  - Is it second or later in a series of code units?
- The character mappings in the 0000–007F range are the same as ASCII, which leads to a degree of backward-compatibility with older software.

Three examples:

| Character | Code point | Code units |
| --- | --- | --- |
| A | 0x0041 | 01000001 |
| π | 0x03C0 | 11001111, 10000000 |
| ☺ | 0x1F642 | 11110000, 10011111, 10011001, 10000010 |

## 17.2 Encodings used in web development: UTF-16 and UTF-8

The Unicode encoding formats, that are used in web development, are: UTF-16 and UTF-8.

### 17.2.1 Source code internally: UTF-16

The ECMAScript specification internally represents source code as UTF-16.

### 17.2.2 Strings: UTF-16

The characters in JavaScript strings are based on UTF-16 code units:

```
• const smiley = '☺';
• smiley.length
2
> smiley === '\uD83D\uDE42' // code units
true
```

For more information on Unicode and strings, consult

§18.6 “Atoms of text: Unicode characters, JavaScript characters, grapheme clusters”.

### 17.2.3 Source code in files: UTF-8

HTML and JavaScript are almost always encoded as UTF-8, these days.

For example, this is how HTML files usually start now:

```
<!doctype html>
<html>
<head>
  <meta charset="UTF-8">
  ...
```

For HTML modules loaded in web browsers, the standard encoding is also UTF-8.

## 17.3 Grapheme clusters – the real characters

The concept of a character becomes remarkably complex, once you consider many of the world's writing systems.

On one hand, there are Unicode characters, as represented by code points.

On the other hand, there are *grapheme clusters*. A grapheme cluster corresponds most closely to a symbol displayed on screen or paper. It is defined as “a horizontally seg-mentable unit of text”. Therefore, official Unicode documents also call it a *user-perceived character*. One or more code point characters are needed to encode a grapheme cluster.

For example, the Devanagari *kshi* is encoded by 4 code points. We use spreading (`...`) to split a string into an Array with code point characters (for details, consult §18.6.1 “Work-ing with code points”):

```
> [...'क्षि']
[ 'क', '्', 'ष', 'ि' ]
```

Flag emojis are also grapheme clusters and composed of two code point characters. For example, the flag of Japan:

```
> [...'🇯🇵']
[ '🇯', '🇵' ]
```

### More information on grapheme clusters

For more information, consult “Let’s Stop Ascribing Meaning to Code Points” by Manish Goregaokar.

### Quiz

See quiz app.

## Chapter 18

# Strings

## Contents

---

Strings are primitive values in JavaScript and immutable. That is, string-related opera-tions always produce new strings and never change existing strings.

## 18.1 Plain string literals

Plain string literals are delimited by either single quotes or double quotes:

```
const str1 = 'abc';
const str2 = "abc";
assert.equal(str1, str2);
```

Single quotes are used more often, because it makes it easier to mention HTML, where double quotes are preferred.

The next chapter covers *template literals*, which give you:

- String interpolation
- Multiple lines
- Raw string literals (backslash has no special meaning)

### 18.1.1 Escaping

The backslash lets you create special characters:

- Unix line break: `'\n'`
- Windows line break: `'\r\n'`
- Tab: `'\t'`
- Backslash: `'\\'`

The backslash also lets you use the delimiter of a string literal inside that literal:

```
assert.equal(
  'She said: "Let\'s go!"',
  "She said: \"Let's go!\"");
```

## 18.2 Accessing characters and code points

### 18.2.1 Accessing JavaScript characters

JavaScript has no extra data type for characters – characters are always represented as strings.

```
const str = 'abc';

• Reading a character
at a given index
assert.equal(str[1],
'b');

• Counting the
characters in a
string:
assert.equal(str.lengt
h, 3);
```

### 18.2.2 Accessing Unicode code point characters via `for-of` and spread-ing

Iterating over strings via `for-of` or spreading (`...`) visits Unicode code point characters. Each code point character is encoded by 1–2 JavaScript characters. For more information, see §18.6 "Atoms of text: Unicode characters, JavaScript characters, grapheme clusters".

This is how you iterate over the code point characters of a string via `for-of`:

```
for (const ch of 'x☺y') {
 console.log(ch);
}
• Output:
• 'x'
• '☺'
• 'y'
```

And this is how you convert a string into an Array of code point characters via spreading:

```
assert.deepEqual([...'x☺y'], ['x', '☺',
'y']);
```

## 18.3 String concatenation via +

If at least one operand is a string, the plus operator (+) converts any non-strings to strings and concatenates the result:

```
assert.equal(3 + ' times ' + 4, '3 times
4');
```

The assignment operator += is useful if you want to assemble a string, piece by piece:

```
let str = ''; // must be `let`!
str += 'Say it';
str += ' one more';
str += ' time';
```

```
assert.equal(str, 'Say it one more time');
```

> **Concatenating via + is efficient**
>
> Using + to assemble strings is quite efficient,
>
> because most JavaScript engines inter-nally optimize
>
> it.

> **Exercise: Concatenating strings**
>
> `exercises/strings/concat_string_array_test.mjs`

## 18.4 Converting to string

These are three ways of converting a value `x` to a string:

- `String(x)`
- `''+x`
- `x.toString()` (does not work for `undefined` and `null`)

Recommendation: use the descriptive and safe String().

Examples:

```
assert.equal(String(undef

ined), 'undefined');

assert.equal(String(null)

, 'null');

assert.equal(String(false), 'false');
assert.equal(String(true), 'true');

assert.equal(String(123.45), '123.45');
```

Pitfall for booleans: If you convert a boolean to a string via String(), you generally can't convert it back via Boolean():

```
> String(false)
'false'
> Boolean('false')
true
```

The only string for which Boolean() returns false, is the empty string.

### 18.4.1 Stringifying objects

Plain objects have a default string representation that is not very useful:

```
> String({a: 1})
'[object Object]'
```

Arrays have a better string representation, but it still hides much information:

```
> String(['a', 'b'])
'a,b'
> String(['a', ['b']])
'a,b'

> String([1, 2])
'1,2'
> String(['1', '2'])
'1,2'

> String([true])
'true'
> String(['true'])
'true'
> String(true)
'true'
```

Stringifying functions, returns their source code:

```
> String(function f() {return 4})
'function f() {return 4}'
```

### 18.4.2 Customizing the stringification of objects

You can override the built-in way of stringifying objects by implementing the method `toString()`:

```
const obj = {
  toString() {
    return 'hello';
  }
};

assert.equal(String(obj), 'hello');
```

### 18.4.3 An alternate way of stringifying values

The JSON data format is a text representation of JavaScript values. Therefore, `JSON.stringify()` can also be used to convert values to strings:

```
> JSON.stringify({a: 1})
'{"a":1}'
> JSON.stringify(['a', ['b']])
'["a",["b"]]'
```

The caveat is that JSON only supports `null`, booleans, numbers, strings, Arrays and ob-jects (which it always treats as if they were created by object literals).

Tip: The third parameter lets you switch on multi-line output and specify how much to indent. For example:

```
console.log(JSON.stringify({first: 'Jane', last: 'Doe'}, null, 2));
```

This statement produces the following output.

```
{
```

```
  "first": "Jane",
  "last": "Doe"
}
```

## 18.5 Comparing strings

Strings can be compared via the following operators:

```
< <= > >=
```

There is one important caveat to consider: These operators compare based on the numeric values of JavaScript characters. That means that the order that JavaScript uses for strings is different from the one used in dictionaries and phone books:

```
> 'A' < 'B' // ok
true
> 'a' < 'B' // not ok
false
```

```
> 'ä' < 'b' // not ok
false
```

Properly comparing text is beyond the scope of this book. It is supported via the ECMA-Script Internationalization API (`Intl`).

## 18.6 Atoms of text: Unicode characters, JavaScript charac-ters, grapheme clusters

Quick recap of §17 "Unicode – a brief introduction":

- Unicode characters are represented by *code points*; numbers which have a range of 21 bits.
- In JavaScript strings, Unicode is implemented via *code units* based on the encoding format UTF-16. Each code unit is a 16-bit number. One to two of code units are needed to encode a single code point.
  - Therefore, each JavaScript character is represented by a code unit. In the JavaScript standard library, code units are also called *char codes*. Which is what they are: numbers for JavaScript characters.
- *Grapheme clusters* (*user-perceived characters*) are written symbols, as displayed on screen or paper. One or more Unicode characters are needed to encode a single grapheme cluster.

The following code demonstrates that a single Unicode character comprises one or two JavaScript characters. We count the latter via `.length`:

- 3 Unicode characters, 3 JavaScript characters:

```
assert.equal('abc'.length, 3);
```

- 1 Unicode character, 2 JavaScript characters:

```
assert.equal('☺'.length, 2);
```

The following table summarizes the concepts we have just explored:

| Entity | Numeric representation | Size | Encoded via |
|---|---|---|---|
| Grapheme cluster | | | 1+ code points |
| Unicode character | Code point | 21 bits | 1–2 code units |
| JavaScript character | UTF-16 code unit | 16 bits | – |

### 18.6.1 Working with code points

Let's explore JavaScript's tools for working with code points.

A *code point escape* lets you specify a code point hexadecimally. It produces one or two JavaScript characters.

```
> '\u{1F642}'
'☺'
```

`String.fromCodePoint()` converts a single code point to 1–2 JavaScript characters:

```
> String.fromCodePoint(0x1F642)
'🙂'
```

`.codePointAt()` converts 1–2 JavaScript characters to a single code point:

```
> '🙂'.codePointAt(0).toString(16)
'1f642'
```

You can *iterate* over a string, which visits Unicode characters (not JavaScript characters).

Iteration is described later in this book. One way of iterating is via a `for-of` loop:

```
const str = '🙂a';
assert.equal(str.length, 3);

for (const codePointChar of str) {
 console.log(codePointChar);
}
```

- Output:
- '🙂'
- 'a'

*Spreading* (`...`) into Array literals is also based on iteration and visits Unicode characters:

```
> [...'🙂a']
[ '🙂', 'a' ]
```

That makes it a good tool for counting Unicode characters:

```
> [...'🙂a'].length
2
> '🙂a'.length
3
```

### 18.6.2 Working with code units (char codes)

Indices and lengths of strings are based on JavaScript characters (as represented by UTF-16 code units).

To specify a code unit hexadecimally, you can use a *code unit escape*:

```
> '\uD83D\uDE42'
'☺'
```

And you can use `String.fromCharCode()`. *Char code* is the standard library's name for *code unit*:

```
> String.fromCharCode(0xD83D) +
String.fromCharCode(0xDE42)
'☺'
```

To get the char code of a character, use `.charCodeAt()`:

```
> '☺'.charCodeAt(0).toString(16)
'd83d'
```

### 18.6.3 Caveat: grapheme clusters

When working with text that may be written in any human language, it's best to split at the boundaries of grapheme clusters, not at the boundaries of Unicode characters.

TC39 is working on `Intl.Segmenter`, a proposal for the ECMAScript Internationaliza-tion API to support Unicode segmentation (along grapheme cluster boundaries, word boundaries, sentence boundaries, etc.).

Until that proposal becomes a standard, you can use one of several libraries that are available (do a web search for "JavaScript grapheme").

## 18.7 Quick reference: Strings

Strings are immutable, none of the string methods ever modify their strings.

### 18.7.1 Converting to string

Tbl. 18.2 describes how various values are converted to strings.

Table 18.2: Converting values to strings.

| • | `String(x)` |
|---|---|
| `undefined` | `'undefined'` |
| `null` | `'null'` |

| Boolean value | `false` → `'false'`, `true` → `'true'` |
|---|---|
| Number value | Example: `123` → `'123'` |
| String value | `x` (input, unchanged) |
| An object | Configurable via, e.g., `toString()` |

### 18.7.2 Numeric values of characters

- **Char code:** represents a JavaScript character numerically. JavaScript's name for *Unicode code unit*.
  - Size: 16 bits, unsigned
  - Convert number to character: `String.fromCharCode()` [ES1]
  - Convert character to number: string method `.charCodeAt()` [ES1]
- **Code point:** represents a Unicode character numerically.
  - Size: 21 bits, unsigned (17 planes, 16 bits each)
  - Convert number to character: `String.fromCodePoint()` [ES6]
  - Convert character to number: string method `.codePointAt()` [ES6]

### 18.7.3 String operators

```
// Access characters via []
const str = 'abc';
assert.equal(str[1], 'b');
```

```
// Concatenate strings via +
assert.equal('a' + 'b' + 'c', 'abc');
assert.equal('take ' + 3 + ' oranges',
'take 3 oranges');
```

### 18.7.4 `String.prototype`: finding and matching

(`String.prototype` is where the methods of strings are stored.)

- `.endsWith(searchString: string, endPos=this.length): boolean` [ES6]

  Returns `true` if the string would end with `searchString` if its length were `endPos`.

  Returns `false`, otherwise.

  ```
  > 'foo.txt'.endsWith('.txt')
  true
  > 'abcde'.endsWith('cd', 4)
  true
  ```

- `.includes(searchString: string, startPos=0): boolean` [ES6]

  Returns `true` if the string contains the `searchString` and `false`, otherwise. The search starts at `startPos`.

  ```
  > 'abc'.includes('b')
  true
  > 'abc'.includes('b', 2)
  false
  ```

- `.indexOf(searchString: string, minIndex=0): number` [ES1]

Returns the lowest index at which `searchString` appears within the string, or `-1`, otherwise. Any returned index will be `minIndex` or higher.

```
> 'abab'.indexOf('a')
0
> 'abab'.indexOf('a', 1)
2
> 'abab'.indexOf('c')
-1
```

- `.lastIndexOf(searchString: string, maxIndex=Infinity): number` [ES1]

  Returns the highest index at which `searchString` appears within the string, or `-1`, otherwise. Any returned index will be `maxIndex` or lower.

  ```
  > 'abab'.lastIndexOf('ab', 2)
  2
  > 'abab'.lastIndexOf('ab', 1)
  0
  > 'abab'.lastIndexOf('ab')
  2
  ```

- [1 of 2] `.match(regExp: string | RegExp): RegExpMatchArray | null` [ES3]

If `regExp` is a regular expression with flag `/g` not set, then `.match()` returns the first match for `regExp` within the string. Or `null` if there is no match. If `regExp` is a string, it is used to create a regular expression (think parameter of `new RegExp()`) before performing the previously mentioned steps.

The result has the following type:

```
interface RegExpMatchArray extends
Array<string> {
  index: number;
  input: string;
  groups: undefined | {
   [key: string]: string
  };
}
```

Numbered capture groups become Array indices (which is why this type extends `Array`). Named capture groups (ES2018) become properties of `.groups`. In this mode, `.match()` works like `RegExp.prototype.exec()`.

Examples:

```
> 'ababb'.match(/a(b+)/)
{ 0: 'ab', 1: 'b', index: 0, input:
'ababb', groups: undefined }
> 'ababb'.match(/a(?<foo>b+)/)
{ 0: 'ab', 1: 'b', index: 0, input:
'ababb', groups: { foo: 'b' } }
> 'abab'.match(/x/)
```

```
null
```

- [2 of 2] `.match(regExp: RegExp): string[] | null` [ES3]

  If flag `/g` of `regExp` is set, `.match()` returns either an Array with all matches or `null` if there was no match.

  ```
  > 'ababb'.match(/a(b+)/g)
  [ 'ab', 'abb' ]
  > 'ababb'.match(/a(?<foo>b+)/g)
  [ 'ab', 'abb' ]
  > 'abab'.match(/x/g)
  null
  ```

- `.search(regExp: string | RegExp): number` [ES3]

  Returns the index at which `regExp` occurs within the string. If `regExp` is a string, it is used to create a regular expression (think parameter of `new RegExp()`).

  ```
  > 'a2b'.search(/[0-9]/)
  1
  > 'a2b'.search('[0-9]')
  1
  ```

- `.startsWith(searchString: string, startPos=0): boolean` [ES6]

  Returns `true` if `searchString` occurs in the string at index `startPos`. Returns `false`, otherwise.

```
> '.gitignore'.startsWith('.')
true
> 'abcde'.startsWith('bc', 1)
true
```

### 18.7.5 String.prototype: extracting

- `.slice(start=0, end=this.length): string` [ES3]

  Returns the substring of the string that starts at (including) index `start` and ends at (excluding) index `end`. If an index is negative, it is added to `.length` before they are used (`-1` means `this.length-1`, etc.).

  ```
  > 'abc'.slice(1, 3)
  'bc'
  > 'abc'.slice(1)
  'bc'
  > 'abc'.slice(-2)
  'bc'
  ```

- `.split(separator: string | RegExp, limit?: number): string[]` [ES3]

  Splits the string into an Array of substrings – the strings that occur between the separators. The separator can be a string:

  ```
  > 'a | b | c'.split('|')
  [ 'a ', ' b ', ' c' ]
  ```

  It can also be a regular expression:

  ```
  > 'a : b : c'.split(/ *: */)
  [ 'a', 'b', 'c' ]
  ```

```
> 'a : b : c'.split(/( *):( *)/)
[ 'a', ' ', ' ', 'b', ' ', ' ', 'c' ]
```

The last invocation demonstrates that captures made by groups in the regular ex-pression become elements of the returned Array.

**Warning: `.split('')` splits a string into JavaScript characters.** That doesn't work well when dealing with astral Unicode characters (which are encoded as two JavaScript characters). For example, emojis are astral:

```
> '☺X☺'.split('')
[ '\uD83D', '\uDE42', 'X', '\uD83D',
'\uDE42' ]
```

Instead, it is better to use spreading:

```
> [...'☺X☺']
>'☺', 'X', '☺' ]
```

- `.substring(start: number, end=this.length): string` [ES1]

Use `.slice()` instead of this method.

`.substring()` wasn't implemented consis-tently in older engines and doesn't support negative indices.

### 18.7.6 `String.prototype`: combining

- `.concat(...strings: string[]): string` [ES3]

  Returns the concatenation of the string and `strings`. `'a'.concat('b')` is equiva-lent to `'a'+'b'`. The latter is much more popular.

  ```
  > 'ab'.concat('cd', 'ef', 'gh')
  'abcdefgh'
  ```

- `.padEnd(len: number, fillString=' '): string` [ES2017]

  Appends (fragments of) `fillString` to the string until it has the desired length `len`.

  If it already has or exceeds `len`, then it is returned without any changes.

  ```
  > '#'.padEnd(2)
  '# '
  > 'abc'.padEnd(2)
  'abc'
  > '#'.padEnd(5, 'abc')
  '#abca'
  ```

- `.padStart(len: number, fillString=' '): string` [ES2017]

  Prepends (fragments of) `fillString` to the string until it has the desired length `len`. If it already has or exceeds `len`, then it is returned without any changes.

  ```
  > '#'.padStart(2)
  ' #'
  ```

```
> 'abc'.padStart(2)
'abc'
> '#'.padStart(5, 'abc')
'abca#'
```

- `.repeat(count=0): string` [ES6]

  Returns the string, concatenated `count` times.

  ```
  > '*'.repeat()
  ''
  > '*'.repeat(3)
  '***'
  ```

### 18.7.7 `String.prototype`: transforming

- `.normalize(form: 'NFC'|'NFD'|'NFKC'|'NFKD' = 'NFC'): string` [ES6]

  Normalizes the string according to the Unicode Normalization Forms.

- [1 of 2] `.replace(searchValue: string | RegExp, replaceValue: string): string` [ES3]

  Replace matches of `searchValue` with `replaceValue`. If `searchValue` is a string, only the first verbatim occurrence is replaced. If `searchValue` is a regular expres-sion without flag `/g`, only the first match is replaced. If `searchValue` is a regular expression with `/g` then all matches are replaced.

```
> 'x.x.'.replace('.', '#')
'x#x.'
> 'x.x.'.replace(/./, '#')
'#.x.'
> 'x.x.'.replace(/./g, '#')
'####'
```

Special characters in replaceValue are:

- $$: becomes $
- $n: becomes the capture of numbered group n (alas, $0 stands for the string '$0', it does not refer to the complete match)
- $&: becomes the complete match
- $`: becomes everything before the match
- $': becomes everything after the match

Examples:

```
> 'a 2020-04 b'.replace(/([0-9]{4})-
([0-9]{2})/, '|$2|')
'a |04| b'
> 'a 2020-04 b'.replace(/([0-9]{4})-
([0-9]{2})/, '|$&|')
'a |2020-04| b'
> 'a 2020-04 b'.replace(/([0-9]{4})-
([0-9]{2})/, '|$`|')
'a |a | b'
```

Named capture groups (ES2018) are supported, too:

- $<name> becomes the capture of named group name

Example:

```
assert.equal(
  'a 2020-04 b'.replace(
```

```
    /(?<year>[0-9]{4})-(?<month>[0-
    9]{2})/, '|$<month>|'),
  'a |04| b');
```

- [2 of 2] `.replace(searchValue: string | RegExp, replacer: (...args: any[]) => string): string` [ES3]
  If the second parameter is a function, occurrences are replaced with the strings it returns. Its parameters `args` are:
  - `matched: string`. The complete match
  - `g1: string|undefined`. The capture of numbered group 1
  - `g2: string|undefined`. The capture of numbered group 2
  - (Etc.)
  - `offset: number`. Where was the match found in the input string?
  - `input: string`. The whole input string

```
const regexp = /([0-9]{4})-([0-9]{2})/;
const replacer = (all, year,
month) => '|' + all + '|';
assert.equal(
  'a 2020-04
  b'.replace(regexp,
  replacer), 'a |2020-
  04| b');
```

Named capture groups (ES2018) are supported, too. If there are any, an argument is added at the end, with an object whose properties contain the captures:

```
const regexp = /(?<year>[0-
9]{4})-(?<month>[0-9]{2})/;
const replacer = (...args) =>
{
  const groups=args.pop();
  return '|' + groups.month + '|';
};
assert.equal(
  'a 2020-04
  b'.replace(regexp,
  replacer), 'a |04|
  b');
```

- `.toUpperCase(): string` [ES1]
  Returns a copy of the string, in which all lowercase alphabetic characters are con-verted to uppercase. How well that works for various alphabets, depends on the JavaScript engine.

  ```
  > '-a2b-'.toUpperCase()
  '-A2B-'
  > 'αβγ'.toUpperCase()
  'ΑΒΓ'
  ```

- `.toLowerCase(): string` [ES1]

Returns a copy of the string, in which all uppercase alphabetic characters are con-verted to lowercase. How well that works for various alphabets, depends on the JavaScript engine.

```
> '-A2B-'.toLowerCase()
'-a2b-'
> 'ΑΒΓ'.toLowerCase()
'αβγ'
```

- `.trim(): string` [ES5]

  Returns a copy of the string, in which all leading and trailing whitespace (spaces, tabs, line terminators, etc.) is gone.

```
> '\r\n#\t '.trim()
'#'
> '  abc  '.trim()
'abc'
```

- `.trimEnd(): string` [ES2019]

  Similar to `.trim()`, but only the end of the string is trimmed:

```
> '  abc  '.trimEnd()
> abc'
```

- `.trimStart(): string` [ES2019]

  Similar to `.trim()`, but only the beginning of the string is trimmed:

```
> '   abc     '.trimStart()
'abc     '
```

### 18.7.8 Sources

- TypeScript's built-in typings
- MDN web docs for JavaScript
- ECMAScript language specification

**Exercise: Using string methods**

`exercises/strings/remove_extension_test.mjs`

**Quiz**

See quiz app.

## Chapter 19

# Using template literals and tagged templates

## Contents

---

Before we dig into the two features *template literal* and *tagged template*, let's first examine the multiple meanings of the term *template*.

## 19.1 Disambiguation: "template"

The following three things are significantly different, despite all having *template* in their names and despite all of them looking similar:

- A *text template* is a function from data to text. It is frequently used in web devel-opment and often defined via text files. For example, the following text defines a template for the library Handlebars:

```
<div class="entry">
  <h1>{{title}}</h1>
  <div class="body">
    {{body}}
  </div>
</div>
```

This template has two blanks to be filled in: `title` and `body`. It is used like this:

```
// First step: retrieve the template text, e.g. from a text file. const tmplFunc = Handlebars.compile(TEMPLATE_TEXT); // compile string const data = {title: 'My page', body: 'Welcome to my page!'}; const html = tmplFunc(data);
```

- A *template literal* is similar to a string literal, but has additional features. For exam-ple, interpolation. It is delimited by backticks:

```
const num = 5;
assert.equal(`Count: ${num}!`, 'Count: 5!');
```

- Syntactically, a *tagged template* is a template literal that follows a function (or rather, an expression that evaluates to a function). That leads to the function being called. Its arguments are derived from the contents of the template literal.

```
const getArgs = (...args) => args;
assert.deepEqual(
  getArgs`Count: ${5}!`,
  [['Count: ', '!'], 5] );
```

Note that `getArgs()` receives both the text of the literal and the data interpolated via `${}`.

## 19.2 Template literals

A template literal has two new features, compared to a normal string literal.

First, it supports *string interpolation*: If you put a dynamically computed value inside a `${}`, it is converted to a string and inserted into the string returned by the literal.

```
const MAX = 100;
function doSomeWork(x) {
  if (x > MAX) {
    throw new Error(`At most ${MAX}
    allowed: ${x}!`);
  }
  // ···
}
assert.throws(
  () => doSomeWork(101),
  {message: 'At most 100 allowed: 101!'});
```

Second, template literals can span multiple lines:

```
const str = `this is
a text with
multiple lines`;
```

Template literals always produce strings.

## 19.3 Tagged templates

The expression in line A is a *tagged template*. It is equivalent to invoking `tagFunc()` with the arguments listed in the Array in line B.

```
function tagFunc(...args) {
  return args;
}

const setting = 'dark mode';
const value = true;

assert.deepEqual(
  tagFunc`Setting ${setting} is ${value}!`,
  // (A)
  [['Setting ', ' is ', '!'], 'dark mode',
  true] // (B)
);
```

The function `tagFunc` before the first backtick is called a *tag function*. Its arguments are:

- *Template strings* (first argument): an Array with the text fragments surrounding the interpolations `${}`.
  – In the example: `['Setting ', ' is ', '!']`
- *Substitutions* (remaining arguments): the interpolated values.
  – In the example: `'dark mode'` and `true`

The static (fixed) parts of the literal (the template strings) are kept separate from the dy-namic parts (the substitutions).

A tag function can return arbitrary values.

### 19.3.1 Cooked vs. raw template strings (advanced)

So far, we have only seen the *cooked interpretation* of template strings. But tag functions actually get two interpretations:

- A *cooked interpretation* where backslashes have special meaning. For example: `\t` produces a tab character. This interpretation of the template strings is stored as an Array in the first argument.
- A *raw interpretation* where backslashes do not have special meaning. For example: `\t` produces two characters – a backslash and a `t`. This interpretation of the tem-plate strings is stored in property `.raw` of the first argument (an Array).

The following tag function `cookedRaw` uses both interpretations:

```
function cookedRaw(templateStrings,
...substitutions) {
 return {
```

```
    cooked: [...templateStrings], // copy
    just the Array elements
    raw: templateStrings.raw,
    substitutions,
  };
}
assert.deepEqual(
  cookedRaw`\tab${'subst'}\newline\\`,
  {
    cooked: ['\tab', '\newline\\'],
    raw: ['\\tab', '\\newline\\\\'],
    substitutions: ['subst'],
  });
```

The raw interpretation enables raw string literals via `String.raw` (described later) and similar applications.

Tagged templates are great for supporting small embedded languages (so-called *domain-specific languages*). We'll continue with a few examples.

### 19.3.2 Tag function library: lit-html

lit-html is a templating library that is based on tagged templates and used by the frontend framework Polymer:

```
import {html, render} from 'lit-html';

const template = (items) => html`
<ul>
  ${
    repeat(items,
      (item) => item.id,
```

```
      (item, index) => html`<li>${index}.
${item.name}</li>`
    )
  }
  </ul>
`;
```

`repeat()` is a custom function for looping. Its 2nd parameter produces unique keys for the values returned by the 3rd parameter. Note the nested tagged template used by that parameter.

### 19.3.3 Tag function library: re-template-tag

re-template-tag is a simple library for composing regular expressions. Templates tagged with `re` produce regular expressions. The main benefit is that you can interpolate regular expressions and plain text via `${}` (line A):

```
const RE_YEAR = re`(?<year>[0-9]{4})`;
const RE_MONTH = re`(?<month>[0-9]{2})`;
const RE_DAY = re`(?<day>[0-9]{2})`;
const RE_DATE = re`/${RE_YEAR}-
${RE_MONTH}-${RE_DAY}/u`; // (A)
```

```
const match = RE_DATE.exec('2017-01-27');
assert.equal(match.groups.year, '2017');
```

### 19.3.4 Tag function library: graphql-tag

The library graphql-tag lets you create GraphQL queries via tagged templates:

```
import gql from 'graphql-tag';

const query = gql`
  {
 user(id: 5) {
     firstName
     lastName
   }
  }
  `;
```

Additionally, there are plugins for pre-compiling such queries in Babel, TypeScript, etc.

## 19.4 Raw string literals

Raw string literals are implemented via the tag function `String.raw`. They are string literals where backslashes don't do anything special (such as escaping characters etc.):

```
assert.equal(String.raw`\back`, '\\back');
```

This helps whenever data contains backslashes. For example, strings with regular expres-sions:

```
const regex1 = /^\./;
const regex2 = new RegExp('^\\.');
const regex3 = new
RegExp(String.raw`^\.`);
```

All three regular expressions are equivalent. With a normal string literal, you have to write the backslash twice, to escape it for that literal. With a raw string literal, you don't have to do that.

Raw string literals are also useful for specifying Windows filename paths:

```
const WIN_PATH = String.raw`C:\foo\bar`;
assert.equal(WIN_PATH, 'C:\\foo\\bar');
```

## 19.5 (Advanced)

All remaining sections are advanced

## 19.6 Multi-line template literals and indentation

If you put multi-line text in template literals, two goals are in conflict: On one hand, the template literal should be indented to fit inside the source code. On the other hand, the lines of its content should start in the leftmost column.

For example:

```
function div(text) {
  return `
    <div>
      ${text}
    </div>
  `;
}
console.log('Output:');
console.log(
  div('Hello!')
  • Replace spaces with mid-dots:
  .replace(/ /g, '·')
  • Replace \n with #\n:
  .replace(/\n/g, '#\n')
);
```

Due to the indentation, the template literal fits well into the source code. Alas, the output is also indented. And we don't want the return at the beginning and the return plus two spaces at the end.

```
Output:
#
```

```
····<div>#
······Hello!#
····</div>#
··
```

There are two ways to fix this: via a tagged template or by trimming the result of the template literal.

### 19.6.1 Fix: template tag for dedenting

The first fix is to use a custom template tag that removes the unwanted whitespace. It uses the first line after the initial line break to determine in which column the text starts and shortens the indentation everywhere. It also removes the line break at the very beginning and the indentation at the very end. One such template tag is `dedent` by Desmond Brand:

```
import dedent from 'dedent';
function divDedented(text) {
 return dedent`
  <div>
   ${text}
  </div>
```

```
    `.replace(/\n/g, '#\n');
  }
  console.log('Output:');
  console.log(divDedented('Hello!'));
```

This time, the output is not indented:

```
Output:
<div>#
 Hello!#
</div>
```

### 19.6.2 Fix: `.trim()`

The second fix is quicker, but also dirtier:

```
function divDedented(text) {
 return `
<div>
 ${text}
</div>
 `.trim().replace(/\n/g, '#\n');
}
console.log('Output:');
console.log(divDedented('Hello!'));
```

The string method `.trim()` removes the superfluous whitespace at the beginning and at the end, but the content itself must start in the leftmost column. The advantage of this solution is that you don't need a custom tag function. The downside is that it looks ugly.

The output is the same as with `dedent`:

```
Output:
```

```
<div>#
 Hello!#
</div>
```

## 19.7 Simple templating via template literals

While template literals look like text templates, it is not immediately obvious how to use them for (text) templating: A text template gets its data from an object, while a template literal gets its data from variables. The solution is to use a template literal in the body of a function whose parameter receives the templating data. For example:

```
const tmpl = (data) => `Hello
${data.name}!`;
assert.equal(tmpl({name: 'Jane'}), 'Hello
Jane!');
```

### 19.7.1 A more complex example

As a more complex example, we'd like to take an Array of addresses and produce an
HTML table. This is the Array:

```
const addresses = [
  { first: '<Jane>', last: 'Bond' },
  { first: 'Lars', last: '<Croft>' },
];
```

The function `tmpl()` that produces the HTML table looks as follows.

```
const tmpl = (addrs) => `
<table>
  ${addrs.map(
4    (addr) => `
5      <tr>
6        <td>${escapeHtml(addr.first)}</td>
7        <td>${escapeHtml(addr.last)}</td>
8      </tr>
9      `.trim()
  ).join('')}
</table>
`.trim();
```

This code contains two templating functions:

- The first one (line 1) takes `addrs`, an Array with addresses, and returns a string with a table.
- The second one (line 4) takes `addr`, an object containing an address, and returns a string with a table row. Note the `.trim()` at the end, which removes unnecessary whitespace.

The first templating function produces its result by wrapping a table element around an Array that it joins into a string (line 10). That Array is produced by mapping the second templating function to each element of `addrs` (line 3). It therefore contains strings with table rows.

The helper function `escapeHtml()` is used to escape special HTML characters (line 6 and line 7). Its implementation is shown in the next subsection.

Let us call `tmpl()` with the addresses and log the result:

```
console.log(tmpl(addresses));
```

The output is:

```
<table>
 <tr>
     <td>&lt;Jane&gt;</td>
     <td>Bond</td>
   </tr><tr>
     <td>Lars</td>
     <td>&lt;Croft&gt;</td>
   </tr>
</table>
```

### 19.7.2 Simple HTML-escaping

The following function escapes plain text so that it is displayed verbatim in HTML:

```
function escapeHtml(str) {
  return str
    .replace(/&/g, '&amp;') // first!
    .replace(/>/g, '&gt;')
    .replace(/</g, '&lt;')
    .replace(/"/g, '&quot;')
    .replace(/'/g, '&#39;')
    .replace(/`/g, '&#96;')
    ;
}
assert.equal(
  escapeHtml('Rock & Roll'), 'Rock &amp; Roll');
assert.equal(
  escapeHtml('<blank>'), '&lt;blank&gt;');
```

> **Exercise: HTML templating**
>
> Exercise with bonus challenge:
> `exercises/template-literals/templating_test.mjs`

> **Quiz**
>
> See quiz app.

## Chapter 20

## Symbols

### Contents



---

Symbols are primitive values that are created via the factory function `Symbol()`:

```
const mySymbol = Symbol('mySymbol');
```

The parameter is optional and provides a description,

which is mainly useful for debug-ging.

On one hand, symbols are like objects in that each value

created by `Symbol()` is unique and not compared by

value:

```
> Symbol() === Symbol()
```

```
false
```

On the other hand, they also behave like primitive values. They have to be categorized via `typeof`:

```
const sym = Symbol();
assert.equal(typeof sym, 'symbol');
```

And they can be property keys in objects:

```
const obj
      = {
  [sym]:
    123,
};
```

169

## 20.1 Use cases for symbols

The main use cases for symbols, are:

- Values for constants
- Unique property keys

### 20.1.1 Symbols: values for constants

Let's assume you want to create constants representing the colors red, orange, yellow, green, blue and violet. One simple way of doing so would be to use strings:

```
const COLOR_BLUE = 'Blue';
```

On the plus side, logging that constant produces helpful output. On the minus side, there is a risk of mistaking an unrelated value for a color, because two strings with the same content are considered equal:

```
const MOOD_BLUE = 'Blue';
assert.equal(COLOR_BLUE, MOOD_BLUE);
```

We can fix that problem via symbols:

```
const COLOR_BLUE = Symbol('Blue');
const MOOD_BLUE = Symbol('Blue');

assert.notEqual(COLOR_BLUE, MOOD_BLUE);
```

Let's use symbol-valued constants to implement a function:

```
const COLOR_RED    = Symbol('Red');
const COLOR_ORANGE = Symbol('Orange');
const        =
COLOR_YELL Symbol('Yel
OW         low');
```

```
const COLOR_GREEN = Symbol('Green');
const COLOR_BLUE = Symbol('Blue');
const COLOR_VIOLET = Symbol('Violet');

function getComplement(color) {
 switch (color) {
  case COLOR_RED:
   return COLOR_GREEN;
  case COLOR_ORANGE:
   return COLOR_BLUE;
  case COLOR_YELLOW:
   return COLOR_VIOLET;
  case COLOR_GREEN:
   return COLOR_RED;
  case COLOR_BLUE:
   return COLOR_ORANGE;
  case COLOR_VIOLET:
   return COLOR_YELLOW;
  default:
```

```
      throw new Exception('Unknown color:
      '+color);
    }
  }
  assert.equal(getComplement(COLOR_YELLOW),
  COLOR_VIOLET);
```

### 20.1.2 Symbols: unique property keys

The keys of properties (fields) in objects are used at two levels:

- The program operates at a *base level*. The keys at that level reflect the problem that the program solves.
- Libraries and ECMAScript operate at a *meta-level*. The keys at that level are used by services operating on base-level data and code. One such key is `'toString'`.

The following code demonstrates the difference:

```
const pt = {
  x: 7,
  y: 4,
  toString() {
    return `(${this.x}, ${this.y})`;
  },
};
assert.equal(String(pt), '(7, 4)');
```

Properties `.x` and `.y` exist at the base level. They hold the coordinates of the point represented by `pt` and are

used to solve a problem – computing with points.
Method

`.toString()` exists at a meta-level. It is used by JavaScript to convert this object to a  string.

Meta-level properties must never interfere with base level properties. That is, their keys must never overlap. That is difficult when both language and libraries contribute to the meta-level. For example, it is now impossible to give new meta-level methods sim-ple names, such as `toString`, because they might clash with existing base level names. Python's solution to this problem is to prefix and suffix special names with two under-scores: `__init__`, `__iter__`, `__hash__`, etc. However, even with this solution, libraries can't have their own meta-level properties, because those might be in conflict with future language properties.

Symbols, used as property keys, help us here: Each symbol is unique and a symbol key never clashes with any other string or symbol key.

#### 20.1.2.1 Example: a library with a meta-level method

As an example, let's assume we are writing a library that treats objects differently if they implement a special method. This is what defining a property key for such a method and implementing it for an object would look like:

```
const specialMethod =
Symbol('specialMethod');
const obj = {
  _id: 'kf12oi',
```

```
  [specialMethod]() { // (A)
   return this._id;
  }
};
assert.equal(obj[specialMethod](),
'kf12oi');
```

The square brackets in line A enable us to specify that the method must have the key `specialMethod`. More details are explained in §25.5.2 "Computed property keys".

## 20.2 Publicly known symbols

Symbols that play special roles within ECMAScript are called *publicly known symbols*. Ex-amples include:

- `Symbol.iterator`: makes an object *iterable*. It's the key of a method that returns an iterator. For more information on this topic, see $full.
- `Symbol.hasInstance`: customizes how `instanceof` works. If an object implements a method with that key, it can be used at the right-hand side of that operator. For example:

```
const PrimitiveNull = {
  [Symbol.hasInstance](x) {
   return x === null;
  }
};
```

```js
assert.equal(null instanceof
PrimitiveNull, true);
```

- `Symbol.toStringTag`: influences the default `.toString()` method.

  ```
  > String({})
  '[object Object]'
  > String({ [Symbol.toStringTag]: 'is
  no money' })
  '[object is no money]'
  ```

  Note: It's usually better to override `.toString()`.

> **Exercises: Publicly known symbols**
>
> - `Symbol.toStringTag`: `exercises/symbols/to_string_tag_test.mjs`
> - `Symbol.hasInstance`: `exercises/symbols/has_instance_test.mjs`

## 20.3 Converting symbols

What happens if we convert a symbol `sym` to another primitive type? Tbl. 20.1 has the answers.

Table 20.1: The results of converting symbols to other primitive types.

| Convert to | Explicit conversion | Coercion (implicit conv.) |
|---|---|---|
| boolean | `Boolean(sym)` → OK | `!sym` → OK |
| number | `Number(sym)` → `TypeError` | `sym*2` → `TypeError` |
| string | `String(sym)` → OK | `''+sym` → `TypeError` |
| | `sym.toString()` → OK | `` `${sym}` `` → `TypeError` |

One key pitfall with symbols is how often exceptions are thrown when converting them to something else. What is the thinking behind that? First, conversion to number never makes sense and should be warned about. Second, converting a symbol to a string is indeed useful for diagnostic output. But it also makes sense to warn about accidentally turning a symbol into a string (which is a different kind of property key):

```
const obj = {};
const sym = Symbol();
assert.throws(
  () => { obj['__'+sym+'__'] = true },
  { message: 'Cannot convert a Symbol value
  to a string' });
```

The downside is that the exceptions make working with symbols more complicated. You have to explicitly convert symbols when assembling strings via the plus operator:

```
• const mySymbol = Symbol('mySymbol');
• 'Symbol I used: ' + mySymbol
TypeError: Cannot convert a Symbol value
to a string
> 'Symbol I used: ' + String(mySymbol)
'Symbol I used: Symbol(mySymbol)'
```

 **Quiz**

See quiz app.

174
*Symbols*

*20*

# Part V

## Control flow and data flow

# Chapter 21

# Control flow statements

## Contents

---

This chapter covers the following control flow statements:

- `if` statement (ES1)
- `switch` statement (ES3)
- `while` loop (ES1)
- `do-while` loop (ES3)

- `for` loop (ES1)
- `for-of` loop (ES6)
- `for-await-of` loop (ES2018)
- `for-in` loop (ES1)

Before we get to the actual control flow statements, let's take a look at two operators for controlling loops.

## 21.1 Controlling loops: `break` and `continue`

The two operators `break` and `continue` can be used to control loops and other statements while you are inside them.

### 21.1.1 `break`

There are two versions of `break`: one with an operand and one without an operand. The latter version works inside the following statements: `while`, `do-while`, `for`, `for-of`, `for-await-of`, `for-in` and `switch`. It immediately leaves the current statement:

```
for (const x of ['a', 'b', 'c']) {
 console.log(x);
 if (x === 'b') break;
 console.log('---')
}
```

- Output:
- 'a'
- '---'
- 'b'

### 21.1.2 `break` plus label: leaving any labeled statement

`break` with an operand works everywhere. Its operand is a *label*. Labels can be put in front of any statement, including blocks. `break foo` leaves the statement whose label is `foo`:

```
foo: { // label
  if (condition) break
  foo; // labeled break
  // ...
}
```

In the following example, we use break with a label to leave a loop differently when we succeeded (line A). Then we skip what comes directly after the loop, which is where we end up if we failed.

```
function findSuffix(stringArray, suffix)
{
  let result;
  search_block: {
    for (const str of stringArray) {
      if (str.endsWith(suffix)) {
```

```
    • Succe
    ss:
    result
    = str;
    break search_block; // (A)
   }
  } // for
  // Failure:
  result = '(Untitled)';
 } // search_block

 return { suffix, result };
  // Same as: {suffix: suffix, result:
  result}
}
assert.deepEqual(
 findSuffix(['foo.txt',
 'bar.html'], '.html'), {
 suffix: '.html', result:
 'bar.html' }
);
assert.deepEqual(
 findSuffix(['foo.txt',
 'bar.html'], '.mjs'), {
 suffix: '.mjs', result:
 '(Untitled)' }
);
```

### 21.1.3 continue

`continue` only works inside `while`, `do-while`, `for`, `for-of`, `for-await-of` and `for-in`. It immediately leaves the current loop iteration and continues with the next one. For example:

```
const lines = [
  'Normal line',
  '# Comment',
  'Another normal line',
];
for (const line of lines) {
  if (line.startsWith('#')) continue;
  console.log(line);
}
• Output:
• 'Normal line'
• 'Another normal line'
```

## 21.2 `if` statements

These are two simple `if` statements: One with just a "then" branch and one with both a "then" branch and an "else" branch:

```
if (cond) {
  // then branch
}
```

```
if (cond) {
  > then
branch }
else {
  > else branch
}
```

Instead of the block, `else` can also be followed by another `if` statement:

```
if (cond1) {
  > ...
} else if (cond2) {
  > ...
}

if (cond1) {
  > ...
} else if (cond2) {
  > ...
} else {
  > ...
}
```

You can continue this chain with more `else if`s.

### 21.2.1 The syntax of `if` statements

The general syntax of `if` statements is:

```
if (cond) «then_statement»
else «else_statement»
```

So far, the `then_statement` has always been a block, but we can use any statement. That statement must be terminated with a semicolon:

```
if (true) console.log('Yes'); else
console.log('No');
```

That means that `else if` is not its own construct, it's simply an `if` statement whose `else_statement` is another `if` statement.

## 21.3 switch statements

A `switch` statement looks as follows:

```
switch («switch_expression») {
 «switch_body»
}
```

The body of `switch` consists of zero or more case clauses:

```
case «case_expression»:
 «statements»
```

And, optionally, a default clause:

```
default:
  «statements»
```

A `switch` is executed as follows:

- It evaluates the switch expression.
- It jumps to the first case clause whose expression has the same result as the switch expression.
- Otherwise – if there is no such clause, it jumps to the default clause.
- Otherwise – if there is no default clause, it does nothing.

### 21.3.1 A first example of a `switch` statement

Let's look at an example: The following function converts a number from 1–7 to the name of a weekday.

```
function dayOfTheWeek(num) {
  switch (num) {
    case 1:
      return 'Monday';
    case 2:
      return 'Tuesday';
    case 3:
      return 'Wednesday';
    case 4:
      return 'Thursday';
    case 5:
      return 'Friday';
    case 6:
      return 'Saturday';
    case 7:
      return 'Sunday';
```

```
  }
}
assert.equal(dayOfTheWeek(5), 'Friday');
```

### 21.3.2 Don't forget to `return` or `break`!

At the end of a case clause, execution continues with the next case clause – unless you `return` or `break`. For example:

```
function englishToFrench(english) {
  let french;
  switch (english) {
    case 'hello':
      french = 'bonjour';
    case 'goodbye':
      french = 'au revoir';
  }
```

```
  return french;
}
// The result should be 'bonjour'!
assert.equal(englishToFrench('hello'),
'au revoir');
```

That is, our implementation of `dayOfTheWeek()` only worked, because we used `return`.

We can fix `englishToFrench()` by using `break`:

```
function englishToFrench(english) {
  let french;
  switch (english) {
    case 'hello':
      french = 'bonjour';
      break;
    case 'goodbye':
      french = 'au revoir';
      break;
  }
  return french;
}
assert.equal(englishToFrench('hello'),
'bonjour'); // ok
```

### 21.3.3 Empty cases clauses

The statements of a case clause can be omitted, which effectively gives us multiple case expressions per case clause:

```
function isWeekDay(name) {
  switch (name) {
```

```
    case 'Monday':
    case 'Tuesday':
    case 'Wednesday':
    case 'Thursday':
    case 'Friday':
   return true;
    case 'Saturday':
    case 'Sunday':
      return false;
  }
}
assert.equal(isWeekDay('
Wednesday'), true);
assert.equal(isWeekDay('
Sunday'), false);
```

### 21.3.4 Checking for illegal values via a `default` clause

A `default` clause is jumped to if the `switch` expression has no other match. That makes it useful for error checking:

```
function isWeekDay(name) {
  switch (name) {
```

```
    case 'Monday':
    case 'Tuesday':
    case 'Wednesday':
    case 'Thursday':
    case 'Friday':
   return true;
    case 'Saturday':
    case 'Sunday':
      return false;
    default:
      throw new Error('Illegal value:
      '+name);
  }
}
assert.throws(
  () => isWeekDay('January'),
  {message: 'Illegal value: January'});
```

> **Exercises: `switch`**
>
> - `exercises/control-flow/number_to_month_test.mjs`
> - Bonus: `exercises/control-flow/is_object_via_switch_test.mjs`

## 21.4 `while` loops

A `while` loop has the following syntax:

```
while («condition») {
  «statements»
}
```

Before each loop iteration, `while` evaluates `condition`:

- If the result is falsy, the loop is finished.
- If the result is truthy, the `while` body is executed one more time.

### 21.4.1 Examples of `while` loops

The following code uses a `while` loop. In each loop iteration, it removes the first element of `arr` via `.shift()` and logs it.

```
const arr = ['a', 'b', 'c'];
while (arr.length > 0) {
 const elem = arr.shift();
 // remove first element
 console.log(elem);
}
```

- Output:
- 'a'
- 'b'

```
// 'c'
```

If the condition always evaluates to `true`, then `while` is an infinite loop:

```
while (true) {
  if (Math.random() === 0) break;
}
```

## 21.5 `do-while` loops

The `do-while` loop works much like `while`, but it checks its condition *after* each loop iteration (not before).

```
let input;
do {
  input = prompt('Enter text:');
  console.log(input);
} while (input !== ':q');
```

`prompt()` is a global function that is available in web browsers. It prompts the user to input text and returns it.

## 21.6 `for` loops

A `for` loop has the following syntax:

```
for («initialization»; «condition»;
«post_iteration») {
  «statements»
}
```

The first line is the *head* of the loop and controls how often the *body* (the remainder of the loop) is executed. It has three parts and each of them is optional:

- `initialization`: sets up variables etc. for the loop. Variables declared here via `let` or `const` only exist inside the loop.
- `condition`: This condition is checked before each loop iteration. If it is falsy, the loop stops.
- `post_iteration`: This code is executed after each loop iteration.

A `for` loop is therefore roughly equivalent to the following `while` loop:

```
«initialization»
while («condition») {
 «statements»
 «post_iteration»
}
```

### 21.6.1 Examples of `for` loops

As an example, this is how to count from zero to two via a `for` loop:

```
for (let i=0; i<3; i++) {
 console.log(i);
}
```

- Output:
- 0
- 1
- 2

This is how to log the contents of an Array via a `for` loop:

```
const arr = ['a', 'b', 'c'];
for (let i=0; i<3; i++) {
 console.log(arr[i]);
}
```

- Output:
- 'a'
- 'b'
- 'c'

If you omit all three parts of the head, you get an infinite loop:

```
for (;;) {
 if (Math.random() === 0) break;
}
```

## 21.7 `for-of` loops

A `for-of` loop iterates over an *iterable* – a data container that supports the *iteration protocol*.

Each iterated value is stored in a variable, as specified in the head:

```
for («iteration_variable» of «iterable») {
```

```
  «statements»
}
```

The iteration variable is usually created via a variable declaration:

```
const iterable = ['hello', 'world'];
for (const elem of iterable) {
  console.log(elem);
}
// Output:
// 'hello'
// 'world'
```

But you can also use a (mutable) variable that already exists:

```
const iterable = ['hello', 'world'];
let elem;
for (elem of iterable) {
```

```
  console.log(elem);
}
```

### 21.7.1 `const`: `for-of` vs. `for`

Note that, in `for-of` loops, you can use `const`. The iteration variable can still be different for each iteration (it just can't change during the iteration). Think of it as a new `const` declaration being executed each time, in a fresh scope.

In contrast, in `for` loops, you must declare variables via `let` or `var`, if their values change.

### 21.7.2 Iterating over iterables

As mentioned before, `for-of` works with any iterable object, not just with Arrays. For example, with Sets:

```
const set = new
Set(['hello',
'world']); for (const
elem of set) {
  console.log(elem);
}
```

### 21.7.3 Iterating over [index, element] pairs of Arrays

Lastly, you can also use `for-of` to iterate over the [index, element] entries of Arrays:

```
const arr = ['a', 'b', 'c'];
```

```
for (const [index, elem]
 of arr.entries()) {
 console.log(`${index} -
 > ${elem}`);
}
• Output:
• '0 -> a'
• '1 -> b'
• '2 -> c'
```

With `[index, element]`, we are using *destructuring* to access Array elements.

> **Exercise: `for-of`**
>
> `exercises/control-flow/array_to_string_test.mjs`

## 21.8 `for-await-of` loops

`for-await-of` is like `for-of`, but it works with asynchronous iterables instead of syn-chronous ones. And it can only be used inside async functions and async generators.

```
for await (const item of asyncIterable)
{
 // ···
}
```

`for-await-of` is described in detail in the chapter on asynchronous iteration.

## 21.9 `for-in` loops (avoid)

> **Recommendation: don't use `for-in` loops** `for-in` has several pitfalls.
>
> Therefore, it is usually best to avoid it.

This is an example of using `for-in` properly, which involves boilerplate code (line A):

```
function getOwnPropertyNames(obj) {
  const result = [];
  for (const key in obj) {
    if ({}.hasOwnProperty.call(obj, key)) {
// (A)
      result.push(key);
    }
  }
  return result;
}
assert.deepEqual(
  getOwnPropertyNames({ a: 1, b:2 }),
  ['a', 'b']);
assert.deepEqual(
  getOwnPropertyNames(['a', 'b']),
  ['0', '1']); // strings!
```

We can implement the same functionality without `for-in`, which is almost always better:

```
function getOwnPropertyNames(obj) {
  const result = [];
```

```
  for (const key of Object.keys(obj)) {
   result.push(key);
  }
  return result;
}
```

### Quiz

See quiz app.

*statements*

## Chapter 22

# Exception handling

## Contents



This chapter covers how JavaScript handles exceptions.

> **Why doesn't JavaScript throw exceptions more often?**

JavaScript didn't support exceptions until ES3. That explains why they are used sparingly by the language and its standard library.

## 22.1 Motivation: throwing and catching exceptions

Consider the following code. It reads profiles stored in files into an Array with instances of class `Profile`:

```
function readProfiles(filePaths) {
  const profiles = [];
  for (const filePath of filePaths) {
    try {
      const profile =
      readOneProfile(filePat
      h);
      profiles.push(profile)
      ;
```

189

```
    } catch (err) { // (A)
      console.log('Error in: '+filePath,
      err);
    }
  }
}
function readOneProfile(filePath) {
  const profile = new Profile();
  const file = openFile(filePath);
  // ··· (Read the data in `file` into
  `profile`)
  return profile;
}
function openFile(filePath) {
  if (!fs.existsSync(filePath)) {
    throw new Error('Could not find file
    '+filePath); // (B)
  }
  // ··· (Open the file whose path is
  `filePath`)
}
```

Let's examine what happens in line B: An error occurred, but the best place to handle the problem is not the current location, it's line A. There, we can skip the current file and move on to the next one.

Therefore:

- In line B, we use a `throw` statement to indicate that there was a problem.
- In line A, we use a `try-catch` statement to handle the problem.

When we throw, the following constructs are active:

```
readProfiles(···)
 for (const filePath of filePaths)
  try
   readOneProfile(···)
    openFile(···)
     if (!fs.existsSync(filePath))
      throw
```

One by one, `throw` exits the nested constructs, until it encounters a `try` statement. Execu-tion continues in the `catch` clause of that `try` statement.

## 22.2 `throw`

This is the syntax of the `throw` statement:

```
throw «value»;
```

Any value can be thrown, but it's best to throw an instance of `Error` or its subclasses.

```
throw new Error('Problem!');
```

### 22.2.1 Options for creating error objects

- Use class `Error`. That is less limiting in JavaScript than in a more static language, because you can add your own properties to instances:

```
const err = new Error('Could not find
the file');
err.filePath = filePath;
throw err;
```

- Use one of JavaScript's subclasses of `Error` (which are listed later).
- Subclass `Error` yourself.

```
class MyError extends Error {
}
function func() {
 throw new MyError('Problem!');
}
assert.throws(
  () => func(),
 MyError);
```

## 22.3 The `try` statement

The maximal version of the `try` statement looks as follows:

```
try {
 «try_statements»
} catch
 (error) {
 «catch_sta
 tements»
} finally {
```

```
  «finally_statements»
}
```

You can combine these clauses as follows:

- `try-catch`
- `try-finally`
- `try-catch-finally`

Since ECMAScript 2019, you can omit the `catch` parameter `(error)`, if you are not inter-ested in the value that was thrown.

### 22.3.1 The `try` block

The `try` block can be considered the body of the statement. This is where we execute the regular code.

### 22.3.2 The `catch` clause

If an exception reaches the `try` block, then it is assigned to the parameter of the `catch` clause and the code in that clause is executed. Next, execution normally continues after the `try` statement. That may change if:

- There is a `return`, `break` or `throw` inside the `catch` block.
- There is a `finally` clause (which is always executed before the `try` statement ends).

The following code demonstrates that the value that is thrown in line A is indeed caught in line B.

```
const errorObject = new Error();
function func() {
 throw errorObject; // (A)
}

try {
 func();
} catch (err) { //
 (B)
 assert.equal(err,
 errorObject);
}
```

### 22.3.3 The `finally` clause

The code inside the `finally` clause is always executed at the end of a `try` statement – no matter what happens in the `try` block or the `catch` clause.

Let's look at a common use case for `finally`: You have created a resource and want to always destroy it when you are done with it – no matter what happens while working with it. You'd implement that as follows:

```
const resource = createResource();
try {
 // Work with `resource`.
Errors may be thrown. }
finally {
 resource.destroy();
}
```

#### 22.3.3.1 `finally` is always executed

The `finally` clause is always executed – even if an error is thrown (line A):

```
let finallyWasExecuted = false;
assert.throws(
() => {
 try {
     throw new Error(); // (A)
    } finally {
     finallyWasExecuted = true;
    }
  },
  Error
);
assert.equal(finallyWasExecuted, true);
```

And even if there is a `return` statement (line A):

```
let finallyWasExecuted = false;
function func() {
  try {
    return; // (A)
  } finally {
    finallyWasExecuted = true;
  }
}
func();
assert.equal(finallyWasExecuted, true);
```

## 22.4 Error classes

`Error` is the common superclass of all built-in error classes. It has the following subclasses (I'm quoting the ECMAScript specification):

- `RangeError`: Indicates a value that is not in the set or range of allowable values.
- `ReferenceError`: Indicate that an invalid reference value has been detected.
- `SyntaxError`: Indicates that a parsing error has occurred.
- `TypeError`: is used to indicate an unsuccessful operation when none of the other *NativeError* objects are an appropriate indication of the failure cause.
- `URIError`: Indicates that one of the global URI handling functions was used in a way that is incompatible with its definition.

### 22.4.1 Properties of error objects

Consider `err`, an instance of `Error`:

```
const err = new Error('Hello!');
assert.equal(String(err), 'Error:
Hello!');
```

Two properties of `err` are especially useful:

- `.message`: contains just the error message.

  ```
  assert.equal(err.message, 'Hello!');
  ```

- `.stack`: contains a stack trace. It is supported by all mainstream browsers.

  ```
  assert.equal(
  err.stack,
  `
  Error: Hello!
    at ch_exception-handling.mjs:1:13
  `.trim());
  ```

> **Exercise: Exception handling**

`exercises/exception-handling/call_function_test.mjs`

 **Quiz**

See quiz app.

# Chapter 23

# Callable values

## Contents

---

## 23.1 Kinds of functions

JavaScript has two categories of functions:

- An *ordinary function* can play several roles:
  - Real function
  - Method
  - Constructor function
- A *specialized function* can only play one of those roles. For example:
  - An *arrow function* can only be a real function.
  - A *method* can only be a method.
  - A *class* can only be a constructor function.

The next two sections explain what all of those things mean.

## 23.2 Ordinary functions

The following code shows three ways of doing (roughly) the same thing: creating an ordinary function.

```
// Function declaration (a statement)
function ordinary1(a, b, c) {
  // ···
}

// const plus anonymous
function expression
const ordinary2 =
function (a, b, c) {
  // ···
};

// const plus named
function expression
const ordinary3 =
```

```
function myName(a, b, c)
{
  // `myName` is only accessible in here
};
```

As we have seen in §10.8 “Declarations: scope and activation”, function declarations are activated early, while variable declarations (e.g. via `const`) are not.

The syntax of function declarations and function expressions is very similar. The context determines which is which. For more information on this kind of syntactic ambiguity, consult §6.5 “Ambiguous syntax”.

### 23.2.1 Parts of a function declaration

Let’s examine the parts of a function declaration via an example:

```
function add(x, y) {
  return x + y;
}
```

- `add` is the *name* of the function declaration.
- `add(x, y)` is the *head* of the function declaration.
- `x` and `y` are the *parameters*.
- The curly braces (`{` and `}`) and everything between them are the *body* of the function declaration.

- The `return` statement explicitly returns a value from the function.

### 23.2.2 Roles played by ordinary functions

Consider the following function declaration from the previous section:

```
function add(x, y) {
  return x + y;
}
```

This function declaration creates an ordinary function whose name is `add`. As an ordinary function, `add()` can play three roles:

- Real function: invoked via a function call.

  ```
  assert.equal(add(2, 1), 3);
  ```

- Method: stored in property, invoked via a method call.

  ```
  const obj = { addAsMethod: add };
  assert.equal(obj.addAsMethod(2, 4), 6);
  ```

- Constructor function/class: invoked via `new`.

  ```
  const inst = new add();
  assert.equal(inst instanceof add,
  true);
  ```

  (As an aside, the names of classes normally start with capital letters.)

> **Ordinary function vs. real function**
>
> In JavaScript, we distinguish:
>
> - The entity *ordinary function*

- The role *real function*, as played by an ordinary function

In many other programming languages, the entity *function* only plays one role – *function*. Therefore, the same name *function* can be used for both.

### 23.2.3 Names of ordinary functions

The name of a function expression is only accessible inside the function, where the func-tion can use it to refer to itself (e.g. for self-recursion):

```
const func = function
funcExpr() { return funcExpr
}; assert.equal(func(),
func);

• The name `funcExpr` only
exists inside the function:
assert.throws(() =>
funcExpr(), ReferenceError);
```

In contrast, the name of a function declaration is accessible inside the current scope:

```
function funcDecl() { return funcDecl }
```

```
• The name `funcDecl` exists
in the current scope
assert.equal(funcDecl(),
funcDecl);
```

## 23.3 Specialized functions

Specialized functions are single-purpose versions of ordinary functions. Each one of them specializes in a single role:

- The purpose of an *arrow function* is to be a real function:

```
const arrow = () => { return 123 };
assert.equal(arrow(), 123);
```

- The purpose of a *method* is to be a method:

```
const obj = { method() { return 'abc'
} };
assert.equal(obj.method(), 'abc');
```

- The purpose of a *class* is to be a constructor function:

```
class MyClass { /* ··· */ }
const inst = new MyClass();
```

Apart from nicer syntax, each kind of specialized function also supports new features, making them better at their jobs than ordinary functions.

- Arrow functions are explained later in this chapter.
- Methods are explained in the chapter on single objects.

- Classes are explained in the chapter on classes.

Tbl. 23.1 lists the capabilities of ordinary and specialized functions.

Table 23.1: Capabilities of four kinds of functions. "Implicit `this`" means that `this` is an implicit parameter.

| | Ordinary function | Arrow function | Method | Class |
|---|---|---|---|---|
| Function call | implicit `this` | ✔ | implicit `this` | ✘ |
| Method call | ✔ | ✘ | ✔ | ✘ |
| Constructor call | ✔ | ✘ | ✘ | ✔ |

### 23.3.1 Specialized functions are still functions

It's important to note that arrow functions, methods and classes are still categorized as functions:

```
> (() => {}) instanceof Function
true
> ({ method() {} }.method) instanceof Function
true
> (class SomeClass {}) instanceof Function
true
```

#### 23.3.2 Recommendation: prefer specialized functions

Normally, you should prefer specialized functions over ordinary functions, especially classes and methods. The choice between an arrow function and an ordinary function is less clear-cut, though:

- Arrow functions don't have `this` as an implicit parameter. That is almost always what you want if you use a real function, because it avoids an important `this`-related pitfall (for details, consult §25.4.6 "Avoiding the pitfalls of `this`").
- However, I like the function declaration (which produces an ordinary function) syntactically. If you don't use `this` inside it, it is mostly equivalent to `const` plus arrow function:

```
function funcDecl(x, y) {
  return x * y;
}
const arrowFunc = (x, y) => {
  return x * y;
};
```

#### 23.3.3 Arrow functions

Arrow functions were added to JavaScript for two reasons:

- To provide a more concise way for creating functions.
- To make working with real functions easier: You can't refer to the `this` of the sur-rounding scope inside an ordinary function (details soon).

#### 23.3.3.1 The syntax of arrow functions

Let's review the syntax of an anonymous function expression:

```
const f = function (x, y, z) { return 123
};
```

The (roughly) equivalent arrow function looks as follows.

Arrow functions are expres-sions.

```
const f = (x, y, z) => { return 123 };
```

Here, the body of the arrow function is a block. But it can also be an expression. The following arrow function works exactly like the previous one.

```
const f = (x, y, z) => 123;
```

If an arrow function has only a single parameter and that parameter is an identifier (not a destructuring pattern) then you can omit the parentheses around the parameter:

```
const id = x => x;
```

That is convenient when passing arrow functions as parameters to other functions or methods:

```
> [1,2,3].map(x => x+1)
[ 2, 3, 4 ]
```

This previous example demonstrates one benefit of arrow functions – conciseness. If we perform the same task with a function expression, our code is more verbose:

```
[1,2,3].map(function (x) { return x+1
});
```

### 23.3.3.2 Arrow functions: lexical `this`

Ordinary functions can be both methods and real functions. Alas, the two roles are in conflict:

- As each ordinary function can be a method, it has its own `this`.
- That own `this` makes it impossible to access the `this` of the surrounding scope from inside an ordinary function. And that is inconvenient for real functions.

The following code demonstrates this issue:

```
const person = {
 name: 'Jill',
 someMethod() {
  const ordinaryFunc = function () {
   assert.throws(
    () => this.name, // (A)
    /^TypeError: Cannot read property
    'name' of undefined$/);
  };
  const arrowFunc = () => {
```

```
      assert.equal(this.name, 'Jill'); //
      (B)
    };

    ordinaryFunc();
    arrowFunc();
  },
}
```

In this code, we can observe two ways of handling `this`:

- Dynamic `this`: In line A, we try to access the `this` of `.someMethod()` from an or-dinary function. There, it is *shadowed* by the function's own `this`, which is `unde-fined` (due the function call). Given that ordinary functions receive their `this` via (dynamic) function or method calls, their `this` is called *dynamic*.
- Lexical `this`: In line B, we again try to access the `this` of `.someMethod()`. This time, we succeed, because the arrow function does not have its own `this`. `this` is resolved *lexically*, just like any other variable. That's why the `this` of arrow func-tions is called *lexical*.

#### 23.3.3.3 Syntax pitfall: returning an object literal from an arrow function

If you want the expression body of an arrow function to be an object literal, you must put the literal in parentheses:

```
const func1 = () => ({a: 1});
assert.deepEqual(func1(), { a: 1 });
```

If you don't, JavaScript thinks, the arrow function has a block body (that doesn't return anything):

```
const func2 = () => {a: 1};
assert.deepEqual(func2(), undefined);
```

`{a: 1}` is interpreted as a block with the label `a:` and the expression statement `1`. Without an explicit `return` statement, the block body returns `undefined`.

This pitfall is caused by syntactic ambiguity: object literals and code blocks have the same syntax. We use the parentheses to tell JavaScript that the body is an expression (an object literal) and not a statement (a block).

For more information on shadowing `this`, consult §25.4.5 "`this` pitfall: accidentally shad-owing `this`".

## 23.4 More kinds of functions and methods

> **This section is a summary of upcoming content**
>
> This section mainly serves as a reference for the current and upcoming chapters.
>
> Don't worry if you don't understand everything.

So far, all (real) functions and methods, that we have seen, were:

- Single-result
- Synchronous

Later chapters will cover other modes of programming:

- *Iteration* treats objects as containers of data (so-called *iterables*) and provides a stan-dardized way for retrieving what is inside them. If a function or a method returns an iterable, it returns multiple values.
- *Asynchronous programming* deals with handling a long-running computation. You are notified, when the computation is finished and can do something else in be-tween. The standard pattern for asynchronously delivering single results is called *Promise*.

These modes can be combined: For example, there are synchronous iterables and asyn-chronous iterables.

Several new kinds of functions and methods help with some of the mode combinations:

- *Async functions* help implement functions that return Promises. There are also *async methods*.
- *Synchronous generator functions* help implement functions that return synchronous iterables. There are also *synchronous generator methods*.
- *Asynchronous generator functions* help implement functions that return asyn-chronous iterables. There are also *asynchronous generator methods*.

That leaves us with 4 kinds (2 × 2) of functions and methods:

- Synchronous vs. asynchronous
- Generator vs. single-result

Tbl. 23.2 gives an overview of the syntax for creating these 4 kinds of functions and meth-ods.

Table 23.2: Syntax for creating functions and methods. The last column specifies how many values are produced by an entity.

| | | Result | Values |
|---|---|---|---|
| **Sync function**<br>`function f() {}`<br>`f = function () {}`<br>`f = () => {}` | **Sync method**<br>`{ m() {} }` | value | 1 |
| **Sync generator function**<br>`function* f() {}`<br>`f = function* () {}` | **Sync gen. method**<br>`{ * m() {} }` | iterable | 0+ |
| **Async function**<br>`async function f() {}`<br>`f = async function () {}`<br>`f = async () => {}` | **Async method**<br>`{ async m() {} }` | Promise | 1 |
| **Async generator function**<br>`async function* f() {}` | **Async gen. method**<br>`{ async * m() {} }` | async iterable | 0+ |

```
f = async
function* ()
{}
```

---

## 23.5 Returning values from functions and methods

(Everything mentioned in this section applies to both functions and methods.)

The `return` statement explicitly returns a value from a function:

```
function func() {
 return 123;
}
assert.equal(func(), 123);
```

Another example:

```
function boolToYesNo(bool) {
 if (bool) {
  return 'Yes';
 } else
  {
  return
  'No';
 }
}
assert.equal(boolToYesNo(true), 'Yes');
assert.equal(boolToYesNo(false), 'No');
```

If, at the end of a function, you haven't returned anything explicitly, JavaScript returns `undefined` for you:

```
function noReturn() {
  // No explicit return
}
assert.equal(noReturn(), undefined);
```

## 23.6 Parameter handling

Once again, I am only mentioning functions in this section, but everything also applies to methods.

### 23.6.1 Terminology: parameters vs. arguments

The term *parameter* and the term *argument* basically mean the same thing. If you want to, you can make the following distinction:

- *Parameters* are part of a function definition. They are also called *formal parameters* and *formal arguments*.
- *Arguments* are part of a function call. They are also called *actual parameters* and *actual arguments*.

### 23.6.2 Terminology: callback

A *callback* or *callback function* is a function that is an argument of a function or method call.

The following is an example of a callback:

```
const myArray = ['a', 'b'];
const callback = (x) => console.log(x);
myArray.forEach(callback);
```

- Output:
- 'a'
- 'b'

**JavaScript uses the term *callback* broadly**

In other programming languages, the term *callback* often has a narrower meaning: It refers to a pattern for delivering results asynchronously, via a function-valued parameter. In this meaning, the *callback* (or *continuation*) is invoked after a function has completely finished its computation.

Callbacks as an asynchronous pattern, are described in the chapter on asynchronous programming.

### 23.6.3 Too many or not enough arguments

JavaScript does not complain if a function call provides a different number of arguments than expected by the function definition:

- Extra arguments are ignored.
- Missing parameters are set to `undefined`.

For example:

```
function foo(x, y) {
 return [x, y];
}

// Too many arguments:
assert.deepEqual(foo('a', 'b', 'c'),
['a', 'b']);

// The expected number of arguments:
assert.deepEqual(foo('a', 'b'), ['a',
'b']);

// Not enough arguments:
assert.deepEqual(foo('a'), ['a',
undefined]);
```

### 23.6.4 Parameter default values

Parameter default values specify the value to use if a parameter has not been provided.

For example:

```
function f(x, y=0) {
 return [x, y];
}

assert.deepEqual(f(1), [1, 0]);
assert.deepEqual(f(), [undefined, 0]);
```

`undefined` also triggers the default value:

```
assert.deepEqual(
```

```
  f(undefined, undefined),
  [undefined, 0]);
```

### 23.6.5 Rest parameters

A rest parameter is declared by prefixing an identifier with three dots (...). During a function or method call, it receives an Array with all remaining arguments. If there are no extra arguments at the end, it is an empty Array. For example:

```
function f(x, ...y) {
  return [x, y];
}
assert.deepEqual(
  f('a', 'b', 'c'),
  ['a', ['b', 'c']]);
assert.deepEqual(
  f(),
  [undefined, []]);
```

#### 23.6.5.1 Enforcing a certain number of arguments via a rest parameter

You can use a rest parameter to enforce a certain number of arguments. Take, for example, the following function.

```
function createPoint(x, y) {
  return {x, y};
    // same as {x: x, y: y}
}
```

This is how we force callers to always provide two arguments:

```
function createPoint(...args) {
  if (args.length !== 2) {
    throw new Error('Please provide exactly
    2 arguments!');
  }
  const [x, y] = args; // (A)
  return {x, y};
}
```

In line A, we access the elements of `args` via *destructuring*.

### 23.6.6 Named parameters

When someone calls a function, the arguments provided by the caller are assigned to the parameters received by the callee. Two common ways of performing the mapping are:

- Positional parameters: An argument is assigned to a parameter if they have the same position. A function call with only positional arguments looks as follows.

```
selectEntries(3, 20, 2)
```

- Named parameters: An argument is assigned to a parameter if they have the same name. JavaScript doesn't have named parameters, but you can simulate them. For example, this is a function call with only (simulated) named arguments:

```
selectEntries({start: 3, end: 20, step:
2})
```

Named parameters have several benefits:

- They lead to more self-explanatory code, because each argument has a descriptive label. Just compare the two versions of `selectEntries()`: With the second one, it is much easier to see what happens.
- The order of the arguments doesn't matter (as long as the names are correct).
- Handling more than one optional parameter is more convenient: Callers can easily provide any subset of all optional parameters and don't have to be aware of the ones they omit (with positional parameters, you have to fill in preceding optional parameters, with `undefined`).

### 23.6.7 Simulating named parameters

JavaScript doesn't have real named parameters. The official way of simulating them is via object literals:

```
function selectEntries({start=0, end=-1,
step=1}) {
 return {start, end, step};
}
```

This function uses *destructuring* to access the properties of its single parameter. The pat-tern it uses is an abbreviation for the following pattern:

```
{start: start=0, end: end=-1, step:
step=1}
```

This destructuring pattern works for empty object literals:

```
> selectEntries({})
{ start: 0, end: -1, step: 1 }
```

But it does not work if you call the function without any parameters:

```
> selectEntries()
TypeError: Cannot destructure property
`start` of 'undefined' or 'null'.
```

You can fix this by providing a default value for the whole pattern. This default value works the same as default values for simpler parameter definitions: If the parameter is missing, the default is used.

```
function
 selectEntries({start=0, end=-
 1, step=1} = {}) { return
 {start, end, step};
}
assert.deepEqual(
 selectEntries(),
```

```
  { start: 0, end: -1, step: 1 });
```

### 23.6.8 Spreading (...) into function calls

If you put three dots (...) in front of the argument of a function call, then you *spread* it. That means that the argument must be an *iterable* object and the iterated values all become arguments. In other words: a single argument is expanded into multiple arguments. For example:

```
function func(x, y) {
  console.log(x);
  console.log(y);
}
const someIterable = ['a', 'b'];
func(...someIterable);
  > same as func('a', 'b')
```

- Output:
- 'a'
- 'b'

Spreading and rest parameters use the same syntax (...), but they serve opposite pur-poses:

- Rest parameters are used when defining functions or methods. They collect argu-ments into Arrays.

- Spread arguments are used when calling functions or methods. They turn iterable objects into arguments.

#### 23.6.8.1 Example: spreading into `Math.max()`

`Math.max()` returns the largest one of its zero or more arguments. Alas, it can't be used for Arrays, but spreading gives us a way out:

```
> Math.max(-1, 5, 11, 3)
11
> Math.max(...[-1, 5, 11, 3])
11
> Math.max(-1, ...[-5, 11], 3)
11
```

#### 23.6.8.2 Example: spreading into `Array.prototype.push()`

Similarly, the Array method `.push()` destructively adds its zero or more parameters to the end of its Array. JavaScript has no method for destructively appending an Array to another one. Once again, we are saved by spreading:

```
const arr1 = ['a', 'b'];
const arr2 = ['c', 'd'];

arr1.push(...arr2);
assert.deepEqual(arr1, ['a', 'b', 'c',
'd']);
```

**Exercises: Parameter handling**

- Positional parameters: `exercises/callables/positional_parameters_test.mjs`
- Named parameters: `exercises/callables/named_parameters_test.mjs`

## 23.7 Dynamically evaluating code: `eval()`, `new Func-tion()` (advanced)

Next, we'll look at two ways of evaluating code dynamically: `eval()` and `new Func-tion()`.

### 23.7.1 `eval()`

Given a string `str` with JavaScript code, `eval(str)` evaluates that code and returns the result:

```
> eval('2 ** 4')
16
```

There are two ways of invoking `eval()`:

- *Directly*, via a function call. Then the code in its argument is evaluated inside the current scope.
- *Indirectly*, not via a function call. Then it evaluates its code in global scope.

"Not via a function call" means "anything that looks different than `eval(···)`":

- `eval.call(undefined, '···')`
- `(0, eval)('···')` (uses the comma operator)
- `window.eval('···')`
- `const e = eval; e('···')`
- Etc.

The following code illustrates the difference:

```
window.myVariable = 'global';
function func() {
 const myVariable = 'local';

 // Direct eval
 assert.equal(eval('myVariable'),
 'local');

 // Indirect eval
 assert.equal(eval.call(undefined,
 'myVariable'), 'global');
}
```

Evaluating code in global context is safer, because then the code has access to fewer in-ternals.

### 23.7.2 `new Function()`

`new Function()` creates a function object and is invoked as follows:

```
const func = new Function('«param_1»',
···, '«param_n»', '«func_body»');
```

The previous statement is equivalent to the next statement. Note that `«param_1»` (etc.) are not inside string literals, anymore.

```
const func = function («param_1», ···,
«param_n») {
 «func_body»
};
```

In the next example, we create the same function twice. First via `new Function()`, then via a function expression:

```
const times1 = new
Function('a', 'b', 'return a *
b'); const times2 = function
(a, b) { return a * b };
```

**new Function() creates non-strict mode functions**

Functions created via `new Function()` are sloppy.

### 23.7.3 Recommendations

Avoid dynamic evaluation of code as much as you can:

- It's a security risk, because it may enable an attacker to execute arbitrary code with the privileges of your code.
- It may be switched off. For example, in browsers, via a Content Security Policy.

Very often, JavaScript is dynamic enough so that you don't need `eval()` or similar. In the following example, what we are doing with `eval()` (line A) can be achieved just as well without it (line B).

```
const obj = {a: 1, b: 2};
const propKey = 'b';

assert.equal(eval('obj.' + propKey), 2);
// (A)
assert.equal(obj[propKey], 2); // (B)
```

If you have to dynamically evaluate code:

- Prefer `new Function()` over `eval()`: It always executes its code in global context and a function provides a clean interface to the evaluated code.
- Prefer indirect `eval` over direct `eval`: Evaluating code in global context is safer.

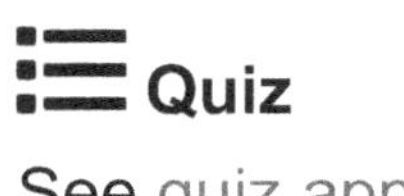

See quiz app.

210 23
*Callable values*

# Part VI

# Modularity

# Chapter 24

# Modules

## Contents

---

## 24.1 JavaScript source code formats

The current landscape of JavaScript modules is quite diverse: ES6 brought built-in mod-ules, but the source code formats that came before them, are still around, too. Under-standing the latter helps understand the former, so let's investigate. The next sections describe the following ways of delivering JavaScript source code:

- *Scripts* are code fragments that browsers run in global scope. They are precursors of modules.
- *CommonJS modules* are a module format that is mainly used on servers (e.g. via Node.js).
- *AMD modules* are a module format that is mainly used in browsers.
- *ECMAScript modules* are JavaScript's built-in module format. It supersedes all pre-vious formats.

Tbl. 24.1 gives an overview of these code formats. Note that, for CommonJS modules and ECMAScript modules, two filename extensions are commonly used. Which one is appropriate depends on how you want to use a file. Details are given later in this chapter.

Table 24.1: Ways of delivering JavaScript source code.

| | Runs on | Loaded | Filename ext. |
|---|---|---|---|
| Script | browsers | async | `.js` |
| CommonJS module | servers | sync | `.js` `.cjs` |
| AMD module | browsers | async | `.js` |
| ECMAScript module | browsers and servers | async | `.js` `.mjs` |

### 24.1.1 Code before built-in modules was written in ECMAScript 5

Before we get to built-in modules (which were introduced with ES6), all code that you'll see, will be written in ES5. Among other things:

- ES5 did not have `const` and `let`, only `var`.
- ES5 did not have arrow functions, only function expressions.

## 24.2 Before we had modules, we had scripts

Initially, browsers only had *scripts* – pieces of code that were executed in global scope. As an example, consider an HTML file that loads script files via the following HTML:

```
<script src="other-
module1.js"></script>
<script src="other-
module2.js"></script>
<script src="my-
module.js"></script>
```

The main file is `my-module.js`, where we simulate a module:

```
var myModule =
 (function () { // Open
 IIFE // Imports (via
 global variables)
 var importedFunc1 =

 otherModule1.importedFunc1

 ; var importedFunc2 =

 otherModule2.importedFunc2

 ;

 // Body
 function internalFunc() {
  // ···
 }
 function exportedFunc() {
  importedFunc1();
  importedFunc2();
  internalFunc();
 }
```

```
  // Exports (assigned to global variable
  `myModule`)
  return {
    exportedFunc: exportedFunc,
  };
})(); // Close IIFE
```

`myModule` is a global variable that is assigned the result of immediately invoking a func-tion expression. The function expression starts in the first line. It is invoked in the last line.

This way of wrapping a code fragment is called *immediately invoked function expression* (IIFE, coined by Ben Alman). What do we gain from an IIFE? `var` is not block-scoped (like `const` and `let`), it is function-scoped: The only way to create new scopes for `var`-declared variables is via functions or methods (with `const` and `let`, you can use either functions, methods or blocks `{}`). Therefore, the IIFE in the example hides all of the following vari-ables from global scope and minimizes name clashes: `importedFunc1`, `importedFunc2`, `internalFunc`, `exportedFunc`.

Note that we are using an IIFE in a particular manner: At the end, we pick what we want to export and return it via an object literal. That is called the *revealing module pattern* (coined by Christian Heilmann).

This way of simulating modules, has several issues:

- Libraries in script files export and import functionality via global variables, which risks name clashes.
- Dependencies are not stated explicitly and there is no built-in way for a script to load the scripts it

depends on. Therefore, the web page has to load not just the scripts that are needed by the page, but also the dependencies of those scripts, the dependencies' dependencies, etc. And it has to do so in the right order!

## 24.3 Module systems created prior to ES6

Prior to ECMAScript 6, JavaScript did not have built-in modules. Therefore, the flexi-ble syntax of the language was used to implement custom module systems *within* the language. Two popular ones are:

- CommonJS (targeting the server side)
- AMD (Asynchronous Module Definition, targeting the client side)

### 24.3.1 Server side: CommonJS modules

The original CommonJS standard for modules was created for server and desktop plat-forms. It was the foundation of the original Node.js module system, where it achieved enormous popularity. Contributing to that popularity were the npm package manager for Node and tools that enabled using Node modules on the client side (browserify, web-pack and others).

From now on, *CommonJS module* means the Node.js version of this standard (which has a few additional features). This is an example of a CommonJS module:

```
// Imports
var importedFunc1 =
require('./other-
module1.js').importedFunc1; var
importedFunc2 = require('./other-
module2.js').importedFunc2;
```

```
// Body
function internalFunc() {
  // ...
}
function exportedFunc() {
  importedFunc1();
  importedFunc2();
  internalFunc();
}

// Exports
module.exports = {
  exportedFunc: exportedFunc,
};
```

CommonJS can be characterized as follows:

- Designed for servers.
- Modules are meant to be loaded *synchronously* (the importer waits while the im-ported module is loaded and executed).
- Compact syntax.

### 24.3.2 Client side: AMD (Asynchronous Module Definition) modules

The AMD module format was created to be easier to use in browsers than the CommonJS format. Its most popular implementation is RequireJS. The following is an example of an AMD module.

```
define(['./other-module1.js',
  './other-module2.js'],
  function (otherModule1,
  otherModule2) {
   var importedFunc1 =
   otherModule1.importedFunc1
   ; var importedFunc2 =
   otherModule2.importedFunc2
   ;

   function internalFunc() {
     // ···
   }
   function exportedFunc() {
     importedFunc1();
     importedFunc2();
     internalFunc();
   }

   return {
     exportedFunc: exportedFunc,
   };
  });
```

AMD can be characterized as follows:

- Designed for browsers.
- Modules are meant to be loaded *asynchronously*. That's a crucial requirement for browsers, where code can't wait until a module has finished

downloading. It has to be notified once the module is available.

- The syntax is slightly more complicated.

On the plus side, AMD modules can be executed directly. In contrast, CommonJS mod-ules must either be compiled before deployment or custom source code must be gener-ated and evaluated dynamically (think `eval()`). That isn't always permitted on the web.

### 24.3.3 Characteristics of JavaScript modules

Looking at CommonJS and AMD, similarities between

JavaScript module systems emerge:

- There is one module per file.
- Such a file is basically a piece of code that is executed:
  - Local scope: The code is executed in a local "module scope". Therefore, by default, all of the variables, functions and classes declared in it, are internal and not global.
  - Exports: If you want any declared entity to be exported, you must explicitly mark it as an export.
  - Imports: Each module can import exported entities from other modules. Those other modules are identified via *module specifiers* (usually paths, occasionally full URLs).
- Modules are *singletons*: Even if a module is imported multiple times, only a single "instance" of it exists.
- No global variables are used. Instead, module specifiers serve as global IDs.

## 24.4 ECMAScript modules

*ECMAScript modules* (short: *ES modules*, *ESM*) were introduced with ES6. They continue the tradition of JavaScript modules and have all of their aforementioned characteristics. Additionally:

- With CommonJS, ES modules share the compact syntax and support for cyclic de-pendencies.
- With AMD, ES modules share being designed for asynchronous loading.

ES modules also have new benefits:

- The syntax is even more compact than CommonJS's.
- Modules have *static* structures (which can't be changed at runtime). That helps with static checking, optimized access of imports, dead code elimination and more.
- Support for cyclic imports is completely transparent.

This is an example of ES module syntax:

```
import {importedFunc1} from

'./other-module1.mjs';

import {importedFunc2} from

'./other-module2.mjs';

function internalFunc() {
  ...
}

export function exportedFunc() {
```

```
    importedFunc1();
    importedFunc2();
    internalFunc();
}
```

From now on, “module” means “ECMAScript module”.

### 24.4.1 ES modules: syntax, semantics, loader API

The full standard of ES modules comprises the following parts:

- Syntax (how code is written): What is a module? How are imports and exports declared? Etc.
- Semantics (how code is executed): How are variable bindings exported? How are imports connected with exports? Etc.
- A programmatic loader API for configuring module loading.

Parts 1 and 2 were introduced with ES6. Work on part 3 is ongoing.

## 24.5 Exporting

### 24.5.1 Named exports

Each module can have zero or more *named exports*.

As an example, consider the following three files:

```
lib/my-math.mjs
main1.mjs
main2.mjs
```

Module `my-math.mjs` has two named exports: `square` and `LIGHTSPEED`.

```
// Not exported, private to module
function times(a, b) {
 return a * b;
}
export function square(x) {
 return times(x, x);
}
export const LIGHTSPEED = 299792458;
```

Module `main1.mjs` has a single named import, `square`:

```
import {square} from './lib/my-math.mjs';
assert.equal(square(3), 9);
```

Module `main2.mjs` has a so-called *namespace import* – all named exports of `my-math.mjs` can be accessed as properties of the object `myMath`:

```
import * as myMath from

'./lib/my-math.mjs';

assert.equal(myMath.squa

re(3), 9);

assert.deepEqual(
 Object.keys(myMath), ['LIGHTSPEED',
 'square']);
```

### Exercise: Named exports

`exercises/modules/export_named_test.mjs`

### 24.5.2 Default exports

Each module can have at most one *default export*. The idea is that the module *is* the default-exported value.

> **Avoid mixing named exports and default exports**
>
> A module can have both named exports and a default export, but it's usually better to stick to one export style per module.

As an example for default exports, consider the following two files:

```
my-func.mjs
main.mjs
```

Module `my-func.mjs` has a default export:

```
const GREETING = 'Hello!';
export default function () {
  return GREETING;
}
```

Module `main.mjs` default-imports the exported function:

```
import myFunc from './my-func.mjs';
assert.equal(myFunc(), 'Hello!');
```

Note the syntactic difference: The curly braces around named imports indicate that we are reaching *into* the module, while a default import *is* the module.

The most common use case for a default export is a module that contains a single function or a single class.

#### 24.5.2.1 The two styles of default-exporting

There are two styles of doing default exports.

First, you can label existing declarations with `export default`:

```
export default function foo() {} // no semicolon!
export default class Bar {} // no semicolon!
```

Second, you can directly default-export values. In that style, `export default` is itself much like a declaration.

```
export default 'abc';
export default foo();
export default /^xyz$/;
export default 5 * 7;
export default { no: false, yes: true };
```

Why are there two default export styles? The reason is that `export default` can't be used to label `const`: `const` may define multiple values, but `export default` needs exactly one value. Consider the following hypothetical code:

```
// Not legal JavaScript!
export default const foo = 1, bar = 2,
baz = 3;
```

With this code, you don't know which one of the three values is the default export.

> **Exercise: Default exports**
>
> `exercises/modules/export_default_test.mjs`

## 24.6 Importing

### 24.6.1 Imports are read-only views on exports

So far, we have used imports and exports intuitively and everything seems to have worked as expected. But now it is time to take a closer look at how imports and exports are really related.

Consider the following two modules:

```
counter.mjs
main.mjs
```

`counter.mjs` exports a (mutable!) variable and a function:

```
export let counter = 3;
export function incCounter() {
  counter++;
}
```

`main.mjs` name-imports both exports. When we use `incCounter()`, we discover that the connection to `counter` is live – we can always access the live state of that variable:

```
import { counter, incCounter } from
'./counter.mjs';

• The imported value
`counter` is live
assert.equal(counter,
3); incCounter();
assert.equal(counter,
4);
```

Note that, while the connection is live and we can read `counter`, we cannot change this variable (e.g. via `counter++`).

There are two benefits to handling imports this way:

- It is easier to split modules, because previously shared variables can become ex-ports.
- This behavior is crucial for supporting transparent cyclic imports. Read on for more information.

### 24.6.2 Syntactic pitfall: importing is not destructuring

Both importing and destructuring look similar:

```
import {foo} from './bar.mjs'; // import
const {foo} = require('./bar.mjs'); //
destructuring
```

But they are quite different:

- Imports remain connected with their exports.
- You can destructure again inside a destructuring pattern, but the `{}` in an import statement can't be nested.
- The syntax for renaming is different:

  ```
  import {foo as f} from './bar.mjs'; //
  importing
  const {foo: f} = require('./bar.mjs');
  // destructuring
  ```

  Rationale: Destructuring is reminiscent of an object literal (incl. nesting), while importing evokes the idea of renaming.

### 24.6.3 ESM's transparent support for cyclic imports (advanced)

ESM supports cyclic imports transparently. To understand how that is achieved, consider the following example: Fig. 24.1 shows a directed graph of modules importing other modules. P importing M is the cycle in this case.

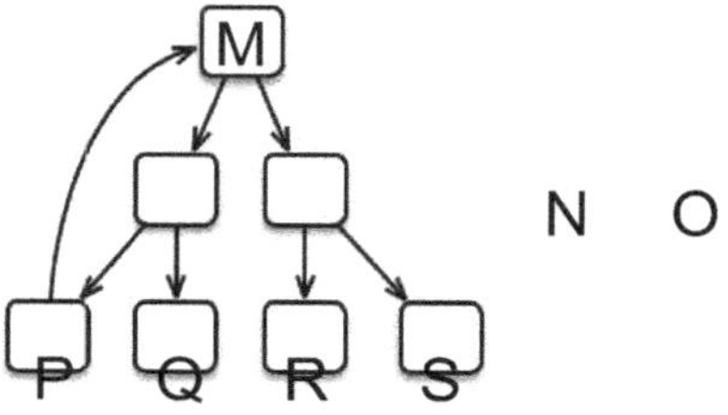


Figure 24.1: A directed graph of modules importing modules: M imports N and O, N imports P and Q, etc.

After parsing, these modules are set up in two phases:

- Instantiation: Every module is visited and its imports are connected to its exports. Before a parent can be instantiated, all of its children must be instantiated.
- Evaluation: The bodies of the modules are executed. Once again, children are eval-uated before parents.

This approach handles cyclic imports correctly, due to two features of ES modules:

- Due to the static structure of ES modules, the exports are already known after pars-ing. That makes it possible to instantiate P before its child M: P can already look up M's exports.

- When P is evaluated, M hasn't been evaluated, yet. However, entities in P can al-ready mention imports from M. They just can't use them, yet, because the imported values are filled in later. For example, a function in P can access an import from M. The only limitation is that we must wait until after the evaluation of M, before calling that function.

  Imports being filled in later is enabled by them being "live immutable views" on exports.

## 24.7 npm packages

The *npm software registry* is the dominant way of distributing JavaScript libraries and apps for Node.js and web browsers. It is managed via the *npm package manager* (short: *npm*). Software is distributed as so-called *packages*. A package is a directory containing arbitrary files and a file `package.json` at the top level that describes the package. For example, when npm creates an empty package inside a directory `foo/`, you get this `package.json`:

```
{
  "name": "foo",
  "version": "1.0.0",
```

```
  "description": "",
  "main": "index.js",
  "scripts": {
   "test": "echo \"Error: no test
   specified\" && exit 1"
  },
  "keywords": [],
  "author": "",
  "license": "ISC"
}
```

Some of these properties contain simple metadata:

- `name` specifies the name of this package. Once it is uploaded to the npm registry, it can be installed via `npm install foo`.
- `version` is used for version management and follows semantic versioning, with three numbers:
  - Major version: is incremented when incompatible API changes are made.
  - Minor version: is incremented when functionality is added in a backward compatible manner.
  - Patch version: is incremented when backward compatible changes are made.
- `description`, `keywords`, `author` make it easier to find packages.
- `license` clarifies how you can use this package.

Other properties enable advanced configuration:

- `main`: specifies the module that "is" the package (explained later in this chapter).
- `scripts`: are commands that you can execute via `npm run`. For example, the script `test` can be executed via `npm run test`.

For more information on `package.json`, consult the npm documentation.

### 24.7.1 Packages are installed inside a directory `node_modules/`

npm always installs packages inside a directory `node_modules`. There are usually many of these directories. Which one npm uses, depends on the directory where one currently is. For example, if we are inside a directory `/tmp/a/b/`, npm tries to find a `node_modules` in the current directory, its parent directory, the parent directory of the parent, etc. In other words, it searches the following *chain* of locations:

- `/tmp/a/b/node_modules`
- `/tmp/a/node_modules`
- `/tmp/node_modules`

When installing a package `foo`, npm uses the closest `node_modules`. If, for example, we are inside `/tmp/a/b/` and there is a `node_modules` in that directory, then npm puts the package inside the directory

```
/tmp/a/b/node_modules/foo/
```

When importing a module, we can use a special module specifier to tell Node.js that we want to import it from an installed package. How exactly that works, is explained later. For now, consider the following example:

```
// /home/jane/proj/main.mjs
import * as theModule from 'the-
package/the-module.mjs';
```

To find `the-module.mjs` (Node.js prefers the filename extension `.mjs` for ES modules),

Node.js walks up the `node_module` chain and searches the following locations:

- `/home/jane/proj/node_modules/the-package/the-module.mjs`
- `/home/jane/node_modules/the-package/the-module.mjs`
- `/home/node_modules/the-package/the-module.mjs`

### 24.7.2 Why can npm be used to install frontend libraries?

Finding installed modules in `node_modules` directories is only supported on Node.js. So how come, we can also use npm to install libraries for browsers?

That is enabled via bundling tools, such as webpack, that compile and optimize code before it is deployed online. During this compilation process, the code in npm packages is adapted so that it works in browsers.

## 24.8 Naming modules

There are no established best practices for naming module files and the variables they are imported into.

In this chapter, I'm using the following naming style:

- The names of module files are dash-cased and start with lowercase letters:

```
./my-module.mjs
./some-func.mjs
```

- The names of namespace imports are lowercased and camel-cased:

```
import * as myModule from './my-module.mjs';
```

- The names of default imports are lowercased and camel-cased:

```
import someFunc from './some-func.mjs';
```

What are the rationales behind this style?

- npm doesn't allow uppercase letters in package names (source). Thus, we avoid camel case, so that "local" files have names that are consistent with those of npm packages. Using only lowercase letters also minimizes conflicts between file sys-tems that are case-sensitive and file systems that aren't: The former distinguish files whose names have the same letters, but with different cases; the latter don't.
- There are clear rules for translating dash-cased file names to camel-cased JavaScript variable names. Due to how we name namespace imports, these rules work for both namespace imports and default imports.

I also like underscore-cased module file names, because you can directly use these names for namespace imports (without any translation):

```
import * as my_module from
'./my_module.mjs';
```

But that style does not work for default imports: I like underscore-casing for namespace objects, but it is not a good choice for functions etc.

## 24.9 Module specifiers

*Module specifiers* are the strings that identify modules. They work slightly differently in browsers and Node.js. Before we can look at the differences, we need to learn about the different categories of module specifiers.

### 24.9.1 Categories of module specifiers

In ES modules, we distinguish the following categories of specifiers. These categories originated with CommonJS modules.

- Relative path: starts with a dot. Examples:

```
'./some/other/module.mjs'
'../../lib/counter.mjs'
```

- Absolute path: starts with a slash. Example:

```
'/home/jane/file-tools.mjs'
```

- URL: includes a protocol (technically, paths are URLs, too). Examples:

```
'https://example.com/some-module.mjs'
'file:///home/john/tmp/main.mjs'
```

- Bare path: does not start with a dot, a slash or a protocol, and consists of a single filename without an extension. Examples:

```
'lodash'
```

```
'the-package'
```

- Deep import path: starts with a bare path and has at least one slash. Example:

```
'the-package/dist/the-module.mjs'
```

### 24.9.2 ES module specifiers in browsers

Browsers handle module specifiers as follows:

- Relative paths, absolute paths and URLs work as expected. They all must point to real files. (In contrast to CommonJS, which lets you omit filename extensions and more.)
- The file name extensions of modules don't matter, as long as they are served with the content type `text/javascript`.
- How bare paths will end up being handled is not yet clear. You will probably eventually be able to map them to other specifiers via lookup tables.

Note that bundling tools such as webpack, which combine modules into fewer files, are often less strict with specifiers than browsers. That's because they operate at build/-compile time (not at runtime) and can search for files by traversing the file system.

### 24.9.3 ES module specifiers on Node.js

> ⚠ **Support for ES modules on Node.js is still new**
> You may have to switch it on via a command line flag. See the Node.js documenta-tion for details.

Node.js handles module specifiers as follows:

- Relative paths are resolved as they are in web browsers – relative to the path of the current module.
- Absolute paths are currently not supported. As a work-around, you can use URLs that start with `file:///`. You can create such URLs via `url.pathToFileURL()`.
- Only `file:` is supported as a protocol for URL specifiers.
- A bare path is interpreted as a package name and resolved relative to the closest `node_modules` directory. What module should be loaded, is determined by looking at property `"main"` of the package's `package.json` (similarly to CommonJS).
- Deep import paths are also resolved relatively to the closest `node_modules` direc-tory. They contain file names, so it is always clear which module is meant.

All specifiers, except bare paths, must refer to actual files. That is, ESM does not support the following CommonJS features:

- CommonJS automatically adds missing filename extensions.
- CommonJS can import a directory `foo` if there is a `foo/package.json` with a `"main"` property.
- CommonJS can import a directory `foo` if there is a module `foo/index.js`.

All built-in Node.js modules are available via bare paths and have named ESM exports.

For example:

```
import * as path from 'path';
import {strict as assert} from 'assert';

assert.equal(
  path.join('a/b/c', '../d'), 'a/b/d');
```

#### 24.9.3.1 Filename extensions on Node.js

Node.js supports the following default filename extensions:

- `.mjs` for ES modules
- `.cjs` for CommonJS modules

The filename extension `.js` stands for either ESM or CommonJS. Which one it is, is config-ured via the "closest" `package.json` (in the current directory, the parent directory, etc.). Using `package.json` in this manner is independent of packages.

In that `package.json`, there is a property `"type"`, which has two settings:

- `"commonjs"` (the default): files with the extension `.js` or without an extension are interpreted as CommonJS modules.
- `"module"`: files with the extension `.js` or without an extension are interpreted as ESM modules.

#### 24.9.3.2 Interpreting non-file source code as either CommonJS or ESM

Not all source code that is executed by Node.js, comes from files. You can also send it code via stdin, `--eval` and `--print`. The command line option `--input-type` lets you specify how such code is interpreted:

- As CommonJS (the default): `--input-type=commonjs`
- As ESM: `--input-type=module`

## 24.10 Loading modules dynamically via `import()`

So far, the only way to import a module has been via an `import` statement. That statement has several limitations:

- You must use it at the top level of a module. That is, you can't, e.g., import some-thing when you are inside a block.
- The module specifier is always fixed. That is, you can't change what you import depending on a

condition. And you can't assemble a specifier dynamically.

The `import()` operator changes that. Let's look at an example of it being used.

### 24.10.1 Example: loading a module dynamically

Consider the following files:

```
lib/my-math.mjs
main1.mjs
main2.mjs
```

We have already seen module `my-math.mjs`:

```
// Not exported, private to module
function times(a, b) {
 return a * b;
}
export function square(x) {
 return times(x, x);
}
export const LIGHTSPEED = 299792458;
```

This is what using `import()` looks like in `main1.mjs`:

```
const dir = './lib/';
const moduleSpecifier = dir + 'my-
math.mjs';
```

```
function loadConstant() {
  return import(moduleSpecifier)
  .then(myMath => {
    const result = myMath.LIGHTSPEED;
    assert.equal(result, 299792458);
    return result;
  });
}
```

Method `.then()` is part of *Promises*, a mechanism for handling asynchronous results, which is covered later in this book.

Two things in this code weren't possible before:

- We are importing inside a function (not at the top level).
- The module specifier comes from a variable.

Next, we'll implement the exact same functionality in `main2.mjs`, but via a so-called *async function*, which provides nicer syntax for Promises.

```
const dir = './lib/';
const moduleSpecifier = dir + 'my-
math.mjs';

async function loadConstant() {
  const myMath = await
  import(moduleSpecifier);
  const result =
  myMath.LIGHTSPEED;
  assert.equal(result,
```

```
    299792458); return
    result;
  }
```

> **(?) Why is `import()` an operator and not a function?**
>
> Even though it works much like a function, `import()` is an operator: In order to resolve module specifiers relatively to the current module, it needs to know from which module it is invoked. A normal function cannot receive this information as implicitly as an operator can. It would need, e.g., a parameter.

### 24.10.2 Use cases for `import()`

#### 24.10.2.1 Loading code on demand

Some functionality of web apps doesn't have to be present when they start, it can be loaded on demand. Then `import()` helps, because you can put such functionality into modules. For example:

```
button.addEventListener('cl
      ick', event => {
  import('./dialogBox.js')
    .then(dialogBox => {
     dialogBox.open();
    })
    .catch(error => {
```

```
    /* Error handling */
  })
});
```

#### 24.10.2.2 Conditional loading of modules

Sometimes you may want to load a module depending on whether a condition is true.

For example, to load a polyfill on legacy platforms. That looks as follows.

```
if (isLegacyPlatform()) {
  import(···)
    .then(···);
}
```

#### 24.10.2.3 Computed module specifiers

For applications such as internationalization, it helps if you can dynamically compute module specifiers:

```
import(`messages_${getLocale()}.js`)
  .then(···);
```

## 24.11 Preview: import.meta.url

"`import.meta`" is an ECMAScript feature proposed by Domenic Denicola. The object `import.meta` holds metadata for the current module.

Its most important property is `import.meta.url`, which contains a string with the URL of the current module file. For example:

```
'https://example.com/code/main.mjs'
```

### 24.11.1 import.meta.url and class URL

Class `URL` is available via a global variable in browsers and on Node.js. You can look up its full functionality in the Node.js documentation. When working with `import.meta.url`, its constructor is especially useful:

```
new URL(input: string, base?: string|URL)
```

Parameter `input` contains the URL to be parsed. It can be relative if the second parameter, `base`, is provided.

On other words – this constructor lets us resolve a relative path against a base URL:

```
> new URL('other.mjs',
'https://example.com/code/main.mjs').href
'https://example.com/code/other.mjs'
> new URL('../other.mjs',
'https://example.com/code/main.mjs').href
'https://example.com/other.mjs'
```

This is how we get a `URL` instance that points to a file `data.txt` that sits next to the current module:

```
const urlOfData =      import.meta.url);
new URL('data.txt',
```

#### 24.11.2 import.meta.url on Node.js

On Node.js, `import.meta.url` is always a string with a `file:` URL. For example:

```
'file:///Users/rauschma/my-module.mjs'
```

##### 24.11.2.1 Example: reading a sibling file of a module

Many Node.js file system operations accept either strings with paths or instances of `URL`.

That enables us to read a sibling file `data.txt` of the current module:

```
import {promises as fs} from 'fs';

async function main() {
 const urlOfData = new URL('data.txt',
 import.meta.url);
 const str = await
 fs.readFile(urlOfData, {encoding:
 'UTF-8'}); assert.equal(str, 'This
 is textual data.\n');
}
main();
```

`main()` is an async function, as explained in $full.

`fs.promises` contains a Promise-based version of the `fs` API, that can be used with async functions.

#### 24.11.2.2 Converting between `file:` URLs and paths

The Node.js module `url` has two functions for converting between `file:` URLs and paths:

- `fileURLToPath(url: URL|string): string`
  Converts a `file:` URL to a path.
- `pathToFileURL(path: string): URL`
  Converts a path to a `file:` URL.

If you need a path that can be used in the local file system, then property `.pathname` of `URL` instances does not always work:

```
assert.equal(
  new
  URL('file:///tmp/with%20spa
  ce.txt').pathname,
  '/tmp/with%20space.txt');
```

Therefore, it is better to use `fileURLToPath()`:

```
import * as url from 'url';
assert.equal(
  url.fileURLToPath('file:///t
  mp/with%20space.txt'),
  '/tmp/with space.txt'); //
  result on Unix
```

Similarly, `pathToFileURL()` does more than just prepend `'file://'` to an absolute path.

## 24.12 Quick reference: exporting and importing

### 24.12.1 Exporting

```
// Re-exporting from another module
export * from './some-module.mjs';
export {foo, b as bar} from './scme-
module.mjs';

// Named exports
export {foo, b as bar};
export function f() {}
export const one = 1;

// Default exports
export default function f() {} //
declaration with optional name //
Replacement for `const` (there must
be exactly one value) export default
123;
```

### 24.12.2 Importing

```
// Empty import (for modules with side
effects)
import './some-module.mjs';

// Default import
import someModule from
'./some-module.mjs'; //
Namespace import
```

```
import * as someModule from
'./some-module.mjs'; //
Named imports
import {foo, bar as b} from './some-
module.mjs';

// Combinations:
import someModule, * as
someModule from './some-
module.mjs'; import someModule,
{foo, bar as b} from './some-
module.mjs';
```

### Quiz

See quiz app.

232

*Modules*

*24*

## Chapter 25

# Single objects

## Contents

---

In this book, JavaScript's style of object-oriented programming (OOP) is introduced in four steps. This chapter covers step 1, the next chapter covers steps 2–4. The steps are (fig. 25.1):

- **Single objects:** How do *objects*, JavaScript's basic OOP building blocks, work in isolation?

- Prototype chains: Each object has a chain of zero or more *prototype objects*. Proto-types are JavaScript's core inheritance mechanism.
- Classes: JavaScript's *classes* are factories for objects. The relationship between a class and its instances is based on prototypal inheritance.
- Subclassing: The relationship between a *subclass* and its *superclass* is also based on prototypal inheritance.

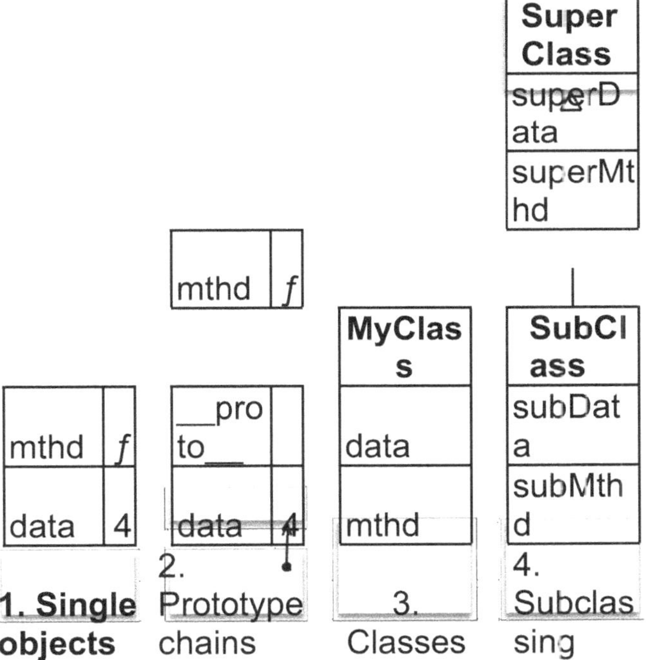


Figure 25.1: This book introduces object-oriented programming in JavaScript in four steps.

## 25.1 What is an object?

In JavaScript:

- An object is a set of *properties* (key-value entries).

- A property key can only be a string or a symbol.

### 25.1.1 Roles of objects: record vs. dictionary

Objects play two roles in JavaScript:

- Records: Objects-as-records have a fixed number of properties, whose keys are known at development time. Their values can have different types.
- Dictionaries: Objects-as-dictionaries have a variable number of properties, whose keys are not known at development time. All of their values have the same type.

These roles influence how objects are explained in this chapter:

- First, we'll explore objects-as-records. Even though property keys are strings or symbols under the hood, they will appear as fixed identifiers to us, in this part of the chapter.
- Later, we'll explore objects-as-dictionaries. Note that Maps are usually better dic-tionaries than objects. However, some of the operations that we'll encounter, can also be useful for objects-as-records.

## 25.2 Objects as records

Let's first explore the role *record* of objects.

### 25.2.1 Object literals: properties

*Object literals* are one way of creating objects-as-records. They are a stand-out feature of

JavaScript: You can directly create objects – no need for classes! This is an example:

```
const jane = {
  first: 'Jane',
  last: 'Doe', // optional trailing comma
};
```

In the example, we created an object via an object literal, which starts and ends with curly braces `{}`. Inside it, we defined two *properties* (key-value entries):

- The first property has the key `first` and the value `'Jane'`.
- The second property has the key `last` and the value `'Doe'`.

We will later see other ways of specifying property keys, but with this way of specifying them, they must follow the rules of JavaScript variable names. For example, you can use `first_name` as a property key, but not `first-name`). However, reserved words are allowed:

```
const obj
  = {
  if: true,
  const: true,
};
```

In order to check the effects of various operations on objects, we'll occasionally use `Ob-ject.keys()` in this part of the chapter. It lists property keys:

```
> Object.keys({a:1, b:2})
[ 'a', 'b' ]
```

### 25.2.2 Object literals: property value shorthands

Whenever the value of a property is defined via a variable name and that name is the same as the key, you can omit the key.

```
function createPoint(x, y) {
 return {x, y};
}
assert.deepEqual(
 createPoint(9, 2),
 { x: 9, y: 2 }
);
```

### 25.2.3 Getting properties

This is how you *get* (read) a property (line A):

```
const jane = {
 first: 'Jane',
 last: 'Doe',
};

// Get property .first
assert.equal(jane.first, 'Jane'); // (A)
```

Getting an unknown property, produces `undefined`:

```
assert.equal(jane.unknownProperty,
undefined);
```

### 25.2.4 Setting properties

This is how you *set* (write to) a property:

```
const obj = {
 prop: 1,
};
assert.equal(obj.prop, 1);
obj.prop = 2; // (A)
assert.equal(obj.prop, 2);
```

We just changed an existing property via setting. If we set an unknown property, we create a new entry:

```
const obj = {}; // empty object
assert.deepEqual(
 Object.keys(obj), []);

obj.unknownProperty = 'abc';
```

```
assert.deepEqual(
  Object.keys(obj), ['unknownProperty']);
```

### 25.2.5 Object literals: methods

The following code shows how to create the method `.says()` via an object literal:

```
const jane = {
  first: 'Jane', // data property
  says(text) {   // method
    return `${this.first} says "${text}"`;
    // (A)
  }, // comma as separator (optional at
  end)
};
assert.equal(jane.says('hello'), 'Jane
says "hello"');
```

During the method call `jane.says('hello')`, `jane` is called the *receiver* of the method call and assigned to the special variable `this`. That enables method `.says()` to access the sibling property `.first` in line A.

### 25.2.6 Object literals: accessors

There are two kinds of accessors in JavaScript:

- A *getter* is a method-like entity that is invoked by getting a property.
- A *setter* is a method-like entity that is invoked by setting a property.

#### 25.2.6.1 Getters

A getter is created by prefixing a method definition with the modifier get:

```
const jane = {
  first: 'Jane',
  last: 'Doe',
  get full() {
    return `${this.first} ${this.last}`;
  },
};

assert.equal(jane.full, 'Jane Doe');
jane.first = 'John';
assert.equal(jane.full, 'John Doe');
```

#### 25.2.6.2 Setters

A setter is created by prefixing a method definition with the modifier set:

```
const jane = {
  first: 'Jane',
  last: 'Doe',
  set full(fullName) {
    const parts = fullName.split(' ');
```

```
    this.first = parts[0];
    this.last = parts[1];
  },
};

jane.full = 'Richard Roe';
assert.equal(jane.first, 'Richard');
assert.equal(jane.last, 'Roe');
```

> **Exercise: Creating an object via an object literal**

`exercises/single-objects/color_point_object_test.mjs`

## 25.3 Spreading into object literals (...)

Inside a function call, spreading (...) turns the iterated values of an *iterable* object into arguments.

Inside an object literal, a *spread property* adds the properties of another object to the current one:

```
> const obj = {foo: 1, bar: 2};
> {...obj, baz: 3}
{ foo: 1, bar: 2, baz: 3 }
```

If property keys clash, the property that is mentioned last "wins":

```
> const obj = {foo: 1, bar: 2, baz: 3};
> {...obj, foo: true}
{ foo: true, bar: 2, baz: 3 }
> {foo: true, ...obj}
{ foo: 1, bar: 2, baz: 3 }
```

### 25.3.1 Use case for spreading: copying objects

You can use spreading to create a copy of an object `original`:

```
const copy = {...original};
```

Caveat – copying is *shallow*: `copy` is a fresh object with duplicates of all properties (key-value entries) of `original`. But if property values are objects, then those are not copied themselves; they are shared between `original` and `copy`. Let's look at an example.

```
const original = { a:
1, b: {foo: true} };
const copy =
{...original};
```

The first level of `copy` is really a copy: If you change any properties at that level, it does not affect the original:

```
copy.a = 2;
assert.deepEqual(
```

```
original, { a: 1, b: {foo: true} }); //
no change
```

However, deeper levels are not copied. For example, the value of `.b` is shared between original and copy.

Changing `.b` in the copy, also changes it in the original.

```
copy.b.foo = false;
assert.deepEqual(
  original, { a: 1, b: {foo: false} });
```

> ⚠ **JavaScript doesn't have built-in support for deep copying**
>
> *Deep copies* of objects (where all levels are copied) are notoriously difficult to do generically. Therefore, JavaScript does not have a built-in operation for them (for now). If you need such an operation, you have to implement it yourself.

### 25.3.2 Use case for spreading: default values for missing properties

If one of the inputs of your code is an object with data, you can make properties optional by specifying default values that are used if those properties are missing. One technique for doing so, is via an object whose properties contain the default values. In the following example, that object is `DEFAULTS`:

```
const DEFAULTS = {foo: 'a', bar: 'b'};
const providedData = {foo: 1};
```

```
const allData =
{...DEFAULTS,
...providedData};
assert.deepEqual(allData,
{foo: 1, bar: 'b'});
```

The result, the object `allData`, is created by copying `DEFAULTS` and overriding its proper-ties with those of `providedData`.

But you don't need an object to specify the default values, you can also specify them inside the object literal, individually:

```
const providedData = {foo: 1};

const allData = {foo: 'a', bar: 'b',
...providedData};
assert.deepEqual(allData, {foo: 1, bar:
'b'});
```

### 25.3.3 Use case for spreading: non-destructively changing properties

So far, we have encountered one way of changing a property `.foo` of an object: We *set* it (line A) and mutate the object. That is, this way of changing a property is *destructive*.

```
const obj = {foo: 'a', bar: 'b'};
obj.foo = 1; // (A)
assert.deepEqual(obj, {foo: 1, bar: 'b'});
```

With spreading, we can change `.foo` *non-destructively* – we make a copy of `obj` where `.foo` has a different value:

```
const obj = {foo: 'a', bar: 'b'};
const updatedObj = {...obj, foo: 1};
assert.deepEqual(updatedObj, {foo: 1,
bar: 'b'});
```

> **Exercise: Non-destructively updating a property via spreading (fixed key)**
>
> `exercises/single-objects/update_name_test.mjs`

## 25.4 Methods

### 25.4.1 Methods are properties whose values are functions

Let's revisit the example that was used to introduce methods:

```
const jane = {
  first: 'Jane',
  says(text) {
    return `${this.first} says "${text}"`;
  },
};
```

Somewhat surprisingly, methods are functions:

```
assert.equal(typeof jane.says,
'function');
```

Why is that? Remember that, in the chapter on callable values, we learned that ordinary functions play several roles. *Method* is one of those roles. Therefore, under the hood, `jane` roughly looks as follows.

```
const jane = {
```

```
  first: 'Jane',
  says: function (text) {
   return `${this.first} says "${text}"`;
  },
};
```

### 25.4.2 `.call()`: specifying `this` via a parameter

Remember that each function `someFunc` is also an object and therefore has methods. One such method is `.call()` – it lets you call a function while specifying `this` via a parameter:

```
someFunc.call(thisValue, arg1, arg2,
arg3);
```

#### 25.4.2.1 Methods and `.call()`

If you make a method call, `this` is an implicit parameter that is filled in via the receiver of the call:

```
const obj = {
 method(x) {
  assert.equal(this, obj); // implicit
  parameter
```

```
    assert.equal(x, 'a');
  },
};

obj.method('a'); // receiver is `obj`
```

The method call in the last line sets up `this` as follows:

```
obj.method.call(obj, 'a');
```

As an aside, that means that there are actually two different dot operators:

- One for accessing properties: `obj.prop`
- One for making method calls: `obj.prop()`

They are different in that (2) is not just (1), followed by the function call operator `()`.

Instead, (2) additionally specifies a value for `this`.

#### 25.4.2.2 Functions and `.call()`

If you function-call an ordinary function, its implicit parameter `this` is also provided – it is implicitly set to `undefined`:

```
function func(x) {
  assert.equal(this,
  undefined); // implicit
  parameter assert.equal(x,
  'a');
}

func('a');
```

The method call in the last line sets up `this` as follows:

```
func.call(undefined, 'a');
```

`this` being set to `undefined` during a function call, indicates that it is a feature that is only needed during a method call.

Next, we'll examine the pitfalls of using `this`. Before we can do that, we need one more tool: method `.bind()` of functions.

### 25.4.3 `.bind()`: pre-filling `this` and parameters of functions

`.bind()` is another method of function objects. This method is invoked as follows.

```
const boundFunc = someFunc.bind(thisValue,
arg1, arg2);
```

`.bind()` returns a new function `boundFunc()`. Calling that function invokes `someFunc()` with `this` set to `thisValue` and these parameters: `arg1`, `arg2`, followed by the parameters of `boundFunc()`.

That is, the following two function calls are equivalent:

```
boundFunc('a', 'b')
someFunc.call(thisValue, arg1, arg2, 'a',
'b')
```

#### 25.4.3.1 An alternative to `.bind()`

Another way of pre-filling `this` and parameters, is via an arrow function:

```
const boundFunc2 = (...args) =>
 someFunc.call(thisValue, arg1, arg2,
 ...args);
```

#### 25.4.3.2 An implementation of `.bind()`

Considering the previous section, `.bind()` can be implemented as a real function as fol-lows:

```
function bind(func,
 thisValue, ...boundArgs)
 { return (...args) =>
  func.call(thisValue, ...boundArgs,
  ...args);
}
```

#### 25.4.3.3 Example: binding a real function

Using `.bind()` for real functions is somewhat unintuitive, because you have to provide a value for `this`. Given that it is `undefined` during function calls, it is usually set to `undefined` or `null`.

In the following example, we create `add8()`, a function that has one parameter, by binding the first parameter of `add()` to `8`.

```
function add(x, y) {
 return x + y;
```

```
}

const add8 = add.bind(undefined, 8);
assert.equal(add8(1), 9);
```

#### 25.4.3.4 Example: binding a method

In the following code, we turn method `.says()` into the stand-alone function `func()`:

```
const jane = {
  first: 'Jane',
  says(text) {
    return `${this.first} says "${text}"`;
    // (A)
  },
};

const func =
jane.says.bind(jane,
'hello');
assert.equal(func(),
'Jane says "hello"');
```

Setting `this` to `jane` via `.bind()` is crucial here. Otherwise, `func()` wouldn't work prop-erly, because `this` is used in line A.

### 25.4.4 `this` pitfall: extracting methods

We now know quite a bit about functions and methods and are ready to take a look at the biggest pitfall involving methods and `this`: function-calling a method extracted from an object can fail if you are not careful.

In the following example, we fail when we extract method `jane.says()`, store it in the variable `func` and function-call `func()`.

```
const jane = {
 first: 'Jane',
 says(text) {
  return `${this.first} says "${text}"`;
 },
};
const func = jane.says;
// extract the method
assert.throws(
  () => func('hello'), // (A)
  {
   name: 'TypeError',
   message: "Cannot read
 property 'first' of
 undefined", });
```

The function call in line A is equivalent to:

```
assert.throws(
  () => jane.says.call(undefined,
 'hello'), // `this` is undefined! {
   name: 'TypeError',
```

```
  message: "Cannot read
 property 'first' of
 undefined", });
```

So how do we fix this? We need to use `.bind()` to extract method `.says()`:

```
const func2 = jane.says.bind(jane);
assert.equal(func2('hello'), 'Jane says
"hello"');
```

The `.bind()` ensures that `this` is always `jane` when we call `func()`.

You can also use arrow functions to extract methods:

```
const func3 = text => jane.says(text);
assert.equal(func3('hello'), 'Jane says
"hello"');
```

#### 25.4.4.1 Example: extracting a method

The following is a simplified version of code that you may see in actual web development:

```
class ClickHandler {
 constructor(id, elem) {
  this.id = id;
  elem.addEventListener('click',
  this.handleClick); // (A)
 }
 handleClick(event) {
```

```
    alert('Clicked ' + this.id);
   }
  }
```

In line A, we don't extract the method `.handleClick()` properly. Instead, we should do:

```
elem.addEventListener('click',
this.handleClick.bind(this));
```

> **Exercise: Extracting a method**
>
> `exercises/single-objects/method_extraction_exrc.mjs`

### 25.4.5 `this` pitfall: accidentally shadowing `this`

> **Accidentally shadowing `this` is only an issue with ordinary functions** Arrow functions don't shadow `this`.

Consider the following problem: When you are inside an ordinary function, you can't access the `this` of the surrounding scope, because the ordinary function has its own `this`. In other words: a variable in an inner scope hides a variable in an outer scope. That is called *shadowing*. The following code is an example:

```
const prefixer = {
 prefix: '==> ',
 prefixStringArray(stringArray) {
  return stringArray.map(
```

```
      function (x) {
       return this.prefix + x; // (A)
      });
    },
  };
  assert.throws(
    () => prefixer.prefixStringArray(['a',
    'b']),
    /^TypeError: Cannot read property
    'prefix' of undefined$/);
```

In line A, we want to access the `this` of `.prefixStringArray()`. But we can't, since the surrounding ordinary function has its own `this`, that *shadows* (blocks access to) the `this` of the method. The value of the former `this` is `undefined` – due to the callback being function-called. That explains the error message.

The simplest way to fix this problem is via an arrow function, which doesn't have its own `this` and therefore doesn't shadow anything:

```
  const prefixer = {
   prefix: '==> ',
   prefixStringArray(stringArray) {
    return stringArray.map(
      • => {
```

```
      return this.prefix + x;
    });
  },
};
assert.deepEqual(
  prefixer.prefixStringArray(['a', 'b']),
  ['==> a', '==> b']);
```

We can also store `this` in a different variable (line A), so that it doesn't get shadowed:

```
prefixStringArray(stringArray) {
  const that = this; // (A)
  return stringArray.map(
    function (x) {
      return that.prefix + x;
    });
},
```

Another option is to specify a fixed `this` for the callback, via `.bind()` (line A):

```
prefixStringArray(stringArray) {
  return stringArray.map(
    function (x) {
      return this.prefix + x;
    }.bind(this)); // (A)
},
```

Lastly, `.map()` lets us specify a value for `this` (line A) that it uses when invoking the callback:

```
prefixStringArray(stringArray) {
  return stringArray.map(
    function (x) {
      return this.prefix + x;
```

```
    },
    this); // (A)
  },
```

### 25.4.6 Avoiding the pitfalls of `this`

We have seen two big `this`-related pitfalls:

- Extracting methods
- Accidentally shadowing `this`

One simple rule helps avoid the second pitfall:

> "Avoid the keyword `function`": Never use ordinary functions, only arrow functions (for real functions) and method definitions.

Following this rule has two benefits:

- It prevents the second pitfall, because ordinary functions are never used as real functions.

- `this` becomes easier to understand, because it will only appear inside methods (never inside ordinary functions). That makes it clear that `this` is an OOP feature.

However, even though I don't use (ordinary) function *expressions*, anymore, I do like func-tion *declarations* syntactically. You can use them safely if you don't refer to `this` inside them. The static checking tool ESLint can warn you during development when you do this wrong, via a built-in rule.

Alas, there is no simple way around the first pitfall:

Whenever you extract a method, you have to be careful and do it properly. For example, by binding `this`.

### 25.4.7 The value of `this` in various contexts

What is the value of `this` in various contexts?

Inside a callable entity, the value of `this` depends on how the callable entity is invoked and what kind of callable entity it is:

- Function call:
  - Ordinary functions: `this === undefined`
  - Arrow functions: `this` is same as in surrounding scope (lexical `this`)
- Method call: `this` is receiver of call
- `new`: `this` refers to newly created instance

You can also access `this` in all common top-level scopes:

- `<script>` element: `this === window`
- ES modules: `this === undefined`
- CommonJS modules: `this === module.exports`

However, I like to pretend that you can't access `this` in top-level scopes, because top-level `this` is confusing and not that useful.

## 25.5 Objects as dictionaries (advanced)

Objects work best as records. But before ES6, JavaScript did not have a data structure for dictionaries (ES6 brought Maps). Therefore, objects had to be used as dictionaries, which imposed a signficant constraint: Keys had to be strings (symbols were also introduced with ES6).

We first look at features of objects that are related to dictionaries, but also useful for objects-as-records. This section concludes with tips for actually using objects as dictio-naries (spoiler: use Maps if you can).

### 25.5.1 Arbitrary fixed strings as property keys

So far, we have always used objects as records.

Property keys were fixed tokens that had to be valid identifiers and internally became strings:

```
const obj = {
 mustBeAnIdentifier: 123,
};
```

```
// Get property
assert.equal(obj.mustBeAnIdentifier, 123);

// Set property
obj.mustBeAnIdentifier = 'abc';
assert.equal(obj.mustBeAnIdentifier,
'abc');
```

As a next step, we'll go beyond this limitation for property keys: In this section, we'll use arbitrary fixed strings as keys. In the next subsection, we'll dynamically compute keys.

Two techniques allow us to use arbitrary strings as property keys.

First – when creating property keys via object literals, we can quote property keys (with single or double quotes):

```
const obj = {
  'Can be any string!': 123,
};
```

Second – when getting or setting properties, we can use square brackets with strings inside them:

```
// Get property
assert.equal(obj['Can be any string!'],
123);

// Set property
obj['Can be any string!'] = 'abc';
assert.equal(obj['Can be any string!'],
'abc');
```

You can also use these techniques for methods:

```
const obj = {
  'A nice method'() {
    return 'Yes!';
  },
};

assert.equal(obj['A nice method'](),
'Yes!');
```

### 25.5.2 Computed property keys

So far, property keys were always fixed strings inside object literals. In this section we learn how to dynamically compute property keys. That enables us to use either arbitrary strings or symbols.

The syntax of dynamically computed property keys in object literals is inspired by dy-namically accessing properties. That is, we can use square brackets to wrap expressions:

```
const obj = {
  ['Hello world!']: true,
  ['f'+'o'+'o']: 123,
  [Symbol.toStringTag]: 'Goodbye', // (A)
```

```
};

assert.equal(obj['Hello world!'], true);
assert.equal(obj.foo, 123);
assert.equal(obj[Symbol.toStringTag],
'Goodbye');
```

The main use case for computed keys is having symbols as property keys (line A).

Note that the square brackets operator for getting and setting properties works with ar-bitrary expressions:

```
assert.equal(obj['f'+'o'+'o'], 123);
assert.equal(obj['==> foo'.slice(-3)],
123);
```

Methods can have computed property keys, too:

```
const methodKey = Symbol();
const obj = {
  [methodKey]() {
   return 'Yes!';
  },
};

assert.equal(obj[methodKey](), 'Yes!');
```

For the remainder of this chapter, we'll mostly use fixed property keys again (because they are syntactically more convenient). But all features are also available for arbitrary strings and symbols.

> **Exercise: Non-destructively updating a property via spreading (computed key)**

exercises/single-objects/update_property_test.mjs

### 25.5.3 The `in` operator: is there a property with a given key?

The `in` operator checks if an object has a property with a given key:

```
const obj = {
 foo: 'abc',
 bar: false,
};

assert.equal('foo' in obj, true);
assert.equal('unknownKey' in obj,
false);
```

#### 25.5.3.1 Checking if a property exists via truthiness

You can also use a truthiness check to determine if a property exists:

```
assert.equal(
 obj.foo ? 'exists' : 'does not exist',
```

```
    'exists');
  assert.equal(
    obj.unknownKey ? 'exists' : 'does not
    exist',
    'does not exist');
```

The previous checks work, because `obj.foo` is truthy and because reading a missing prop-erty returns `undefined` (which is falsy).

There is, however, one important caveat: Truthiness checks fail if the property exists, but has a falsy value (`undefined`, `null`, `false`, `0`, `""`, etc.):

```
  assert.equal(
    obj.bar ? 'exists' : 'does not exist',
    'does not exist'); // should be: 'exists'
```

### 25.5.4 Deleting properties

You can delete properties via the `delete` operator:

```
const obj
    = {
    foo: 123,
  };
  assert.deepEqual(Object.keys(obj),
  ['foo']);

  delete obj.foo;

  assert.deepEqual(Object.keys(obj), []);
```

### 25.5.5 Listing property keys

Table 25.1: Standard library methods for listing *own* (non-inherited) prop-erty keys. All of them return Arrays with strings and/or symbols.

| | enumerable | non-e. | string | symbol |
|---|---|---|---|---|
| `Object.keys()` | ✔ | | ✔ | |
| `Object.getOwnPropertyNames()` | ✔ | ✔ | ✔ | |
| `Object.getOwnPropertySymbols()` | ✔ | ✔ | | ✔ |
| `Reflect.ownKeys()` | ✔ | ✔ | ✔ | ✔ |

Each of the methods in tbl. 25.1 returns an Array with the own property keys of the parameter. In the names of the methods, you can see that the following distinction is made:

- A *property key* can be either a string or a symbol.
- A *property name* is a property key whose value is a string.
- A *property symbol* is a property key whose value is a symbol.

*Enumerability* is an *attribute* of a property. Non-enumerable properties are ignored by some operations. For example, by `Object.keys()` (see table) and by spread properties.

By default, most properties are enumerable. The next example shows how to change that.

It also demonstrates the various ways of listing property keys.

```
const enumerableSymbolKey =
Symbol('enumerableSymbolKey');
const nonEnumSymbolKey =
Symbol('nonEnumSymbolKey');

// We create enumerable
properties via an object
literal const obj = {
 enumerableStringKey: 1,
 [enumerableSymbolKey]: 2,
}

• For non-enumerable properties, we
need a more powerful tool
Object.defineProperties(obj, {
 nonEnumStri
  ngKey: {
  value: 3,
  enumerable
  : false,
 },
 [nonEnumSym
 bolKey]: {
  value: 4,
```

```
    enumerable: false,
  },
});

assert.deepEqual(
  Object.keys(obj),
  • 'enumerableStr
ingKey' ]);
assert.deepEqual
(
  Object.getOwnPropertyNames(obj),
  • 'enumerableStringKey',
'nonEnumStringKey' ]);
assert.deepEqual(
  Object.getOwnPropertySymbols(obj),
  • enumerableSymbolKey,
nonEnumSymbolKey ]);
assert.deepEqual(
  Reflect.ownKeys(obj),
•
    'enumerableStringKey',
    'nonEnumStringKey',
    enumerableSymbolKey,
    nonEnumSymbolKey,
  ]);
```

`Object.defineProperties()` is explained later.

### 25.5.6 Listing property values via `Object.values()`

`Object.values()` lists the values of all enumerable properties of an object:

```
const obj = {foo: 1, bar: 2};
assert.deepEqual(
 Object.values(obj),
 [1, 2]);
```

### 25.5.7 Listing property entries via `Object.entries()`

`Object.entries()` lists key-value pairs of enumerable properties. Each pair is encoded as a two-element Array:

```
const obj = {foo: 1, bar: 2};
assert.deepEqual(
  Object.entries(obj),
  [
    ['foo', 1],
    ['bar', 2],
  ]);
```

> **Exercise: `Object.entries()`**
>
> `exercises/single-objects/find_key_test.mjs`

### 25.5.8 Properties are listed deterministically

Own (non-inherited) properties of objects are always listed in the following order:

- Properties with string keys that contain integer indices (that includes Array in-dices): In ascending numeric order
- Remaining properties with string keys: In the order in which they were added
- Properties with symbol keys: In the order in which they were added

The following example demonstrates how property keys are sorted according to these rules:

```
> Object.keys({b:0,a:0, 10:0,2:0})
[ '2', '10', 'b', 'a' ]
```

> **The order of properties**
>
> The ECMAScript specification describes in more detail how properties are ordered.

### 25.5.9 Assembling objects via `Object.fromEntries()`

Given an iterable over [key,value] pairs, `Object.fromEntries()` creates an object:

```
assert.deepEqual(
  Object.fromEntries([['foo',1],
  ['bar',2]]),
  {
   foo: 1,
   bar: 2,
  }
);
```

`Object.fromEntries()` does the opposite of `Object.entries()`.

To demonstrate both, we'll use them to implement two tool functions from the library Underscore in the next subsubsections.

#### 25.5.9.1 Example: `pick(object, ...keys)`

`pick` returns a copy of `object` that only has those properties, whose keys are mentioned as arguments:

```
const address = {
  street: 'Evergreen Terrace',
  number: '742',
  city: 'Springfield',
  state: 'NT',
  zip: '49007',
};
assert.deepEqual(
  pick(address, 'street', 'number'),
  {
    street: 'Evergreen Terrace',
    number: '742',
  }
);
```

We can implement `pick()` as follows:

```
function pick(object, ...keys) {
  const filteredEntries =
  Object.entries(object)
```

```
    .filter(([key, _value]) =>
   keys.includes(key)); return
   Object.fromEntries(filtered
   Entries);
  }
```

#### 25.5.9.2 Example: `invert(object)`

`invert` returns a copy of `object` where the keys and values of all properties are swapped:

```
assert.deepEqual(
  invert({a: 1, b: 2, c: 3}),
  {1: 'a', 2: 'b', 3: 'c'}
);
```

We can implement `invert()` like this:

```
function invert(object) {
  const mappedEntries =
  Object.entries(object)
    .map(([key, value]) => [value, key]);
  return
  Object.fromEntries(mappedEntries);
}
```

#### 25.5.9.3 A simple implementation of `Object.fromEntries()`

The following function is a simplified version of `Object.fromEntries()`:

```
function fromEntries(iterable) {
  const result = {};
  for (const [key, value] of iterable) {
    let coercedKey;
    if (typeof key === 'string' ||
      typeof key === 'symbol') {
      coercedKey = key;
    } else {
      coercedKey = String(key);
    }
    result[coercedKey] = value;
  }
  return result;
}
```

The npm package `object.fromentries` is a *polyfill* for `Object.entries()`: it installs its own implementation if that method doesn't exist.

> **Exercise: `Object.entries()` and `Object.fromEntries()`**
>
> `exercises/single-objects/omit_properties_test.mjs`

### 25.5.10 The pitfalls of using an object as a dictionary

If you use plain objects (created via object literals) as dictionaries, you have to look out for two pitfalls.

The first pitfall is that the `in` operator also finds inherited properties:

```
const dict = {};
assert.equal('toString' in dict, true);
```

We want `dict` to be treated as empty, but the `in` operator detects the properties it inherits from its prototype, `Object.prototype`.

The second pitfall is that you can't use the property key `__proto__`, because it has special powers (it sets the prototype of the object):

```
const dict = {};

dict['__proto__'] = 123;
// No property was added to dict:
assert.deepEqual(Object.keys(dict), []);
```

So how do we avoid these pitfalls?

- Whenever you can, use Maps. They are the best solution for dictionaries.
- If you can't: use a library for objects-as-dictionaries that does everything safely.
- If you can't: use an object without a prototype.

The following code demonstrates using objects without prototypes as dictionaries:

```
const dict = Object.create(null); // no prototype

assert.equal('toString' in dict, false); // (A)

dict['__proto__'] = 123;
assert.deepEqual(Object.keys(dict), ['__proto__']);
```

We avoided both pitfalls: First, a property without a prototype does not inherit any properties (line A). Second, in modern JavaScript, `__proto__` is implemented via `Ob-ject.prototype`. That means that it is switched off if `Object.prototype` is not in the prototype chain.

> **Exercise: Using an object as a dictionary**
>
> `exercises/single-objects/simple_dict_test.mjs`

## 25.6 Standard methods (advanced)

`Object.prototype` defines several standard methods that can be overridden to configure how an object is treated by the language. Two important ones are:

- `.toString()`
- `.valueOf()`

### 25.6.1 `.toString()`

`.toString()` determines how objects are converted to strings:

```
> String({toString() { return 'Hello!'
}})
'Hello!'
> String({})
'[object Object]'
```

### 25.6.2 `.valueOf()`

`.valueOf()` determines how objects are converted to numbers:

```
> Number({valueOf() { return 123 }})
123
> Number({})
NaN
```

## 25.7 Advanced topics

The following subsections give brief overviews of a few advanced topics.

### 25.7.1 `Object.assign()`

`Object.assign()` is a tool method:

```
Object.assign(target, source_1, source_2,
···)
```

This expression assigns all properties of `source_1` to `target`, then all properties of `source_2`, etc. At the end, it returns `target`. For example:

```
const target = { foo: 1 };

const result = Object.assign(
  target,
  {bar: 2},
  {baz: 3, bar: 4});

assert.deepEqual(
  result, { foo: 1, bar: 4, baz: 3 });
• target was
modified and
returned:
assert.equal(result,
target);
```

The use cases for `Object.assign()` are similar to those for spread properties. In a way, it spreads destructively.

### 25.7.2 Freezing objects

`Object.freeze(obj)` makes `obj` completely immutable: You can't change properties, add properties or change its prototype. For example:

```
const frozen =
Object.freeze({ x: 2, y:
5 }); assert.throws(
  () => { frozen.x = 7 },
  {
   name: 'TypeError',
   message: /^Cannot assign to
  read only property 'x'/, });
```

There is one caveat: `Object.freeze(obj)` freezes shallowly. That is, only the properties of `obj` are frozen, but not objects stored in properties.

### 25.7.3 Property attributes and property descriptors

Just as objects are composed of properties, properties are composed of *attributes*. The value of a property is only one of several attributes. Others include:

- `writable`: Is it possible to change the value of the property?
- `enumerable`: Is the property considered by `Object.keys()`, spreading, etc.?

When you are using one of the operations for handling property attributes, attributes are specified via *property descriptors*: objects where each property represents one attribute. For example, this is how you read the attributes of a property `obj.foo`:

```
const obj = { foo: 123 };
assert.deepEqual(
 Object.getOwnPropertyDescriptor(obj,
 'foo'),
 {
  value: 123,
  writable: true,
  enumerable: true,
  configurable: true,
 });
```

And this is how you set the attributes of a property `obj.bar`:

```
const obj = {
 foo: 1,
 bar: 2,
};

assert.deepEqual(Object.keys(obj),
['foo', 'bar']);

• Hide property `bar`
from Object.keys()
Object.defineProperty(o
bj, 'bar', {
 enumerable
: false,
});

assert.deepEqual(Object.keys(obj),
['foo']);
```

For more information on property attributes and property descriptors, consult “Speaking JavaScript”.

# Chapter 65

# Prototype chains and classes

## Contents

---

In this book, JavaScript's style of object-oriented programming (OOP) is introduced in four steps. This chapter covers steps 2–4, the previous chapter covers step 1. The steps are (fig. 26.1):

- Single objects: How do *objects*, JavaScript's basic OOP building blocks, work in isolation?
- **Prototype chains:** Each object has a chain of zero or more *prototype objects*. Proto-types are JavaScript's core inheritance mechanism.
- **Classes:** JavaScript's *classes* are factories for objects. The relationship between a class and its instances is based on prototypal inheritance.
- **Subclassing:** The relationship between a *subclass* and its *superclass* is also based on prototypal inheritance.

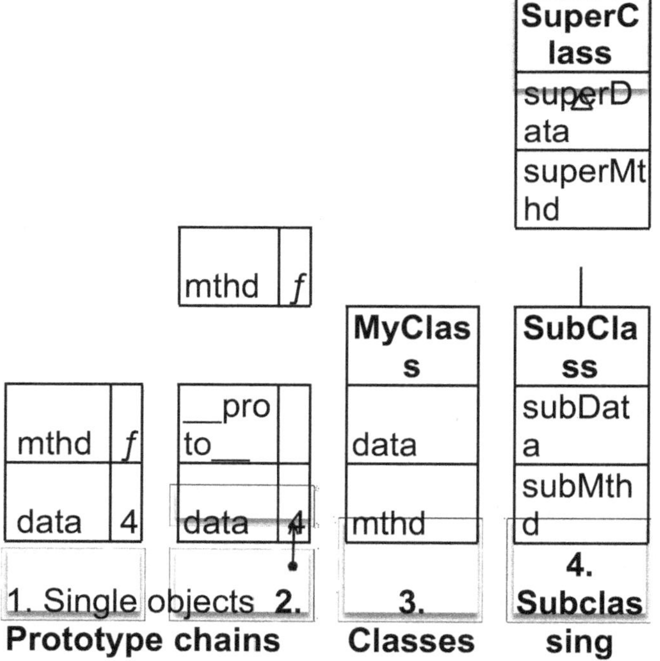


Figure 26.1: This book introduces object-oriented programming in JavaScript in four steps.

## 26.1 Prototype chains

Prototypes are JavaScript's only inheritance mechanism: Each object has a prototype that is either `null` or an object. In the latter case, the object inherits all of the prototype's properties.

In an object literal, you can set the prototype via the special property `__proto__`:

```
const proto = {
  protoProp: 'a',
};
const obj = {
  __proto__: proto,
  objProp: 'b',
};

• obj inherits
.protoProp:
assert.equal(obj.proto
Prop, 'a');
assert.equal('protoPro
p' in obj, true);
```

Given that a prototype object can have a prototype itself, we get a chain of objects – the so-called *prototype chain*. That means that inheritance gives us the impression that we are dealing with single objects, but we are actually dealing with chains of objects.

Fig. 26.2 shows what the prototype chain of `obj` looks like.

Non-inherited properties are called *own properties*. `obj` has one own property, `.objProp`.

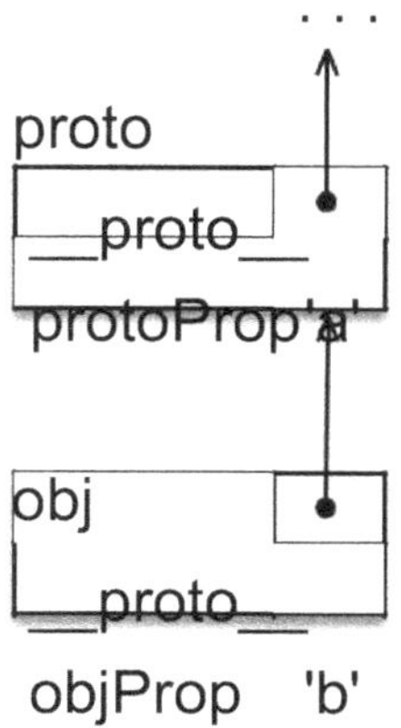


Figure 26.2: `obj` starts a chain of objects that continues with `proto` and other objects.

### 26.1.1 JavaScript's operations: all properties vs. own properties

Some operations consider all properties (own and

inherited). For example, getting prop-erties:

```
• const obj = { foo: 1 };
• typeof obj.foo // own
'number'
> typeof obj.toString // inherited
'function'
```

Other operations only consider own properties. For example, `Object.keys()`:

```
> Object.keys(obj)
[ 'foo' ]
```

Read on for another operation that also only considers own properties: setting properties.

### 26.1.2 Pitfall: only the first member of a prototype chain is mutated

One aspect of prototype chains that may be counter-intuitive is that setting *any* property via an object – even an inherited one – only changes that very object – never one of the prototypes.

Consider the following object `obj`:

```
const proto = {
  protoProp: 'a',
};
const obj = {
  __proto__: proto,
  objProp: 'b',
};
```

In the next code snippet, we set the inherited property `obj.protoProp` (line A). That "changes" it by creating an own property: When reading obj.protoProp, the own prop-erty is found first and its value *overrides* the value of the inherited property.

```
• In the beginning, obj has one own
  property
assert.deepEqual(Object.keys(obj),
['objProp']);

obj.protoProp = 'x'; // (A)

// We created a new own property:
assert.deepEqual(Object.keys(obj),
['objProp', 'protoProp']);

• The inherited property

itself is unchanged:

assert.equal(proto.protoP

rop, 'a');

• The own property overrides

the inherited property:

assert.equal(obj.protoProp,

'x');
```

The prototype chain of obj is depicted in fig. 26.3.

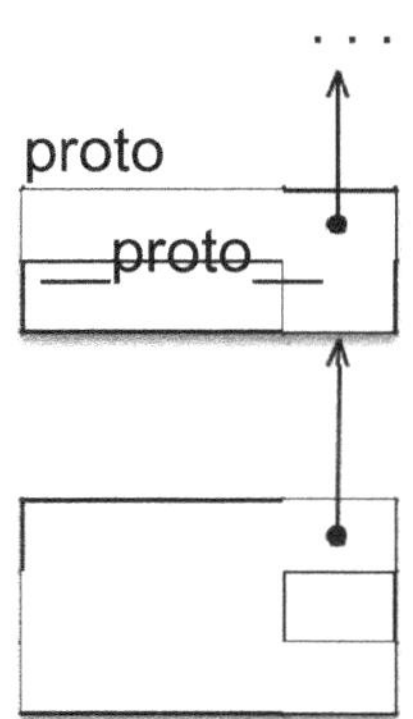

protoProp 'a'

obj

__proto__

objProp 'b'

protoProp 'x'

Figure 26.3: The own property `.protoProp` of `obj` overrides the property inherited from `proto`.

### 26.1.3 Tips for working with prototypes (advanced)

#### 26.1.3.1 Best practice: avoid `__proto__`, except in object literals

I recommend to avoid the pseudo-property `__proto__`:

As we will see later, not all objects have it.

However, `__proto__` in object literals is different.

There, it is a built-in feature and always available.

The recommended ways of getting and setting prototypes are:

- The best way to get a prototype is via the following method:

```
Object.getPrototypeOf(obj: Object) :
Object
```

- The best way to set a prototype is when creating an object – via `__proto__` in an object literal or via:

  ```
  Object.create(proto: Object) : Object
  ```

  If you have to, you can use `Object.setPrototypeOf()` to change the prototype of an existing object. But that may affect performance negatively.

This is how these features are used:

```
const proto1 = {};
const proto2 = {};

const obj = Object.create(proto1);
assert.equal(Object.getPrototypeOf(obj),
proto1);

Object.setPrototypeOf(obj, proto2);
assert.equal(Object.getPrototypeOf(obj),
proto2);
```

#### 26.1.3.2 Check: is an object a prototype of another one?

So far, "`p` is a prototype of `o`" always meant "`p` is a *direct* prototype of `o`". But it can also be used more loosely and mean that `p` is in the prototype chain of `o`. That looser relationship can be checked via:

```
p.isPrototypeOf(o)
```

For example:

```
const a = {};
const b = {__proto__: a};
const c = {__proto__: b};

assert.equal(a.isPrototypeOf(b), true);
assert.equal(a.isPrototypeOf(c), true);

assert.equal(a.isProto

typeOf(a), false);

assert.equal(c.isProto

typeOf(a), false);
```

### 26.1.4 Sharing data via prototypes

Consider the following code:

```
const jane = {
 name: 'Jane',
 describe() {
  return 'Person named '+this.name;
 },
};
const tarzan = {
 name: 'Tarzan',
```

```
  describe() {
   return 'Person named '+this.name;
  },
};

assert.equal(jane.describe(),
'Person named Jane');
assert.equal(tarzan.describe()
, 'Person named Tarzan');
```

We have two objects that are very similar. Both have two properties whose names are `.name` and `.describe`. Additionally, method `.describe()` is the same. How can we avoid that method being duplicated?
We can move it to an object `PersonProto` and make that object a prototype of both `jane` and `tarzan`:

```
const PersonProto = {
 describe() {
  return 'Person named ' + this.name;
 },
};
const jane = {
 __proto__: PersonProto,
 name: 'Jane',
};
const tarzan = {
 __proto__: PersonProto,
 name: 'Tarzan',
};
```

The name of the prototype reflects that both `jane` and `tarzan` are persons.

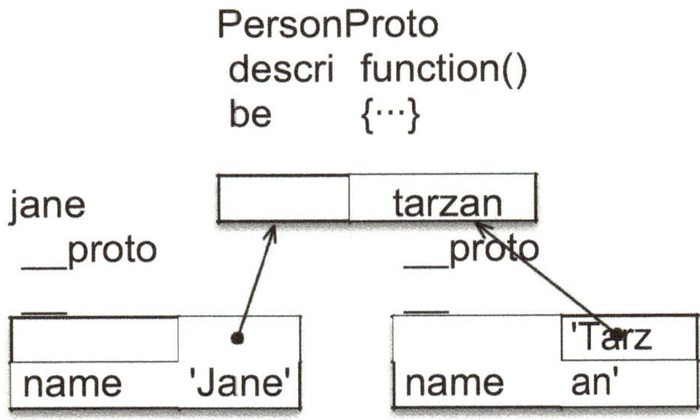


Figure 26.4: Objects `jane` and `tarzan` share method `.describe()`, via their common pro-totype `PersonProto`.

The diagram in fig. 26.4 illustrates how the three objects are connected: The objects at the bottom now contain the properties that are specific to `jane` and `tarzan`. The object at the top contains the properties that are shared between them.

When you make the method call `jane.describe()`, `this` points to the receiver of that method call, `jane` (in the bottom left corner of the diagram). That's why the method still works. `tarzan.describe()` works similarly.

```
assert.equal(jane.describe(),
'Person named Jane');
assert.equal(tarzan.describe()
, 'Person named Tarzan');
```

## 26.2 Classes

We are now ready to take on classes, which are basically a compact syntax for setting up prototype chains. Under the hood, JavaScript's classes are unconventional. But that is something you rarely see when working with them. They should normally feel familiar to people who have used other object-oriented programming languages.

### 26.2.1 A class for persons

We have previously worked with `jane` and `tarzan`, single objects representing persons.
Let's use a *class declaration* to implement a factory for person objects:

```
class Person {
 constructor(name) {
  this.name = name;
 }
 describe() {
  return 'Person named '+this.name;
 }
}
```

`jane` and `tarzan` can now be created via `new Person()`:

```
const jane = new Person('Jane');
assert.equal(jane.name, 'Jane');
assert.equal(jane.describe(), 'Person
named Jane');

const tarzan = new Person('Tarzan');
assert.equal(tarzan.name, 'Tarzan');
assert.equal(tarzan.describe(), 'Person
named Tarzan');
```

#### 26.2.1.1 Class expressions

There are two kinds of *class definitions* (ways of defining classes):

- *Class declarations*: which we have seen in the previous section.
- *Class expressions*: which we'll see next.

Class expressions can be anonymous and named:

```
// Anonymous class expression
const Person = class { ··· };

// Named class expression
const Person = class MyClass { ··· };
```

The name of a named class expression works similarly

to the name of a named function expression.

This was a first look at classes. We'll explore more features soon, but first we need to learn the internals of classes.

### 26.2.2 Classes under the hood

There is a lot going on under the hood of classes. Let's look at the diagram for `jane` (fig. 26.5).

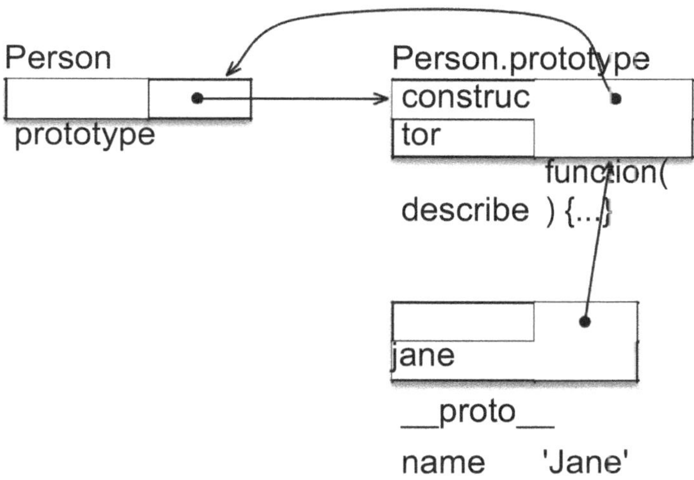


Figure 26.5: The class `Person` has the property `.prototype` that points to an object that is the prototype of all instances of `Person`. `jane` is one such instance.

The main purpose of class `Person` is to set up the prototype chain on the right (`jane`, followed by `Person.prototype`). It is interesting to note that both constructs inside class `Person` (`.constructor` and

`.describe()`) created properties for `Person.prototype`, not for `Person`.

The reason for this slightly odd approach is backward compatibility: Prior to classes, *constructor functions* (ordinary functions, invoked via the `new` operator) were often used as factories for objects. Classes are mostly better syntax for constructor functions and therefore remain compatible with old code. That explains why classes are functions:

```
> typeof Person
'function'
```

In this book, I use the terms *constructor (function)* and *class* interchangeably.

It is easy to confuse `.__proto__` and `.prototype`.

Hopefully, the diagram in fig. 26.5 makes it clear, how they differ:

- `.__proto__` is a pseudo-property for accessing the prototype of an object.
- `.prototype` is a normal property that is only special due to how the `new` operator uses it. The name is not ideal: `Person.prototype` does not point to the prototype of `Person`, it points to the prototype of all instances of `Person`.

#### 26.2.2.1 `Person.prototype.constructor` (advanced)

There is one detail in fig. 26.5 that we haven't looked at, yet: `Person.prototype.constructor` points back to `Person`:

```
>
Person.prototype.constr
uctor === Person true
```

This setup also exists due to backward compatibility. But it has two additional benefits.

First, each instance of a class inherits property `.constructor`. Therefore, given an in-stance, you can make "similar" objects via it:

```
const jane = new Person('Jane');

const cheeta = new
jane.constructor('Cheeta');
• cheeta is also an instance of Person
• (the instanceof operator

is explained later)

assert.equal(cheeta

instanceof Person, true);
```

Second, you can get the name of the class that created a given instance:

```
const tarzan = new Person('Tarzan');

assert.equal(tarzan.constructor.name,
'Person');
```

### 26.2.3 Class definitions: prototype properties

All constructs in the body of the following class declaration, create properties of `Foo.prototype`.

```
class Foo {
constructor(p
      rop) {
 this.prop =
       prop;
 }
 protoMethod() {
  return 'protoMethod';
 }
 get protoGetter() {
  return 'protoGetter';
 }
}
```

Let's examine them in order:

- `.constructor()` is called after creating a new instance of `Foo`, to set up that in-stance.
- `.protoMethod()` is a normal method. It is stored in `Foo.prototype`.
- `.protoGetter` is a getter that is stored in `Foo.prototype`.

The following interaction uses class `Foo`:

- `const foo = new Foo(123);`
- `foo.prop`

```
123

> foo.protoMethod()
'protoMethod'
> foo.protoGetter
'protoGetter'
```

### 26.2.4 Class definitions: static properties

All constructs in the body of the following class declaration, create so-called *static* prop-erties – properties of `Bar` itself.

```
class Bar {
 static staticMethod() {
  return 'staticMethod';
 }
 static get staticGetter() {
  return 'staticGetter';
 }
}
```

The static method and the static getter are used as follows.

```
> Bar.staticMethod()
'staticMethod'
> Bar.staticGetter
'staticGetter'
```

### 26.2.5 The `instanceof` operator

The `instanceof` operator tells you if a value is an instance of a given class:

```
> new Person('Jane') instanceof Person
true
> ({}) instanceof Person
false
> ({}) instanceof Object
true
> [] instanceof Array
true
```

We'll explore the `instanceof` operator in more detail later, after we have looked at sub-classing.

### 26.2.6 Why I recommend classes

I recommend using classes for the following reasons:

- Classes are a common standard for object creation and inheritance that is now widely supported across frameworks (React, Angular, Ember, etc.). This is an improvement to how things were before, when almost every framework had its own inheritance library.

- They help tools such as IDEs and type checkers with their work and enable new features there.
- If you come from another language to JavaScript and are used to classes, then you can get started more quickly.
- JavaScript engines optimize them. That is, code that uses classes is almost always faster than code that uses a custom inheritance library.
- You can subclass built-in constructor functions such as `Error`.

That doesn't mean that classes are perfect:

- There is a risk of overdoing inheritance.
- There is a risk of putting too much functionality in classes (when some of it is often better put in functions).
- How they work superficially and under the hood is quite different. In other words, there is a disconnect between syntax and semantics. Two examples are:
  - A method definition inside a class `C` creates a method in the object
  - Classes are functions.

  The motivation for the disconnect is backward compatibility. Thankfully, the dis-connect causes few problems in practice; you are usually OK if you go along what classes pretend to be.

> **Exercise: Writing a class**
>
> `exercises/proto-chains-classes/point_class_test.mjs`

## 26.3 Private data for classes

This section describes techniques for hiding some of the data of an object from the outside. We discuss them in the context of classes, but they also work for objects created directly, e.g. via object literals.

### 26.3.1 Private data: naming convention

The first technique makes a property private by prefixing its name with an underscore. This doesn't protect the property in any way; it merely signals to the outside: "You don't need to know about this property."

In the following code, the properties `._counter` and `._action` are private.

```
class Countdown {
 constructor(counter, action) {
  this._counter = counter;
```

```
    this._action = action;
  }
  dec() {
    this._counter--;
    if (this._counter === 0) {
      this._action();
    }
  }
}
```

- The two properties aren't really private:

```
assert.deepEqual(
  Object.keys(new Countdown()),
  ['_counter', '_action']);
```

With this technique, you don't get any protection and private names can clash. On the plus side, it is easy to use.

### 26.3.2 Private data: WeakMaps

Another technique is to use WeakMaps. How exactly that works is explained in the chap-ter on WeakMaps. This is a preview:

```
const _counter = new WeakMap();
const _action = new WeakMap();
```

```
class Countdown {
 constructor(counter, action) {
  _counter.set(this, counter);
  _action.set(this, action);
 }
 dec() {
  let counter = _counter.get(this);
  counter--;
  _counter.set(this, counter);
  if (counter === 0) {
   _action.get(this)();
  }
 }
}
```

- The two pseudo-properties are truly private:

```
assert.deepEqual(
 Object.keys(new
 Countdown()),
 []);
```

This technique offers you considerable protection from outside access and there can't be any name clashes. But it is also more complicated to use.

### 26.3.3 More techniques for private data

This book explains the most important techniques for private data in classes. There will also probably soon be built-in support for it. Consult the ECMAScript proposal "Class Public Instance Fields & Private Instance Fields" for details.

A few additional techniques are explained in "Exploring ES6".

## 26.4 Subclassing

Classes can also subclass ("extend") existing classes. As an example, the following class `Employee` subclasses `Person`:

```
class Person {
 constructor(name) {
  this.name = name;
 }
 describe() {
  return `Person named ${this.name}`;
 }
 static logNames(persons) {
  for (const person of persons) {
   console.log(person.name);
  }
 }
}

class Employee extends Person {
 constructor(name, title) {
  super(name);
```

```
    this.title = title;
  }
  describe() {
    return super.describe() +
      ` (${this.title})`;
  }
}

const jane = new
Employee('Jane',
'CTO'); assert.equal(
  jane.describe(),
  'Person named Jane (CTO)');
```

Two comments:

- Inside a `.constructor()` method, you must call the super-constructor via `super()`, before you can access `this`. That's because `this` doesn't exist before the super-constructor was called (this phenomenon is specific to classes).
- Static methods are also inherited. For example, `Employee` inherits the static method

```
.logNames():

  > 'logNames' in Employee
  true
```

**Exercise: Subclassing**

`exercises/proto-chains-classes/color_point_class_test.mjs`

### 26.4.1 Subclasses under the hood (advanced)

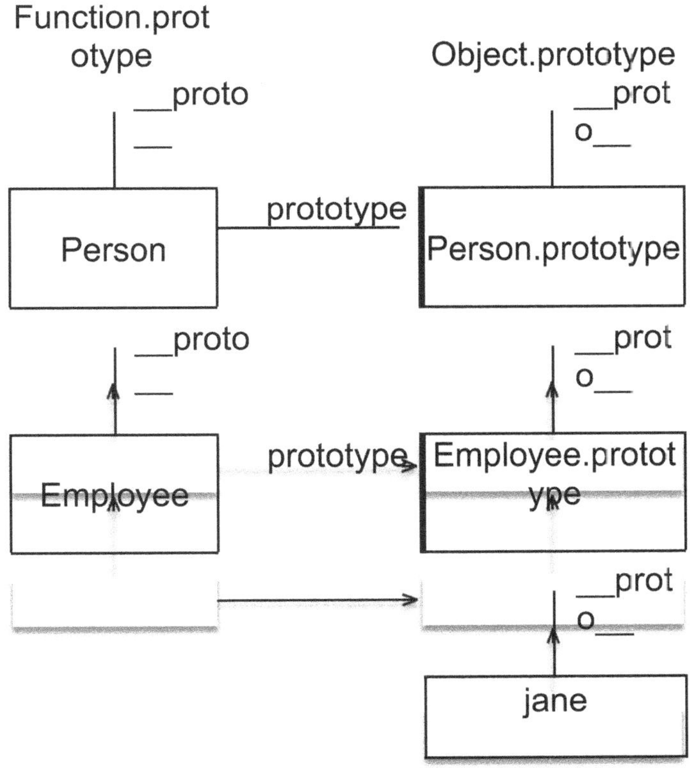


Figure 26.6: These are the objects that make up class `Person` and its subclass, `Employee`. The left column is

about classes. The right column is about the `Employee` instance `jane` and its prototype chain.

The classes `Person` and `Employee` from the previous section are made up of several objects (fig. 26.6). One key insight for understanding how these objects are related, is that there are two prototype chains:

- The instance prototype chain, on the right.
- The class prototype chain, on the left.

#### 26.4.1.1 The instance prototype chain (right column)

The instance prototype chain starts with `jane` and continues with `Employee.prototype` and `Person.prototype`. In principle, the prototype chain ends at this point, but we get one more object: `Object.prototype`. This prototype provides services to virtually all objects, which is why it is included here, too:

```
>
Object.getPrototypeOf(Person.proto
type) === Object.prototype true
```

#### 26.4.1.2 The class prototype chain (left column)

In the class prototype chain, `Employee` comes first, `Person` next. Afterwards, the chain continues with `Function.prototype`, which is only there, because `Person` is a function and functions need the services of `Function.prototype`.

```
>
Object.getPrototypeOf(Person)
=== Function.prototype true
```

### 26.4.2 `instanceof` in more detail (advanced)

We have not yet seen how `instanceof` really works. Given the expression:

```
x instanceof C
```

How does `instanceof` determine if `x` is an instance of `C` (or of a subclass of `C`)? It does so by checking if `C.prototype` is in the prototype chain of `x`. That is, the following expression is equivalent:

```
C.prototype.isPrototypeOf(x)
```

If we go back to fig. 26.6, we can confirm that the prototype chain does lead us to the following correct answers:

```
> jane instanceof Employee
true
> jane instanceof Person
true
> jane instanceof Object
```

```
true
```

### 26.4.3 Prototype chains of built-in objects (advanced)

Next, we'll use our knowledge of subclassing to understand the prototype chains of a few built-in objects. The following tool function `p()` helps us with our explorations.

```
const p =
Object.getPrototypeOf.bind(Object);
```

We extracted method `.getPrototypeOf()` of `Object` and assigned it to `p`.

#### 26.4.3.1 The prototype chain of `{}`

Let's start by examining plain objects:

```
> p({}) === Object.prototype
true
> p(p({})) === null
true
```

Fig. 26.7 shows a diagram for this prototype chain. We can see that `{}` really is an instance of `Object` – `Object.prototype` is in its prototype chain.

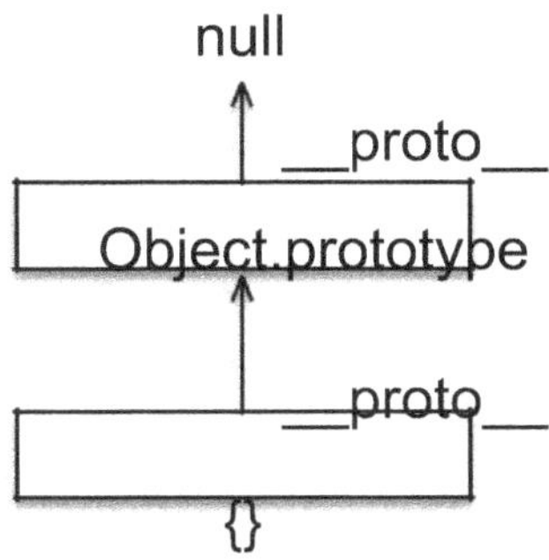


Figure 26.7: The prototype chain of an object created via an object literal starts with that object, continues with `Object.prototype` and ends with `null`.

#### 26.4.3.2 The prototype chain of `[]`

What does the prototype chain of an Array look like?

```
> p([]) === Array.prototype
true
> p(p([])) === Object.prototype
true
> p(p(p([]))) === null
true
```

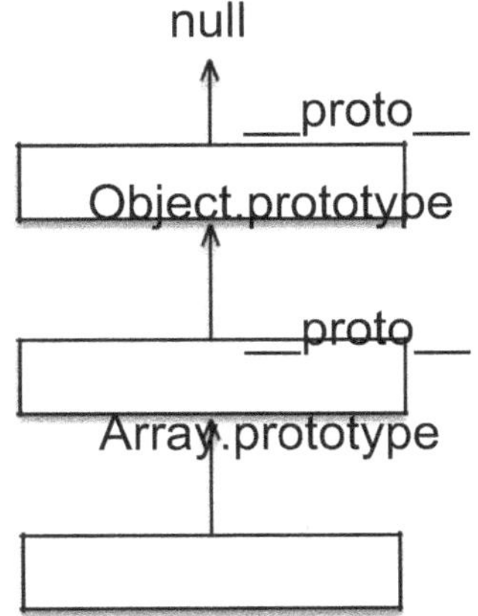

__proto__

[]

Figure 26.8: The prototype chain of an Array has these members: the Array instance, `Array.prototype`, `Object.prototype`, `null`.

This prototype chain (visualized in fig. 26.8) tells us that an Array object is an instance of `Array`, which is a subclass of `Object`.

#### 26.4.3.3 The prototype chain of `function () {}`

Lastly, the prototype chain of an ordinary function tells us that all functions are objects:

```
> p(function () {}) === Function.prototype
true
> p(p(function () {})) ===
Object.prototype
true
```

#### 26.4.3.4 Objects that aren't instances of `Object`

An object is only an instance of `Object` if `Object.prototype` is in its prototype chain.

Most objects created via various literals are instances of `Object`:

```
> ({}) instanceof Object
true
> (() => {}) instanceof Object
true
> /abc/ug instanceof Object
true
```

Objects that don't have prototypes are not instances of `Object`:

```
> ({ __proto__: null })
instanceof Object false
```

`Object.prototype` ends most prototype chains. Its prototype is `null`, which means it isn't an instance of `Object`, either:

```
> Object.prototype instanceof Object
false
```

#### 26.4.3.5 How exactly does the pseudo-property `.__proto__` work?

The pseudo-property `.__proto__` is implemented by class `Object`, via a getter and a setter.

It could be implemented like this:

```
class Object {
  get __proto__() {
    return Object.getPrototypeOf(this);
  }
  set __proto__(other) {
    Object.setPrototypeOf(this, other);
  }
  // ···
}
```

That means that you can switch `.__proto__` off, by creating an object that doesn't have

`Object.prototype` in its prototype chain (see previous section):

```
> '__proto__' in {}
true
> '__proto__' in { __proto__: null }
false
```

### 26.4.4 Dispatched vs. direct method calls (advanced)

Let's examine how method calls work with classes. We are revisiting `jane` from earlier:

```
class Person {
  constructor(name) {
    this.name = name;
  }
  describe() {
    return 'Person named '+this.name;
  }
}
const jane = new Person('Jane');
```

Fig. 26.9 has a diagram with `jane`'s prototype chain.

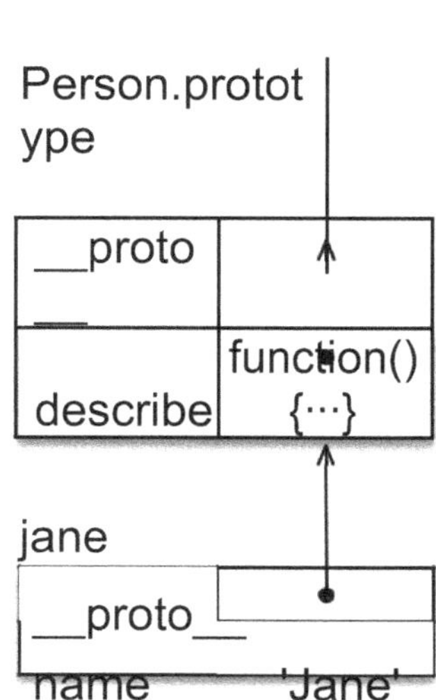


Figure 26.9: The prototype chain of `jane` starts with `jane` and continues with `Per-son.prototype`.

Normal method calls are *dispatched* – the method call `jane.describe()` happens in two steps:

- Dispatch: In the prototype chain of `jane`, find the first property whose key is `'de-scribe'` and retrieve its value.

  ```
  const func = jane.describe;
  ```

- Call: Call the value, while setting `this` to `jane`.

  ```
  func.call(jane);
  ```

This way of dynamically looking for a method and invoking it, is called *dynamic dispatch*.

You can make the same method call *directly*, without dispatching:

```
Person.prototype.describe.call(jane)
```

This time, we directly point to the method, via `Person.prototype.describe` and don't search for it in the prototype chain. We also specify `this` differently, via `.call()`.

Note that `this` always points to the beginning of a prototype chain. That enables `.de-scribe()` to access `.name`.

#### 26.4.4.1 Borrowing methods

Direct method calls become useful when you are working with methods of `Ob-ject.protctype`. For example, `Object.prototype.hasOwnProperty(k)` checks if `this` has a non-inherited property whose key is `k`:

```
• const obj = { foo: 123 };
• obj.hasOwnProperty('foo')
true
> obj.hasOwnProperty('bar')
false
```

However, in the prototype chain of an object, there may be another property with the key `'hasOwnProperty'`, that overrides the method in `Object.prototype`. Then a dispatched method call doesn't work:

```
• const obj = { hasOwnProperty: true };
• obj.hasOwnProperty('bar')
TypeError: obj.hasOwnProperty is not a
function
```

The work-around is to use a direct method call:

```
>
Object.prototype.hasOwnProperty.call(obj,
'bar')
false
```

```
> Object.prototype.hasOwnProperty.call(obj, 'hasOwnProperty')
true
```

This kind of direct method call is often abbreviated as follows:

```
> ({}).hasOwnProperty.call(obj, 'bar')
false
> ({}).hasOwnProperty.call(obj, 'hasOwnProperty')
true
```

This pattern may seem inefficient, but most engines optimize this pattern, so that perfor-mance should not be an issue.

### 26.4.5 Mixin classes (advanced)

JavaScript's class system only supports *single inheritance*. That is, each class can have at most one superclass. One way around this limitation is via a technique called *mixin classes* (short: *mixins*).

The idea is as follows: Let's say we want a class `C` to inherit from two superclasses `S1` and `S2`. That would be *multiple inheritance*, which JavaScript doesn't support.

Our work-around is to turn `S1` and `S2` into *mixins*, factories for subclasses:

```
const S1 = (Sup) => class extends Sup { /*···*/ };
const S2 = (Sup) => class extends Sup { /*···*/ };
```

Each of these two functions returns a class that extends a given superclass `Sup`. We create class `C` as follows:

```
class C extends S2(S1(Object)) {
  /*···*/
}
```

We now have a class `C` that extends a class `S2` that extends a class `S1` that extends `Object` (which most classes do, implicitly).

#### 26.4.5.1 Example: a mixin for brand management

We implement a mixin `Branded` that has helper methods for setting and getting the brand of an object:

```
const Branded = (Sup) =>
  class extends Sup {
    setBrand(brand) {
      this._brand = brand;
      return this;
    }
    getBrand() {
      return this._brand;
    }
  };
```

We use this mixin to implement brand management for a class `Car`:

```
class Car extends Branded(Object) {
  constructor(model) {
```

```
    super();
    this._model = model;
  }
  toString() {
    return `${this.getBrand()}
    ${this._model}`;
  }
}
```

The following code confirms that the mixin worked: `Car` has method `.setBrand()` of `Branded`.

```
const modelT = new
Car('Model
T').setBrand('Ford');
assert.equal(modelT.toString
(), 'Ford Model T');
```

#### 26.4.5.2 The benefits of mixins

Mixins free us from the constraints of single inheritance:

- The same class can extend a single superclass and zero or more mixins.
- The same mixin can be used by multiple classes.

www.ingramcontent.com/pod-product-compliance
Lightning Source LLC
Chambersburg PA
CBHW031216050326
40689CB00009B/1357

* 9 7 8 1 0 7 5 6 3 0 6 9 9 *